THE LIVES OF

Studies in Continental Thought

John Sallis, general editor

Consulting Editors

The Lives
of Things

❧

CHARLES E. SCOTT

INDIANA
University Press
Bloomington & Indianapolis

This book is a publication of

Indiana University Press
601 North Morton Street
Bloomington, IN 47404-3797 USA

http://iupress.indiana.edu

Telephone orders   800-842-6796
Fax orders   812-855-7931
Orders by e-mail   iuporder@indiana.edu

The paper used in this publication meets the minimum
requirements of American National Standard for Information
Sciences—Permanence of Paper for Printed Library Materials,
ANSI Z39.48-1984.

MANUFACTURED IN THE UNITED STATES OF AMERICA

Library of Congress Cataloging-in-Publication Data

Scott, Charles E.
The lives of things / Charles E. Scott.
p. cm. — (Studies in Continental thought)
Includes bibliographical references and index.
ISBN 0-253-34068-3 (cloth : alk. paper) — ISBN 0-253-21514-5 (pbk. :
alk. paper)
1. Philosophy of nature. I. Title. II. Series.
BD581 .S375 2002
113—dc21
2001005670

1 2 3 4 5   07 06 05 04 03 02

*This book is dedicated
to the people of Staniel Cay*

CONTENTS

PREFACE / VII

Part I

PHYSICALITY

1. Facts and Astonishments   3

2. What's the Matter with "Nature"?   22

3. *Phusis* and Its Generations   54

Part II

TOPICS AT "NATURE'S" EDGE

4. Physical Memories   85

5. Starlight in the Face of the Other   99

6. Physical Weight on the Edge of Appearing   113

7. Lightness of Mind and Density   125

8. Feeling, Transmission, *Phusis:* A Short Genealogy of "Immanence"   144

9. Psalms, Poems, and Morals with Celestial Indifference   175

10. The *Phusis* of Nihil: The Sight and Generation of Nihilism   184

INDEX / 195

PREFACE

But if literature is not enough to assure me that I am not just
chasing dreams, I look to science to nourish my visions in
which all heaviness disappears. Today every branch of science
seems intent on demonstrating that the world is supported by
the most minute entities, such as messages of DNA, the im-
pulses of neurons, and quarks, and neutrinos wandering
through space since the beginning of time. . . .
                                                        —Italo Calvino

I found the words that begin this preface in *Six Memos for the Next Millen-
nium*.[1] Calvino speaks in these memos of lightness, quickness, exactitude,
visibility, multiplicity, and, had he lived long enough to finish them, con-
sistency. He does not speak of Nature, Substance, Origin, or Universe. He
uses words, rather, in "pursuit of things, as a perpetual adjustment to their
infinite variety" (26). Words, for him—and thoughts and perceptions,
too—in their transformative, levitational energy, can lighten the weight of
living. Full buckets, he observes, do not fly (29). To perceive things with
lightness we need empty spaces, the fantasies of desires, the velocity of
lively rhythms that break our hold on whatever we cling to. We need the
distances and incompletions that give us occasions for another look, another observation, another fantasy—we need the "privation of life that is
transformed into lightness" (28).

In such lightness we might speak of the lives and densities of things,
their "unpredictable deviations and infinite, unexpected possibilities." We
might speak of the "dissolving . . . solidity of the world" (9). Addressing
Lucretius, Calvino says, "even the poetry of nothingness . . . issues from a
poet who had no doubts whatever about the physical reality of the world"
(9). Indeed, in their invisible mobilities and visible, passing distinctness—
in their very physicality—the lives of things encourage the philosopher as
well as the poet, in speaking of them, to speak also at once of nothing.

Were I to continue this preface on the airy avenues and byways that
Calvino's words provide, I would engage, in addition to many of his other

---

1. Italo Calvino, *The Charles Eliot Norton Lectures, 1985–86,* trans. Patrick Creagh (Cambridge,
Mass.: Harvard University Press, 1988).

observations and references, his quotation from Carlo Emilio Gadda's *That Awful Mess on Via Merulana* that includes this observation: "we must 'reform *within ourselves* the meaning of the category of cause' as handed down by the philosophers from Aristotle to Immanuel Kant, and replace cause with causes" (104, emphasis added). But these byways would then turn my beginning into something improperly long. My intention now is no more than to introduce the tone and predisposition of this book and to speak appreciatively of those who have provided ballast and light for me during this work.

Susan Schoenbohm introduced me to "physicality" as a translation for *phusis.* That word and its variations play a major role in this book. Michael Bray and Wendy Hamblet helped with the research that informs Part 1. Dr. Hamblet also provided, with exceptional kindness, order and connection for me at Penn State when I was away and writing for extended periods of time. Omar Rivera gave me exceptionally adept editorial assistance, insight, and suggestions as the book neared completion. As I think of those whose thought, work, and support form part of the book's intangibility, I return to Calvino (whom I read because of the encouragement of Daniela Vallega-Neu and Alejandro Vallega): "Who are we, who is each one of us, if not a combinatory of experiences . . . ? Each life an encyclopedia, a library, an inventory of objects, a series of styles, and everything can be constantly shuffled and reordered in every way conceivable. . . . But perhaps the answer that stands closest to my heart is something else: think of what it would be to have a work . . . that would let us escape the limited perspective of the individual ego, not only to enter into selves like our own but to give speech to that which has no language, to the bird perching on the edge of the gutter, to the tree in spring and the tree in fall, to stone, to cement, to plastic" (124). While I do not presume to give speech to other people or to things, I would like to speak appropriately in their regard, to use language so that in it, in moments of success, I am able "to approach things (present or absent) with discretion, attention, and caution, with respect for what things (present or absent) communicate without words" (77). I am indeed "a combinatory" of many influences, often bespoken in this book, often kindly given, frequently insufficiently noted, by friends and critics. I wish that I could name them all. These influences, in the airiness of their transformations in my writing, are lightly and persistently present. I am grateful for the differences that they make.

I note in the dedication the people of Staniel Cay. They will have no interest in this book. But the people I know there begin—always it seems to me—with the life of whatever is before them, whether it be a fish, a machine, a wind, or a man with a basket, begin with its particular density, movement, and manner, with its uselessness or usefulness in their environment. I am not especially useful in their environment. I am rather an odd particular in a world saturated by practical know-how. But their hospitality and support have not wavered before the singularity of this intellectual, and they too have helped to form some of the experiences that guide my efforts toward what Calvino calls a certain extraction of weight from our language regarding the lives of things.

Part I

PHYSICALITY

ONE

Facts and Astonishments

I was right when I thought that two friends, a poet and an artist, would think less well of me if I told them that facts are as effective as "poetic experiences" in occasioning astonishment and a sense of wonder. I did not doubt that they were correct in referring to wordless experiences of wonder in which a mountain or a human face or an infinity of other things stands out with awesome singularity and power and escapes conceptual grasp. I am familiar with such events. But when I said that the "facts" of evolution, high-energy physics, biochemistry, or astronomy can have much the same effect, they could not hide their disappointment. The poet's eyes narrowed slightly, the edges of his lips dropped fractionally, and the veins in his forehead that were standing out with engorged excitement a moment earlier waned in deflation. The artist just looked at the floor and tapped his index finger on the chair arm in a way that reminded me of my high school principal tapping his fingers just before he passed sentence on some of us who had successfully penetrated the inside of the girls' empty dressing room. (We had wanted to see what it was like in the mystical presence of their absent bodies.) The poet, artist, and I had been talking about vividness in experience, about the importance of not succumbing to the lure of everyday life with its mundane demands—indeed about the importance of freeing ourselves from the crassness of popular culture, for the sake of a pristine astonishment before the lives of things. I recalled reading an article about the size of the universe when I was seventeen and sitting in my hometown barber's chair. The point of the article was that the "known" universe is so immense that it exceeds the reach of human imagination and that scientific facts help people to extend their imaginative range before this immensity. And, the article continued, seeing how mysteriously big the universe is according to astronomers, imagine how mysteriously huge, how inconceivable is the creative power of God. The intervening years have considerably rusted the latter thought, but the first observation about fact, immensity, and wonder struck home. I even found a certain poetic quality in the notion of facts' engendering a sense of astonishment and wonder without injury to the facts or the wonder. Why shouldn't actual events in their recognition give rise to astonishment?

But the intrusion of such objective, if suspiciously speculative, factuality struck my friends as a kind of betrayal. Isn't that the very kind of objectivity and scientific technological mentality that we must resist in order to see things with astonished attention to their lives? Doesn't wonder arise in connection with "something" beyond the reach of facts?

I didn't think so. At least the "something beyond the reach of facts" that gives rise to wonder struck me as a statement of at least proposed actuality, i.e., a proposed fact. I reported that the gargantuan amount of unperceived "matter" that "had" to be in the "universe" according to calculations that I do not understand gave rise to astonishment as far as I was concerned—not to mention the reported actuality of supernovas, galaxies, light years, and the beginning of gravity. I said that I was even thrown into astonishment when I looked at infrared pictures of one galaxy eating another. It's not only a matter of intense surprise *about* the facts and speculations. It's also a state of mind to which, in my case at least, the facts and speculations led, and in which the occurrences of barbershops and of us in them felt astonishing.

That's not the point, the poet said. You're talking about your reaction to the size and distance of the universe. I'm talking, he said, about the mystery in and with the life of each thing, in a bridge or an old barn, or in the face of a child.

Well, I wondered, what about a plastic spoon, litter in the street, a McDonald's sign, or a pimple?

He didn't care much for what he detected in my attitude, but he was about to respond in a guardedly positive direction, I thought, when the artist said enthusiastically, "Yes! Yes, that too and so much more. It all depends on how you see pimples and plastic spoons. They too can be beautiful—not pretty, but *beautiful,* if you can really see them, really experience their texture and color in their striking presence." I took his point, although I wondered about a lyric to the purple pimple upon her nose. (See! How she flourishes! / See! How she grows! . . .) Wonder has an originary quality that exceeds facts. ("Is that a fact?" I said to myself, silently.)

Okay, I said. But now let's say that someone gives an account of the life of a pimple, the facts of its bacteria and other microscopic elements, its cellular origins and processes of formation, an account of the very building of this pimple—all that happened and happens in its coming into being and its being able to come into being. I believe that the account would need to tell us about the "making" of some of those microscopic elements in the explosion of stars billions of years ago, their movements through space and their splattering over the earth, their endurance during the earth's own formation as well as the development of cells and cellular organizations that "know" when and how to produce pimples. Wouldn't that be simply astonishing? Isn't it a question of learning how to read with your intellect, feeling, and imagination as you are guided by those perceived processes that come to fruition (as it were) in these pussy beings on this nose? Seeing it by means of a history of facts would fill a book. Aren't we talking about a possible story that could give rise to astonishment? A story built on facts, no matter how tentative and culturally determined those facts might be? Doesn't scientific objectivity carry with it a high potential for eliciting and expressing astonishment?

The conversation did not stop there because both the poet and the artist thought that I was not giving due consideration to the fallout of scientific objectivity in a society that is mesmerized by facts and the technology that, depending on your perspective, makes them or uncovers them. They thought that the overall effect of scientific objectivity is found in the loss of a state of mind that is predisposed to astonishment and wonder, one more given to everyday preoccupations—in short, a predisposition to banality. I, on the other hand, thought that their perspective might be predisposed by a quasi-religious belief that "real" astonishment (its very fact) requires a sense of transcendent mystery, a predisposition that places a person in a virtually worshipful state of mind, one that divides and opposes at least quasi-sacred and profane realms. When all hints of divinity, "calling," and exceptional perceptiveness dissolve, what would be left other than a profane sense of magnitude and meaningless force? Astonishment and wonder would be left, I thought, and left without disappointment over the loss of "the sacred" and without diminishment of attentiveness to the unspeakable wonder of lives, even when these lives are also measured. Lives are, as a matter of fact, forever breaking the measurements and shining in their passing intensities.

I wish that I had also said to my friends that astonishment, too, is a fact, if "fact" means an occurrence that is communicably recognized in the occurrence's appearing. And I might have said, too, that "facts" means statements about what happens (as well as other actual happenings) that can change as knowledge and perceptions change, that facts are social events and bear all manner of mutable elements, and that factual certainty is, in fact, fairly changeable over time. But at least I got this much articulated in our conversation: astonishment and facts—mundane facts—can be friends; there appears to be no necessary reason why various disciplined knowledges—"the" sciences among them—should be antidotes to astonishment and wonder or why people who prize astonishment and come to ideas, poems, and paintings in its inspiration should view scientific knowledge and mentality with suspicion, as though such knowledge and mentality were somehow hostile aliens to people of wonder—unless, of course, wonder must have a quasi-worshipful basis to be wonder at all. Then, I suppose, that factual claim about wonder would eliminate from consideration a lot of other facts and their combinations from being able to generate wonder.

I would like now to pursue further some of these observations about astonishment with the intention of showing that an inclination toward astonishment inheres in some people's physicality and is manifest in the very situations that are presented by mundane facts. If I carry out this intention successfully, I will also eliminate a certain loftiness and an image of transcendence that often attaches to interpretations of astonishment. The emotional overtones that sometimes come with experiences of mystery will be lowered a notch or two and brought back into the everyday world. Astonishment, I wish to propose, is for many people part of the everyday occurrences of their lives. It belongs together with facts. The cost of separating it from the everyday is found in senses of special qualities in those people who enjoy astonishment as well as in judgments of decadence regarding those who do not pay much attention to it. By emphasizing the physicality, contingency, and worldliness of astonishment, its "at homeness" with facts, I believe that we can dispense with judgments of privilege and transcendent regions of reality that have traditionally often swarmed around it.

Let's begin again, this time with ears and sounds instead of poets and artists. No matter how intricate and complex the occurrences of hearing are, the waves, intensities, vibrations, amplifications, and cellular transfers in ears do not by themselves compose even one meaning, much less astonishment. Perceptive meaning and astonishment come from elsewhere. But consider the metaphors and allusions that "we" use in speaking of the physiology of hearing. People have "inherited" auditory "equipment" from their aquatic "ancestors." The outer ear is "gathering equipment." The ear as a whole is an "energy transformation system." Composing the ear are canals, drums, tubes, and cavities; ossicles, chains, anvils, stirrups, and mallets; vestibules, windows, rooms, and labyrinths; codes, waves, hydraulic systems, analyzers, envelopes, and even a superior olive—words that mean several different things and that in this application transfer and accrue both ordinary scientific and unscientific meanings. As we learn to speak of the ear's anatomy, we are in a remarkably rich metaphorical field that speaks of the pre-meaning processes of sounding. I will return in a moment to this strange juxtaposition of meanings, metaphors, and processes that appear to be outside of the range of meaning and metaphor.

By means of a package not much larger than a sugar cube, ears hear sounds that are found by transmissions of waves of air pressure, which are transformed into waves of liquid, which in turn produce miniscule movements in tiny hair cells, which excite neurons and bio-electric energy. No meaning yet in that astonishing process. Nor is there meaning as our ears establish a sense of balance and our brains calibrate intensities, coordinate patterns, and match sounds. After all of that and much more happen, a person can hear the sounds and still ask, "What did you say?" Or, "What was that noise?" Or not hear with alertness anything at all.

The facts of ears and auditory functions appear in these words and concepts richly endowed with meaning, fully connected with wide ranges of experiences and established recognitions (e.g., windows, waves, and olives). And in their meaningful appearances a dimension of their occurrence can be discerned that, while meaningfully recognized, considerably exceeds their meaning. Such excess of meaning in the meaningful appearance strikes me as an important component in the astonishing factuality of hearing. An excess with the worldly, textured, and meaningful occurrence and the complex transfers of meanings in metaphorical language altogether compose the factual understanding of hearing. And while people certainly do not need that understanding to hear, the mechanical, metaphorically transforming language that figures their understanding can help in an allowance of sounding's difference from heard meanings. The instrumental, equipmental, and mechanical usage refers meaningfully to dimensions of sounding occurrences that sound outside of the boundaries of meaningful alertness as they are converted to significant perceptions. Heard meanings, in other words, cover over considerably with *meaning* the impersonal, pre-significant goings-on in hearing that our instrumental metaphors call attention to. It's this difference in hearing between meaning and no meaning that facts of physiology bring out and that I find ingredient in the possibility for one kind of astonishment.

To speak of the instrumentality of a loving whisper or of the sounds of Mahler's First Symphony or of the modulations in a subtle suggestion can sharpen our alertness to the completely impersonal, utterly corporeal, and "other" dimension in even our most stirring auditory experiences. This is a dimension that can noisily qualify, like a galactic wind, our sense of familiarity and purpose in our hearing. It can give reticence to feelings of full and encompassing meaning and allow us to "overhear," perhaps, in our understanding of sound the minuscule slosh of salty solution in our inner ears, a solution that came out of the sea with our amphibious predecessors as nothing more (nor less) than a balancing mechanism. Our humanity and meaning stretch only so far in our lives, and the human meanings of sound come through "tunnels," "caves," and "electromagnetic fields" that compose our lives as much as the values by which we make our way in the world.

The metaphorically expressed, culturally evolved, scientifically construed facts of hearing make stark the awesome, impersonal complexity of this tiny organ and set an interpretive stage for experiences of the astonishing occurrence of meanings and all else by which we communicate with sound.

Consider these bits of information about ears. They detect soft sounds that move the eardrum one tenth of the diameter of a molecule and loud sounds that are ten trillion times stronger than that. The balance system that aquatic animals brought with them from the sea to the land remains a vital function in human inner ears. The fluid in the middle ear now transfers degrees of amplified vibration into tiny wave actions, and the mechanical linkage of vibration and waves provides the hydraulic movement that passes on in cellular movements in minuscule hairs that activate neurological responses (bio-electric energy) in the brain. Such highly tuned transferal activity takes place before patterns of sound are available for the brain's decoding and people have something that appears meaningfully. If our ears were more sensitive we could hear the random movements of molecules in the air, a cacophony of sounds that would drastically alter human perceptions and, I assume, our entire orientation in the world as well as our ordinary understanding of it—a continuous sounding without ordered patterns that would constitute a backdrop in the brain's perception of everything it hears and hence in everything that it experiences.

Even without this extreme sensitivity, the patterns and orders of sounds that we hear are nonetheless given randomness with their enormous range of frequencies, intensities, directions, sources, and interspersing silences. When I stop for a moment and listen to all that I can hear, I do not have the impression of an ordered piece of music, even like that of George Gershwin's symphonies of city sounds or of Dmitri Shostakovich's transpositional, atonal string quartets. These sounds that I hear are not authored to hang together nor are they in any sense "written." They do have this ear's location as a site of hearing, and they are ordered only somewhat by the ear's complex limits. But the silences among them and the randomness of their trajectories and frequencies give a fading and ephemeral quality to the limits of hearing what I hear where I happen at the moment to be. In order to hear *something* we "block out" sounds, cock our ears as it were, and add the forces of concentration to the silence-pervaded mess of waves that wafts and sloshes and beeps through our hammers, stirrups, and hydraulic systems to the fringes of our consciousness where they appear in their distinctions.

When I process this physiological dimension of hearing, a dimension of experience that is not heard with immediate explicitness as I hear, I feel a sense of limit in heard meanings, a sense of strange and radical difference in auditory occurrences. I generalize beyond my experiences and feel the marvel of hearing sounding things, of their appearing as they do, of being able to listen—an ability that appears to me all the more striking because of my partial deafness. The "merely" physical facts seem to erase part of their metaphorical composition. They return me to a dimension that is not quite a fact and to the verge of astonishment. Sounding comes with a dimension of "merely there," excessive to meaning, a bluntness of happening that impacts and staggers even its factuality.

Astonishment comes at intervals of familiarity, utter strangeness, and renewed recognition. Indeed, the recognition accompanies the interval and follows itself, as it were, to its own exhaustion, awake to the end as it ceases before something too "dense" for recognition. Astonishment happens as a feeling in this interval. It happens like a high frequency of surprise that stops, turns to itself in its extremity, and in that turning perceives everything within its purview as there, utterly there, and, intervalled and passing, as not having to be.

How, then, might we understand the *appearance* of astonishment?

While I have emphasized up to this point the nonsubjective locale of sounding, its difference from human character, value, and consciousness, its difference that seeps into anatomical interpretations as mechanical metaphors transfer their meanings in an almost absurd composition—a stirrup in the ear and an olive in the brain?! While I have emphasized this general, instrumental nonsubjective, corporeal locale, the physiological site is nonetheless highly individualized by its physical placement. The early stages of hearing occur with all the specific determinations that characterize any other corporeal thing: all the specifics of spatial and temporal location that define particular corporeal events such as, in the case of hearing, humidity that muffles some sounds and enhances others, stillness with a slight breeze from the south that carries sounds from far away, the age of the impacted bones, tissues, and fluids, speed and rhythm of movements in an open clearing, etc. If this dimension is not subjective in the sense that it is not structured by self-conscious activity, it is nonetheless highly individualized in the specificity of its determinations. We might say that what I can hear here and what you can hear there were subjectively determined *if* ears in their physical activity were identified as individual sites that are inclusive of a sounding environment and *if* we interpreted, as I believe we should, their activity as extended to include their environmental sites. But "subjective" would not be exactly right to describe hearing in this dimension. It might rather be characterized as individualizing within a heard, auditory site. I would like to emphasize that the extensiveness in sounding—an individualization of sound—is open-ended. For no matter how individualized, the instrumental goings-on of ears constitute an auditory happening of a physical place or region, not just the murmurings and bangings of a mechanical-hydraulic-electro-dynamic system. An extensive and fairly open auditory environment of airy disturbances happens in the soundings of ears.

When we include spatial siting as an aspect of initial sounding, we will find instrumental and mechanical language, even in its metaphorical and transferring quality, limited in its power of description. Ears hear *in site,* not only on the sides of heads at the tops of human shapes (not on feet, for example. We can imagine the differences of sound if our ears were placed differently on our bodies—one, say, on our right hand and another on our right knee). Ear activity also occurs *with* sites that are *in* the sounds—the frequencies and vibrations in a cave—the soundings of a cave—happen differently from those underwater or on top of a hill. There are uncountable variations in the sounds of sites, and the specifics of such extensiveness in sounds come in the sounds and are not fully recognized if our recognition is circumscribed by instrumental language. Such language pays attention primarily to the ways waves, frequencies, and energy are received, held, and transferred—to what happens "automatically" as hearing. Rudimentary sounding, however, carries out into a site, and a site comes with the sounding. As the facts have it, distance and place sound with and in the vibrations that touch eardrums, remain alive in the liquid waves, and carry through neuro-electric energy. The marvel of it is found not only in the size and working of this little system but also in the ear's entertainment of sites in which a spatial location happens with the complexity of directions, proximities, volumes, ups, downs, and all arounds, none of which are in the ears and all of which sound with them, come to them, and are carried by them.

Ears are thus not just remarkable instrumental events—although they are that too, as I have said, and in their instrumentality, they contribute to occasions of astonishment. They are auditory site events, events of reach that are comprised of the stirrings, air currents, moving, molecular interruptions of other molecular movements, and uncountable "frequencies," none of which ears make on their own and all of which constitute living interconnections in a place. Ears are occasions of site presentation. Ears do not hear themselves. They hear the sounds of motors, of the horn, the screech of tires, the cry of a voice, and the dull thump of two bodies colliding.

But I am close to overstating my point in this respect: in rudimentary sounding, the meanings of the words I have been using do not happen. I was careful to say "*sounds* of motors" and not just "motors," because ears do not, I think, identify that sound as motors. A lot more instrumentality and a much wider and more complex region is needed to bring soundings to worldly meanings, and I expect many layers of meaning are also needed, from mere registration, shift of attention, or "automatic" response (like getting out of the way of something or turning to look at something) to sophisticated discrimination and interpretation. I find this process all the more surprising for its gradations from registration and transfer of frequencies to transfers of inchoate images to meanings and transfers of meanings to other meanings and images. Transfers constitute these processes, and there appears to be no still point from which the transfers proceed or to which they non-transferentially refer: continuous movements and their dissipations, like waves rollicking to a rocky shore, striking the boulders, and ending their miles of coastward movement in passing sounds and spumes of mist shooting upward and carried off by a breeze.

The differences of meaning and non-meaning that the transfers figure in the happening of meaningful sounds strike me as occasions for astonishment. When, as I listen, I pay attention to hearing by means of even elementary facts and when I pay attention to the enormous differences from meanings that compose the full range of a meaningful event, I am astonished. I admit that I do not need a whole lot of mystery to excite astonishment. Mystery is fine when it happens, and if by "mystery" we mean a dimension of occurrences that does not seem to have parts and seems to fall outside of the explanatory power of all the facts that accompany it, then, okay, mystery and astonishment can be friends. But as I think of the fact of astonishment, its quality of attention to events in the full range of their dimensionality, its extraordinary intensity of surprise (sometimes shock) and joy (sometimes anxiety), and its predisposition to behold and not to settle or solve or analyze anything—as I think of its happening, astonishment seems to do well without being connected to any talk about mystery. The problem with "mystery" is found in its history of heavy connotation. The word suggests people's being struck dumb before revelations that they cannot understand except on the basis of special knowledge that comes from the revelations themselves.[1] The word suggests a source that says itself in its event and is lost to all other expressions. Before it we are to keep silent. "Secret," "holy," and "rites" are closely associated with a dimensionality that is not only not subject to sufficient explanation but that also calls out a state of mind that is not looking for explanation. But occurrences of astonishment do not need to be focused by the meaning of "revelation." While many astonished persons are too

---

1. *Mysterium: mystos* (keeping silent) and *mystes* (mute).

surprised to talk during their astonishment, they are not so likely to be predisposed by their experience to think of secrecy and holiness, as they would be if they were within the force and meaning of "mystery." (I have known people who in their astonishment could not stop talking. I experience irritation if I am sharing in those occasions, but I am the silent-astonishment type.)

Astonishment, unlike mystery, also comes with many different intensities. The word is designed in part to name a whole lot of intense surprises, and it applies to events of strong surprise as well as to those that are too startling to call "surprise," and to those of stunned, quiet awe that are too far from surprise to be linked directly to the word. These gradients can have more or less intellectual input, as we have seen, and can move people on a scale from, say, jarred to stunned to rapt attention.

There is also a scale of response to astonishment. For some people take even rapt attention in stride in their lives. They know that such experience is a part of their lives. They live with a continuing sense of it, often. But they do not make a big deal out of it. For other people, however, astonishment can have an enormous impact, especially, I think, on people who are more given to judgmental perception and analytical intelligence than to nonrational occurrences or the meaningless dimensions of events. They (or we) have little practice in dealing with astonishment up close, are not predisposed to expect it to occur (at least to them), and can be inclined to excited exaggeration after an engagement with it—something like seeing a bear up close and in the wild for the first time. I think that this is especially true for people who are usually tied down by the honest confines of this or that rationality, like Rudolf Otto (who wrote *The Idea of the Holy*), whose account of awe I will address in a moment. They (or we) can be shocked right out of our honest rationality, at least for a moment, by a strong encounter of astonishment, and sometimes that shock does come to expression in stories about holy divinities or other big things—glorious things that express the surprising, almost overwhelming exception in their ordinary and ordered lives. But I think that such interpretations can be credited to unfamiliarity with astonishment that is often combined with a need for big justifications for dimensions of ungraspable, non-objective unmeaning in the face of our orders of meaning and that is also combined with a lack of appreciation for astonishment's everyday quality.

For astonishment can happen as a feeling component in people's encounters with the occurrences of meanings, a happening conditioned and made stark by a dimension of no meaning and hence no order of meaning in ordered meanings' very happenings. Hearing sounds in their meaningful specificity and interconnections is astonishing, and all the more so in the absence of any clear necessity that auditory meaning happen at all. I can report that the more intense my astonishment grows, the more I pay attention to hearing things as things, hearing them in their presentation; I am more inclined to pay attention to the happenings of meanings in and with meaningless sounding—sounding where no meaning appears to sound. And that astonishment puts me in a position to encounter things quite differently from the ways in which I encounter them in the ordinary course of instrumental and routine engagements with them.

We do justice to astonishment when we emphasize its perceptive quality. In astonishment or wonder people perceive something not quite perceptible outside of astonishment. For Rudolf Otto, for example, awe composes an experience of what he calls an inexpressible "*mysterium tremendum.*" It comprises an apprehending and apprehensive response to the wholly Other.[2] And for Martin Heidegger, astonishment is perceptive in the sense that the questionableness of being—its non-necessity—appears with astonishment and through it. Aristotle's observation that philosophy begins in wonder suggests that in wonder people perceive "something" about life that they do not grasp or understand, and this event sets them to asking questions and exploring the nature of reality. In such accounts, astonishment is not only a state of mind that arises *because* of specific perceptions. Things occur differently in astonished people's perceptions from the ways they occur in more routine perceptive connections.

Astonishment can also be perceptive in the sense that in it and the rapt attention that goes with it people can sense a dimensionality of ungraspable non-meaning that considerably startles any complacency they might have concerning the dominance of meaning and value in the events of their lives. Astonished people not only perceive differently from when they are not astonished but can also perceive in a manner different from perceiving things in the dominance of their meanings. I can, for example, appreciate the anatomical accounts of ears, enjoy the metaphors in these accounts, and undergo surprise when I learn something new from them. But when I am astonished, I am not simply surprised by *something* new or unusual. I am, in the instances that I have noted, in the midst of an event that calls for neither belief nor skepticism nor analysis nor resolution—not even for elaboration. I am before no meaningful thing at all at the same time that I am with meaningful things. I am before non-meaning in meaning, before fragility and departure of meanings that do not even have the meanings I just invoked to describe them. In such occurrences people can perceive and engage things as the things surpass their meanings when they appear

2. Rudolf Otto, *The Idea of the Holy* (Oxford: Oxford University Press, 1958), chaps. 3–5. While my account of astonishment leads in a very different direction from Otto's account of awe, both descriptions appreciate the perceptive aspect of astonishment and awe.

meaningfully. I will say more about this kind of perceptive occurrence. For now, I note that things seem to shimmer or shine in their differences as they slip out of the dominance of their meanings. And the fact of meaning can appear quite wonderfully—as there and recognizable with no apparent necessity.

The combination in astonishment of the predispositions found in specific knowledges, a culture's consciousness, and an individual's sensuous perception and beliefs, together with the appearing departure of things from meaning and identity in the events of their meaning and identity—I am tempted to say that this combination is astonishing too. When I hear, for example, the cry of a squirrel in the quiet of a late autumn afternoon, shortly after the oak and maple leaves have dropped and when the time is close to early darkness, my experience—which on occasions has been one of astonishment—includes not only my attitudes toward decline and death, most of which I have inherited, and past experiences of mourning but also what I know about death, autumn, and shorter days, what I imagine to be the squirrel's sense of the coming of winter, my own moods at the moment, how I feel generally (whether I am tired or energized, etc.), the events that have recently affected me, whether I am alone or with someone (and the relationship I have with the person or persons I might be with), and, I believe, the state of mind that I share with my culture and species.

One of several experiences of this kind occurred in an afternoon in Connecticut outside of a winterized beach cottage that I had rented for my first year in graduate school—a time of anxiety, anticipation, and exceptional vulnerability. I had been reading with considerable impact Heidegger's *Being and Time* and "The Origin of the Work of Art." I did not recognize the sound that I heard one afternoon and went outside to investigate. There, toward the top of a bare and swaying oak tree, was a squirrel crying—or it sounded to me like a cry, mournfully repeated. As I stood in the chilly air looking up, I smelled the salt air from the sea and heard the waves lapping on the shore. I had been impressed during the previous days by the slate-colored ocean's indifference to human life and value, and that perception had combined with a sense of loneliness that surrounded the cottage in the departure of the area's summer residents and with awareness that I alone had to survive the new rigors of graduate education. My active convictions about a personal, caring God were eroding, and a vague projection of "nature" in the image of mothering that had exercised a considerable pre-reflective power in my life had come to full awareness and lost its force.

At that time, I thought that squirrels hibernated throughout the winter, and that bit of mistaken knowledge led me to think of this squirrel as preparing for a long withdrawal from the world beyond some empty limb or attic. All of that plus my now distant childhood experiences with a pet squirrel and many other associations and bits and pieces of information figured in a moment of perception in which each "thing" that I saw and heard stood out with intense vividness and happened with intervals of empty space and nothing determinate—something not wholly other but quite ordinary, personal and impersonal at once, appearing and simultaneously leaving—like a projection of withdrawal. I was astonished.

That event was, of course, meaningful and significant for me. Had I been astonished in the midst of a battle or while gazing at a painting or in an attitude of reverence—or if someone else had reported seeing and hearing that squirrel in that tree in Connecticut—the experience would have had different meanings and would have been determined in extremely different ways.[3] And if you say that you have been astonished with no sense at all of meaninglessness and no projection of withdrawal in the event, I will believe you. Astonishment can come in the context of many different lives, beliefs, and knowledges, and with many different perceptions, all of which depend on the circumstances of the event. It can happen like the effect of an unexpected clap of thunder or a quiet, intense surprise, but, however it is occasioned, its event exceeds a person's expectations at the moment, comes usually without warning, takes over one's affections, commands attention, surpasses considerably the reach of calculations, is without boredom, and happens exorbitantly with all of the events' meanings and determinations. As I interpret it, included in the fact of astonishment are a person's experiences, things in their own eventfulness, and the very eventfulness of things—the happening of what happens. Neither this experience nor the eventfulness is captured by any of the meanings that take place or by a subjective structure of experience. Astonishment is, as it were, an awareness of an escape from meanings and completed totalities.

The extraordinary quality of astonishment, however, is also ordinary in the sense that it requires no special knowledge or moral accomplishment and takes place with ordinary people in the midst of their ordinary lives. It is ordinary like lightning or shock or the feelings of falling in love are ordinary. It certainly interrupts routine perceptions and expectations and sets its moments apart from the lack of attention that often characterizes people's daily lives. But illnesses, childbirths, car wrecks, intense joy, and extreme danger can also interrupt our rote orders of life. Interruptions of the ordinary are not especially unusual, and I take this fact to mean that "ordinary" in our present context describes an attitude more than it describes frequency or likelihood of occurrence—the attitude of routine

---

3. When I discovered thirty-six years later and after I wrote this account that my current graduate dean now was then, as I looked up at the squirrel, my backdoor neighbor, I was at least on the edge of astonishment. Astonishment in the midst of accidental coincidence would be another topic for consideration.

living. So I am inclined to say that astonishment, which is not contrary to any facts that I am aware of, is in its happening quite at home in factual and ordinary worlds—astonishment is just not "contained" or pinned down by our ordinary, fuzzy recognitions and limited factual designations. It enjoys a surprising freedom with them and from them. That kind of freedom (or excess, if you prefer that word) appears with the happenings of worldly things, although we do not ordinarily notice it. Perhaps it is good that we do not notice such freedom a lot of the time since it is so impractical in its departure from our ordinary expectations as we go about doing what we need to do to survive. But when we undergo astonishment, ordinary orders, limits, and identities can be rattled for a while, and people are then often prone to rearrange some parts of their lives, think again about what they are doing and why, and, when good fortune is having a good day, become less dogmatic about what they ordinarily believe and know.

Astonishment occurs as a physical event. I am emphasizing its physicality and factuality (an emphasis that I will say more about) because I think that this fairly common and important experience has been so spiritualized in interpretations and responses to it, so separated from flesh, liquids, neurological transfers, chemical constitutions and effects, so drained of blood, serotonin, and metabolic juices that you would think that astonishment and wonder were not physical at all. I will carry out in the next two chapters the observation that "physicality" is not circumscribed by what people usually mean by "body" or "flesh," but that "physicality" can indeed rightfully include in its meanings those largely non-conscious processes and organs that constitute our lives and place limits on the range of meaning in our lives. There is no good reason that I can find to respond to astonishment as though it did not occur in skin (and sometimes with goose bumps), pumping hearts, and a reptilian layer of the brain. If we engage astonishment as though it, and we in it, were a "purely" spiritualized state of being, we probably would be operating with assumptions that present astonishment and spirit without corporeality and hence presenting them dangerously. "Dangerously" because people's spirituality is then presented as though it does not bleed or defecate, as though it were not an occurrence of brains and ears, arms and hands and lungs—as though it were not physical. Then it might seem as though nutrition, medicine, means of production, buying and selling, housing, and other influences in and on organic life were not spiritual matters, as though physicality were essentially different from spirituality, as though the "merely" operational parts of our lives were not ingredient in our most moving and inspirational moments. Such assumptions can lead to attitudes that leave bodies to bleed while spirits soar and that divide the things of the world, including ourselves, according to degrees of the "spiritual," with those who are most conspicuous in their spiritual accomplishments at the top. It would seem as though people had to withdraw from physicality to cultivate spirituality, as though the physical constituted a lower form of life than the spiritual. That would be dangerous for people's physical lives.

With these assumptions people could well think that the sub-cortical structures of the brain—the limbic system—were not a defining aspect of astonishment, that the operations of neurotransmitters made no difference *in* the event. Astonishment might seem totally separated from evolutionary formations and from inbred interest in survival and nourishment. One might think that the occurrences of astonishment were not intrinsically dependent as well on agricultural production, functional kidneys, and a culture's history. With such assumptions that hold astonishment apart from these elements, the excessiveness to meaning that comes with astonishment would not seem physical and some people might take comfort in believing that astonishment made available to them *something* without physicality and beyond human meaning, something spiritual that was even higher and loftier than their own spirits. That would constitute a symbolic gesture at the edge and loss of meaning that appears in astonishment—a gesture, I believe, that usually aims to preserve meaning at the border where meaning ceases to have control of appearances. When it is interpreted as though it were not physical, astonishment's meaning figures an event that does not happen within the circumference of the physical world, and, as I shall show in greater detail in the following chapters, the lives of things suffer a demotion in human valuation.

If the meaning of "physical" were circumscribed only by organic functions and their "objective" and instrumental facts, it too would miss dangerously the range that "physical" rightfully can name. We saw in the discussion of ears that sounding happens "extensively." An environment comes to bear in sounds. Ears, I noted, do not just hear themselves. All manner of things, spaces, and dimensions sound. "Physicality," of course, comes from *phusis,* which suggests growth; *phuein,* to bring forth, and *phunai,* to be born. *Ta phusika* refers to growing things that are subject to generation (and hence, decay). (I am avoiding here the words "nature" and "natural" for reasons that I will discuss in the next chapter.) I wish now to underscore a group of meanings in the stem *physic* that will help preliminarily to indicate the extensive meaning that physicality can have, meaning that will define many of the claims in this book. The observations that I will develop in the context of the occurrences of astonishment are that things, in their physicality, are intrinsically and extensively connected with other things and that to understand physical things well we need to consider them in their eventuation, their coming forth, in appearances as well as in their physical "refusal" to appear. In this way I hope to set a broader context for interpreting the physicality of astonishment than the anatomical, chemical, and neurological accounts by themselves can provide. I also wish to indicate a context that continues to proceed along lines that bring us, by way of astonishment, to dimensions of earthly events that are wonderful as well as chemical and neurological operations.

I have noted frequently that everything that constitutes an event composes part of the event's character—its definition. That means that the definition of astonishment *includes* in its happening—astonishment is corporeal in the sense of "is composed by"—mechanical, elemental operations and ingredients. Its definition, in other words, is not found in something that discloses itself from outside of corporeal events as "mystery" in and only in the event (or as mechanical operations, either). That kind of thing—elevation to a mystery or reduction to a mechanism—arrives with beliefs or other types of experiences and may certainly be imported into an experience of astonishment *as* a belief and even asserted as the event's essence: "I beheld the Face of God" or "And before me there was only infinite Mystery, Beyond Being," etc., etc. Some people are even moved to say that the question of being is the "essence" of astonishment. But when we see that astonishment can be described in part by reference to its corporeality and a withdrawal of meaning as well as with reference to all manner of beliefs and values, I expect that, as we describe events of astonishment, whether we are seeing squirrels or mysteries does not compose a central problem. With practiced patience, we will see either dissolve in its import, thanks to astonishment's way of displacing meaning's circumscription of events, and leave us with a perceptive happening that is defined by the way it happens—by *its* life—rather than primarily by the characters in the event.

One of the ways astonishment happens is with interconnections with interconnected things: it happens as a worldly event. Events of astonishment appear, and I will use "physicality" to address ways in which such events appear. I assume that we may describe only appearances and their borders and that in astonishment we find its own appearance as well as that of multiple things. In other parts of this book I write of the density of things in their appearing: of their gravity, for example, in the language of Jean-Luc Nancy, of otherness in the context of Emmanuel Levinas' thought, and of being in the context of Martin Heidegger's work. In these and other instances that I address, the issue is one of finding words and concepts that address in the appearing of things the dimensionality that is neither discursive nor conceptual. In this chapter I have noted in this regard the excess of meaning—the non-meaning—that appears with recognizable sounds, with anatomical language, and with astonishment. I am attempting to make clear *that* such density happens in appearances as well as *how* it happens in astonishment. In this process I find no basis for saying that the one essence of appearances is found in structures and patterns of subjectivity or in those of mechanical, organic operations. Neither the concept of a unified essence nor the idea of one sufficient kind of knowledge suffices to describe what appears.

"Physicality" describes the appearing of things in what I shall call their lightness: in their richly open-ended and meaningful interconnections and in their density that is like a withdrawal of meaning and a limit to meaning.

When a sound appears as something, as the sound of the squirrel's cry, for example, it is figured by all manner of worldly connections. It arose and came to appear in the sounds of the sea close by, in the salty cool air, in the height of the tree over the cabin, in the fall of a year, from a squirrel (and not from an uncountable number of other things, including hippopotamuses), away from a big city. The worldly texture of the event would take pages to describe, and even then the description would be only partial. Although the anatomy of the sounding and the uncountable points of transfer are happening in this arising of the appearance, and although they and my own body of figuring experiences, beliefs, and knowledge contextualize and individualize the event, I am not hearing only myself and the instrumental functions of my ears and brain. I am hearing a physical world of things together in the physical appearing of the sound. In the squirrel's sound a physical event arises. Something aborning comes to pass of which I am a part, something vast in its intricacy of differences, something worldly and vastly excessive with and to my part within it.

Throughout this physical event are many, many meanings, shades of meaning, echoes of meanings, each with cultural histories—meanings lodged in words, practices, predispositions, and institutions. These meanings have no one subject or origin but bring with them in their appearing a bewildering array of trajectories and mutations, patterns made up of other broken and re-stitched patterns, strange fusions of religious and scientific values, and pre-reflective, tacit dimensions of cultural moods and dispositions. Sea, wind, and ground. Cry, autumn, death. Cabin, beach, school. Animal, philosophy, alone. A world of interwoven meanings comes tumbling in with the *phusis,* the bringing forth, of this appearance of this sound.

This sound also brings out and presents unencompassable differences. Meanings seem to lapse before them like waves hitting a breaker on a shore. The "there" quality of things is not simply an "out there." It happens in the extensiveness, in the spatial locations and mechanisms, in the ears, of a sound. People in their physicality happen as and with the sounding extensiveness as well as in and with the welter of meanings. As things appear meaningfully in their interconnections, they constitute in people's events a draw to lapses—to borders where there is a mere density of this presence, a location where they and only they can suffer injury or change or nurturance, a still point of difference in their arising to appear as they happen, richly textured in meanings and yet enowned by *their* occurrences, by the un-replaceable events of their own lives that is neither metaphor nor symbol nor anything other than their happening. There. This life. A limit of difference with everything else. When people note this "still point of difference," they can engage the singularity of things, their immense vulnerability, their lives beyond the meanings that situate them in multiple ways in the experienced world. I take this to be a fact.

"Physicality" describes and names, then, the appearing of things that, by appearing, are things of the world and, in their appearing, surpass the compass of meanings that composes them. "Physicality" further describes the occurrence of appearing in reference to organic functions, such as those of ears and brains, which also happen beyond the compass of meanings and in the "arising" of things. There is in appearances a strange and, when I think about it, surprising silence with these organic functions—the silence of location and of all of the nonvoluntary signals that keep the ears and other organs doing what they do, the silence of the metabolic and neuro- logical network that makes the stomach and intestines second only to the brain as a center of transfer and initiation. You might list a hundred other "silences" in our physicality that affect and effect the appearing of what ap- pears. I collect them together by identifying them in a dimension of silence, constitutive and nonvoluntary, in the appearing of squirrels and gods and everything else that composes the human world. These silences appear indi- rectly—like gravity, for example, appears as something falls to the ground. They are not obviously apparent but, in their appearances, compose set- tings, moodal tones, flows, networks, functions, movements, ingredients, vibrations, divisions, economies of energy that give physical vitality, join- ture, and senses of organizational unity. These unobvious "things" are hid- den in their appearances unless the occurrences of appearances appear by means of specific investigation, analysis, and discourse. They comprise a nonhuman dimension in the sense that silent functions are not necessarily dependent in their occurrences on human meaning. But they nonetheless compose and limit, largely silently and not altogether humanly, events of appearing.

In this context, "physicality" names the occurring of at once richly and historically textured meanings, density that lightly surpasses meaning, and organic functioning in the appearing of whatever appears. Since the word connotes birth and bringing forth, growth and passage, it allows me to address the corporeality of coming to presence in appearing without suggesting a reduction to either essence or matter. The eventuation of appearing happens physically, i.e., historically, meaningfully, densely (non- meaningfully) and with organic functions. My reasons for using this word with these connotations are to emphasize the nonreducible differentiations in appearing and, in this chapter, to emphasize the physicality of astonishment. With these emphases I am able to appreciate the worldly and "mechanical" aspects of astonishment in its power to let things stand out in their own meanings, density, and non-meaning. They, in their happening as they come forth, happen physically and thus with their meanings surpassing their non-meaning and their non-meaning surpassing their meanings. Their continuing and relatively stable aspects are at once broken and destabilized by differences within their presencing. "Surpassing" in this context does not suggest another region of reality. It suggests constitutive differences and relations in the *phusis* of things. The "thereness" of appearing things happens as they appear together in nonreducible fissures of differences.

Astonishment thus holds people in the strangeness of their places with things in the startlingly fragmentary and elusive character of a given world of reference. Things happen *there* with specificities that lack one defining essence. In astonishment the world is open with incompleteness and differentiation as things appear, never to be fully seized, always at once dense and resonant with passing life.

TWO

What's the Matter with "Nature"?

It could be like that then the beloved
old dog finding it harder and harder
to breathe and understanding but coming
to ask whether there is something that can be done about it coming again to
ask and then standing there without asking.

          —W. S. Merwin, "The Name of the Air"

I find myself ambiguously drawn by statements like Henry Beston's in *The Outermost House:*

> When the Pleiades and the wind in the grass are no longer a part of the human spirit, a part of the very flesh and bone, man becomes, as it were, a kind of cosmic outlaw, having neither the completeness and integrity of the animal nor the birthright of a true humanity. [By the sea] . . . the great rhythms of nature, today so dully disregarded, wounded even, have here their spacious and primeval liberty; cloud and shadow of cloud, wind and tide, tremor of night and day. Journeying birds alight here and fly away again all unseen. . . .
>
> The fortnight ending, I lingered on, and as the year lengthened into autumn, the beauty and mystery of this earth and outer sea so possessed and held me that I could not go. The world today is sick to its blood for lack of elemental things . . . the flux and reflux of ocean, the incoming of the waves, the gatherings of birds, the pilgrimages of the peoples of the sea, winter storm.[1]

In this draw I gravitate beyond statements and texts toward palpable things and their impalpable, appearing aspects, to the rhythms, birds, tides, and storms of which Beston speaks, as well as of things about which he does not speak, such as withdrawal from appearing, density in appearing, and nonmeaning with meaning. You saw evidence of this draw in the last

---

1. Henry Beston, *The Outermost House* (New York: Henry Holt and Co., 1977; first published in 1928), pp. xxxv–10.

chapter as I addressed "sounding," which I could not speak or read, in an attitude of astonishment. The differential distance of the unappropriable quality of events in their volatile presence with us plays a significant role in that attitude. This "else-than" quality is like a dimension of appearing things—one that is often "disregarded, wounded even"—but one that is an intrinsic part of people's lives. The extensiveness of sounding, I said, manifests a kind of openness in the world that the language of simple mechanisms or of perceiving subjectivity cannot adequately handle. I mean by that observation that "our flesh and bone" are involved and interconnected with events that are so much themselves as to constitute unsurpassable boundaries in people's flesh and blood—something like the gravitational draw of a weighty body in a shared space. I have felt drawn to what Beston calls the integrity of an animal and the spacious and primeval rhythms of nature, integrity, and rhythms that inhabit and compose our own living events and that outstrip the tropes and images that address them and call attention to them.

"Nature," however, appears to have meanings in which a disregard and wounding of the primeval dimension happen. I have in mind a degree of abstraction and subjectification, perhaps inevitable abstraction and subjectification, which takes place with the word's meanings. The issue is not that abstraction and subjectification inevitably happen as we name things or write and speak of them—that is surely the case. The issue, rather, is that while "nature" might intend the concrete and shared specificity of things and organizations of things in *their* occurrences, the meanings of "nature" also include a broad experience of drawing away from the concrete specificity of things and their happenings. The word's meanings often draw us to an abstracting process rather than to the lives of things in their nondiscursive, dynamic interactions. I do not mean that our use of "nature" always does that. The word is often used with the opposite intention, and I will elaborate that point with appreciation in this chapter. But a main current of intention runs in the word's meaning that draws our attention away from living situations, away from their lives, and that powerful cross-purpose is what is wrong with "nature": it often signifies a kind of subjectivity as well as a seemingly timeless coherence and continuity, a purposive process that manifests something either whole or striving for wholeness, a process that has completion in, as it were, mind. Or it can signify something systematically comprehensible; something with a definitive beginning that is compatible with intelligent observations and articulation.

The broad philosophical tradition in which I usually work, phenomenology, is not immune to this cross-purpose in spite of its emphasis on the specificity of occurrences and its struggle to depart from such traditional abstractions as mind-matter and subject-object. The phenomenological attention to appearances and disclosures and the enlargement of this attention to systems of signs, to behavior instead of transcendental consciousness, to the incompleteness, elusiveness, and elliptical quality of texts, the strange, alluring eventuation of non-presence—this emphasis in the phenomenological tradition that gives primary attention to ways things happen nonetheless frequently turns away from dimensions that are without meaning, text, or utterance in the occurrences of things. There is "something" non-phenomenological, "something" without appearance or disclosure or sign that accompanies appearances, disclosures, and signs and that happens in lives. Or at least words like "appearance," "disclosure," and "sign" do not quite address the "else-than" of dynamic events. Have you ever been in a current of water or a wind so powerful that there was nothing you could do but go helter-skelter with it? Have you felt space so vast or so minuscule that all you felt was noncomprehension? Radical transformation? Loss of orientation and all sense of order? Death?

I refer to these ordinary, if radical, experiences in which recognition, meaning, and textuality are exceeded and occasionally demolished—traumas of the gut for many of us—to indicate weighty events for which "appearance" or "sign" will not do. Sometimes in reference to such things we say "wild" or "mystical" or "horror." But the larger observation that I want to underscore is that the dimensions that they make stark never leave us; they are the dimensions that "nature," in spite of its good intentions, often loses track of or obscures by recognitions.

The word "nature," which has the root *nasci,* to be born, to give birth to, to originate, should be a fine word. It suggests birth and begetting, kinship and commonality, a gift of being the ways we are. It also suggests something like a birthright or inevitability in our being as well as in the ways all other things are. It *could* mean no more than the ways in which we and things come to be in the makeup of our lives. "Nature" also has the ability to name very general conditions, not just mutable structures and dispositions but ones that are permanent as far as individual lives go. And it has the disadvantage of getting locked into a frame of mind that links together permanence, coherence, *uni*versality, *uni*verse, and inevitability and that attaches poor "nature" to the value of "unchanging." It would be different if we thought of "nature" as naming commonalities that are for all practical purposes permanent for us now, for *us* and our environments that have been like we and they are for a considerable stretch of time and that will likely be this way long after we specific individuals are gone. But the meaning of identity as such can look fragile when the commonalities that define us as "we humans" and that make other lives around us recognizable in a recognizable whole are known as impermanent, as phases in an "unwhole" without identity. A "whole" and "its" parts that are mutable and passing organizations? Nature not permanent in its essence? I believe that many people do indeed accept as reasonable the observation that all things change, but somewhere deep inside our feelings (as well as in the traditional intentions of "nature") many of us nonetheless assume and perhaps need to assume that in our commonalities something persists timelessly and that that "something" is tied to "nature." This meaning of persistent timelessness, unity, purpose, and coherence that attaches to "nature" detaches "nature" in a strange way from astonishing, singular, ordinary, and unspeakable events.

I do not mean to say that detachment like that is caused primarily by the meaning of the word. But I do want to point out that "nature" has a complex ambiguity among its several meanings that allows people to mean by its use that the "real" essence of things is neither physical nor a thing, that when the meaning of nature is either explicitly or subliminally associated with images and meanings of subjectivity, coherent intention, rationality, or timeless constancy, that meaning directs people away from a severity of difference from the meaning that composes physical events.

The Latin *natura,* like "nature," however, *can* mean simply the defining way in which some things happen. In that case, *natura* or "nature" can place emphasis on the thing's happening—"it's its nature to grow tall," for example—and place emphasis on what some philosophers call a thing's immanent cause, not on factors that act on it externally. I have already noted that a thing's happening—its physical eventuation—includes in its "immanence" uncountable historical and worldly aspects, that such happening *is* extensive *in* its event and not at all a thing alone in its immanence.[2] But even granting this considerable difference in claims, this first sense of nature puts the spotlight on things' own dispositions and leaves out any decision about a "higher" essence of things.

"Nature," in its linkage to *natura,* can also name the originary aspects of something—that it was born, for example, and not made by manual production: natural and not artifactual, or natural and not artificial. But the word can go considerably beyond such limited meaning. It can name the power of life (e.g., "the nature of being" or even the being of all things) as well as a way of life. It can name the identifying form (the nature of humanity) as well as animation and movement (a natural rhythm). And it can bring together animation and form by the image of a principle of animation—the law of life, for example. So "nature" can suggest with varying degrees of emphasis bringing to birth, having been born, identity, manner of production, growth, and manner of growth.

The size and inclusiveness of nature has been a subject of considerable speculation among people in the West. Many Stoics thought of "nature,"

---

2. See chapter 8 for an account of several interpretations of immanence in our philosophical tradition.

for example, as an all-inclusive term. Everything—all infinite things and all finite things—are in the system of nature. Once we figure out how that system works, we will have a good handle on the limits, possibilities, and proper placement of all lives. In this context anything that opposes the natural would be a contradiction to its own life and would be unspeakably perverted. On the other hand, such all-inclusiveness suggests strongly that all differential aspects and different natures—the differences among humans, the heavens, giraffes, and gods, for example—share a primordial, systematically interconnected commonality. If not one big happy family, at least all living things enjoy a universal community with a basis for establishing appropriate, worldwide regulation for actions, ranks, laws, and procedures. And once we find out what kind of people are the natural leaders, find out how to educate them so that they want to obey and know how to obey the natural laws, and give them the power of governance, we will have things pretty well set up for a good life. Until then, exceptional individuals will have to satisfy themselves by ordering their own lives according to nature as best they can.

In our tradition many thinkers have had "nature" doing things, mostly creating, which strikes me as artistic and interesting, and sustaining what it creates, which is, as I see it, the more onerous job of management and one that is often left to creatures to take care of within strict guidelines. In its divine, creative, continuously sustaining functions, "nature" becomes "Nature" and does what Nature does best, which is Naturing: Nature does its thing and Natures. And created beings do the best they can by way of naturing in their finitude and carry forth naturally, if limitedly, as creatures. The extent to which God is in nature, is Nature, or dwells outside of it has been from time to time a big issue. I will avoid that controversy, however, and note that when Nature is viewed as self-enacting, regardless of its connection to divinity, it behaves to some degree like a defining subject, and in that case we would need to pay a lot of attention to Nature to find out about physical things. That's part of what I mean when I say that in many interpretations of "nature," things are detached from their own astonishing, singular, and unspeakable events: we interpret *them* by reference to something that they in their singularity are not, or are only a subsidiary part of. In that case we often know things best when we look away from them to something that is their "essence."

That's not, however, the full story of their detachment. In the last two paragraphs, I did not mention any uses of *phusis* in Greek. Translators frequently use "nature" to transfer the Greek meanings for *phusis* into English. My reservations about these translations have something to do with the history of the detachment that I am addressing. I do not mean that translating *phusis* as "nature" is inaccurate. *Phusis* and "nature" share senses of birth, animation, and inborn qualities in things. But *phusis* has the advantage of lacking some of the interpretive historical formation of "nature" in Western culture, and so I would like to highlight its meaning for the strategic purpose of avoiding some of the meanings that almost inevitably attach to "nature" and its history of detachment from the singular complexity of living things (in spite of intentions to the contrary).

One of those meanings is wholeness. By emphasizing the meaning of *phusis* as the springing up of individual things, I can at least hold at bay a further move to an image of a whole process that provides a definitive origin and a definitive end for things and that thus defines them. I have no doubt that things begin and end and that their manners of being are describable in many ways. But I doubt that the idea and image of a whole of all things will help us in our descriptions. Such an image can give us a feeling, if not of definitive completion, then at least one of potential definitive completion. This imagery is one of the things that is wrong with some of the suggestions in traditional uses of "nature." But if we valorize *phusis* as meaning a thing's coming to be and persisting for a while as the thing that it is, a meaning primary for *phusis,* we need not make the enormous jump to a definitive and unifying whole of all things. We then leave open the possibility that *phusis* is not any particular thing and that it does not have a "nature."

Another meaning that is closely associated with wholeness, and one that we might avoid, is the unitary nature of life. *Phusis* can suggest origin in the sense of coming to be and rising up in living—that astonishing happening of something's coming to life and continuing to live, as though the thing were imbued with an inner fire that rises up out of mere inertia and nonbeing and occurs as an animated being, a real event. *This* real event! The one that makes *this* difference, here, now! *Phusis!* While we may well wish to speak of various contexts in which things occur with interconnected significance, nothing needs to be said about unity beyond the temporal and situated event of the thing's happening and continuing to happen. It's not that *phusis* provides unity or is itself unified and shares its unity with things. It's rather that in being what it is, *a* thing is *this* event and not any of the other events. And we stop there. No speculative explanations, no ultimate structure, no subtraction of "attributes" to reach a general defining "essence," no thought of some "higher" nature. The issue is not one of making another ontological claim. It is rather one of a different discipline in thinking in which people direct their attention primarily to the happenings of things in their multiple and interconnected aspects and do not look above or below them or add or subtract qualities to find out what they are or mean.

It's hard to stop like that, short of further narratives or unifying additions. I think it's hard because it leaves so much outside of our interpretive and cognitive grasp. And that's the point: so much of what happens in lives and singularities is beyond our grasp. Even when we connect with living occurrences imaginatively or mathematically, so much of what happens remains in its eventuation different from all the interesting, imaginative, and systematic activity that produces lively images and concepts in its regard. The thing is there, real and exposed, not only a perception or an object of perception, but appearing physically—lively and, as long as it's there, seeming to start up continuously, persisting—something that can draw, obstruct, perhaps sound, float, sink, or cut, what *ever,* for now. It might well be the case that mortal time has been a source of major and defining anxiety in Western culture, but I expect that another source of anxiety has to do with physical happenings that seldom arrive with explanations or meanings greater than their events. They arrive singularly and with an immense complexity of interconnections without systematic completion or unity—those happenings have composed an anxious quandary in the gut of Western experience as people have applied all manner of narratives to the occurrences in and of their lives. Many of these narratives are indeed wonderful and illuminating in themselves, spelling out mathematical systems, magnificent origins with human-like or very un-human agencies, presenting histories of people's experiences with boredom, terror, need for recognition and order on a people's scale, senses of mystery, and desires for dominance or cosmic influence. But these applications, frequently in the structure of "nature's" meaning, have left underattended things with their powerful ignorance of meanings. They have formed human beings who are more attentive to their imaginative abstractions than to the other occurrences in their lives. The trouble with "nature" is consequently that some of its meanings smudge and even deny this dimension of physical occurrences. Rhythms in environments without a greater whole, hard events without much to support them but other hard events, radical transitions without a greater unity except that of post-transition perspectives, losses without restorations, enchantments that fade and pass away, meanings in our lives that find resonance only in the living of our lives: such physical things challenge the circumscriptive package of "nature" when it suggests a unified whole that infuses and provides definitive limits for everything all of the time. I doubt that "nature" can be used constructively without invoking in us the powerful, affective history of desire, far from voluntary in many societies, for such definitive wholeness, unity, and purpose in life "as such."

When people think of physical events as self-enclosed units, hardly porous, or as organisms that contain their own "principles" and resources for persistence and growth, they often have an image that is similar to that of a mini-*uni*verse, a reasonably self-contained unity of processes. I believe that the "uni-image," that of one or oneness, is part of the problem. It's as though "one" were a self-subsisting unit, in no sense not "one" even when it connects with other units and forms relations; in its relations, we might say, a unit is not two or three, etc., and that this "not" that preserves singularity somehow resides in "one." *Phusis,* however, need not name any one thing and need not suggest unity in living occurrences. Rather, it can name a thing's coming to be, its continuing animation and becoming. *Phusis* may name only the coming to persisting life of what happens, and what happens, in its physicality, may be experienced as not exactly a unit or not a unit but as different from what "unit" and "uni" generally suggest. At best, when *phusis* is considered, people stop counting and do not begin to count for a while, for physical events are not like units, singly or collectively, are said to be. Or at least that's the way physical events seem to me. They are interactive happenings, porous and mutable, and I would like to find the words and phrases that lend support to those strands of our culture that seek to encounter things in their happenings. Happenings in this context take us in our recognitions of them beyond our recognitions of them to their own occurrences. They confirm a perhaps indelible sense that we are in open-ended worlds that are not ours. They are events whose lives are not graspable, that belong to no one, that are careless of us, and that inspire us implacably even when we run from them or seek shelter from their terrors.

I will say in following chapters more about the dimensions of meaning in *phusis* that appear to us foreign in a context of "nature's" meanings. For now I will accept the possibility that there is a considerable gap between the limits that *phusis* can place in our thought and the range of narration that often comes with "nature." A compelling account can be given, I am sure, that shows that through a history of translation and interpretation *phusis* came to be linked to a broad Western understanding of nature. But I would like to highlight a considerable distance between the two words' suggestions in order to give attention to a very different predisposition (from that instigated by "nature"), one that also composes our inherited ways of experiencing things. That difference is one between an inclination toward abstract, theoretical, mythical, or mystical completion of things by reference to "nature" and another toward open engagements that are oriented by historically and socially formed events that have a palpable dimension of occurrence that "is" without meaning, intelligibility, or narrativity.

Jean-Paul Sartre articulated one broad experience of such exposure when he described the sense of nausea that he felt before what he termed (ill-advisedly, I believe) the sheer in-itself quality of things. That is something like an experience of a border of consciousness at which nothing conscious happens in a thing's presence to consciousness. Many other people have spoken of a stark boredom that occupies human consciousness at this level of "mere" existence. If my account of astonishment in the last chapter is persuasive for you, you will agree with me that such experiences of nausea and boredom are not "ontologically" necessary any more than depression is. The problem with Sartre's description of nausea, and with others similar to his, is that he experiences things so much in terms of conscious autonomy and of consciousness' opposition to anything that is not conscious that he finds the borders of difference to constitute negation and something like death. In technical words, he did not experience consciousness as being-in-the-world, and thus he could not experience the world except by reference to a relatively isolated subjectivity. As he finds the limits of conscious intention and reflection, the world "there" loses a sense of living event, and he apparently has no feeling of kinship in the sheer physicality of things. Outside of consciousness, things go flat, nonresonant, rather like a succubus effect that takes away the very breath of life.

There are, however, options to this kind of experience, options that are not anthropological reductions of things to human dimensions. I am thinking of events of rapt attention, recurrent surprise, appreciation, beauty, senses of rejuvenation and beginning, as well as those of terror, limitation, and mere difference, none of which requires certainty, prediction, or completion in their recognition. Such experiences point us toward a body of possible expectations quite different from those that are engendered by fixations on human uniqueness and privilege in the cosmos, priority of subjective enactment, rational explanation, human intention, or extraterrestrial meaning and guidance.

When we have a "*phusis* sensibility," one without expectations for any kind of holistic determination or teleology, one that is not governed by a prioritized kind of being or a unifying theoretical authority, we can find ourselves in a region of predisposition that is quite different from those that produce "nature." It is a sensibility in which "determination" does not necessarily mean "definition," one, indeed, in which definitions often open to engagements that are as incompletely defined as they are ordinary. This body of predispositions will not, I think, produce the senses of complete human difference that are ingredient in desires for holistic meaning or human privilege in some experience of "nature." Nor will it produce the consequent deep and nonvoluntary disappointment, sense of threat, or feelings of isolation that can spin off of those inbred senses and desires concerning human privilege and cosmic significance. If people do not experience a deficiency of energy in their neurotransmitting activity and if they are not otherwise oppressed, why would they be bored and not enlivened by the lively occurrences in their environments? Are we moved in those instances by dispositions that require lively stories of "natural" meanings and purposes to make things appear genuinely lively and life-enhancing for people?

My hope is that as we focus on the differences from "nature" that we find in *phusis* we will be more attuned to the singularities of things and their unspeakable differences as we recognize and attend to them. This composes a strategy that might also enable us to call into question a group of intentions that have invested "nature" with lively, experience-forming predispositions and that at the same time obscure some of the processes that they attempt to make clear.

Consider the following broad sensibilities concerning "nature."

There is, some people feel, something perpetually disappointing about "nature." On good days, we go, if not to her then to it, with such expectations! Expectations of beauty, resonance in "nature" with at least a few of our deepest values, frequently with expectations for religious inspiration, with a vague sense that either God or "His" hand is there or was there or is Himself or Itself "Nature," and more often than not with expectations for a whole, living order of systematic connections, a *uni*-verse. "Nature" *means* a lot in such a serious, imaginative, and mythical world. The fecundity of earth and sea, the vulnerability of the land, the splendor of sunrises and sunsets and wide and starry nights in their awesome precision can send even scientifically dried and cured minds into spasms of religious and theological vitality. But in the face of our images, cries, and meanings, "nature" is also confusing. "*It*" is supposed to mean a lot but all the energy for inspiration seems to come from us. *We* are attentive. *We* give our accounts. *We* find the metaphors that carry "natural" things over to human likeness. *We* provide the names. (Maybe, just maybe, Nature shows Itself in our "We." Maybe Nature is most self-revelatory and incarnate in human creativity. Maybe we can understand "Nature" by understanding ourselves! Let's call this an ancient dream, not entirely mistaken but inherently disappointing.)

But the waves roll on and the flies continue to swarm, and when people's energy flags the twinkling stars are just mere interruptions in the non-responsive night. When we mourn, "nature" can turn flat, and frequently, as people die, "nature" doesn't mean much. It's all a matter of the energy with which we meet "nature," greet the day, create our stories, compose our calculations, and engender what we call spirit. But in spite of our goodwill and effort—I believe that Sartre was right in this observation—"nature" leaks and loses on the sides and at the bottom of its meanings all signs of value, spirit, and resonance. With "nature" we confront human culture and our personal enactments of it along with something else that appears to withdraw from our meanings. "Nature" in our lineage often appears to stand over and against us in our joinings with it, not to mean what it seems to mean, to promise and not to promise at the same time, to show something like divinity and not to show it, to give unity and to take it away in tumults of lives and forms, to give us to be creators, and not to care at all about our creations.

In some of these thoughts and images, "Nature" appears with an implicit call to self-sacrifice: "Nature" seems in its promise to require that people give up themselves and sacrifice their self-centered interests in order to hear the "foreign" in themselves, as though proper resonance with "Nature itself" demands a sacrifice of the small and mortal familiarities of selfhood. That demand appears to be an effect of the hidden, deathless, nonhuman foreignness of "Nature," and human selfhood appears to be (or almost to be) an embodiment of meanings that "Nature" both sustains and obliterates. "Nature," in this sensibility, appears to constitute unreconciled tensions between determined and accountable human inaugurative production and energy beyond any appearance, between the "spiritual" work of people that makes "It" meaningful and a mere absence of human "spirit" in "Nature's" animation. To put this thought most provisionally and in "natural" terms, "Nature's" life does not long sustain "Nature's" forms. In different terms, "Nature" appears as a crafted work that signifies or symbolizes crafted, nonhuman work. Even if the human spirit's work is like "Nature's" animation, people sometimes feel that the difference between them is so huge that human spirit faces the necessity of concealing its own mortal power to allow "Nature" to appear in its awesome dimension.

In its self-sameness, its "secret," "Nature" requires the human agency of creating and crafting to "deny" itself or at least to adopt a very humble attitude toward those very activities that seem to be like "Nature's" productivity. "Nature," in this case, spins itself out in a drawing-repelling likeness to human spirit, almost like a vacuum that takes and disperses all air that approaches it, gives spirit to evacuate itself, empty itself, give itself up before its infinite difference, its immortal ken. "Nature" continuously removes itself from specificity, inspiring self-removal on the part of people who would be conscious with "It." Self-removal and "Nature's" withdrawal from adequacy of presentation sometimes appear to be strongly coordinated, as though people were "naturally" made for self-renunciation. Their very own-ness and singularity, themselves works of spirit, pose the sites of people's suffering their inadequacy of being partial before an absolute Source that breathes life into them. This composes the site for a very heavy work.

In such sensibility, "Nature," this most worldly production, appears to be a non-worldly force that is most manifest by means of sacrifice. "Nature" and people stand at once together and apart. "Nature" appears to express itself in transcendence of human effort, and only if people turn away from the absorbing pull of living things and their own interests can they follow in the wake of this transcendence. "Nature" appears as though it were a self-sustaining organism with secret purposes that are hidden from all but a self-transcending few: it appears as though people must transcend themselves to be in tune with it. "Nature" thus appears as immanent transcendence, and "Nature-attuned" artists or teachers appear as special self-sacrificers who bring to expression transcendent truth, like the Pythagorean seers, like those, in Hölderlin's phrase, who bring to word the fire from heaven.

But "Nature" in this configuration disappoints. While union with it presumably burns out the merely human, gives people to suffer, empties out mortal creative energy by its own force, consumes and returns no thanks to its worshipers, people in the bonds of such sensibility often do marvelous, creative work. They seem inspired as they write and paint and think and generally find considerable, if agonized, self-expression in their times and locations. They embody this sacrifice to "Nature" in their day-to-day lives and assume roles as prophets and saints of a "natural" religiousness. (Sir Laurence Olivier reportedly suggested to Dustin Hoffman, who was incorporating into his off-set lifestyle the agony and pain of a part he was playing, "Dear boy, why don't you consider acting your part instead of suffering it?") It seems that there can be an impressive payoff if you are talented in this sensibility and given to certain myths. That is, the self-sacrifice appears to boomerang into successful self-expression—maintaining the illusion of sacrificing one's self to "Nature," in such instances, strikes me as requiring a good bit of dissembling energy and a will not to see. (But I write in quite a different sensibility.)

Setting aside my skepticism, however, on this view, "Nature" gives a completion to the sacrifices of its most dedicated creators: to be near it is to lose oneself in a transcendent work; to commune with it is like poetizing one's struggle and silence before it. In such experiences of "Nature" people can truly revere it only by debasing themselves, thereby receiving a wise peace of mind that comes with self-sacrificial self-transcendence in "Nature's" animation. Perhaps more than a dash of a tradition that values self-sacrifice before the sacred has been added to "Nature" in such experiences.[3] In the face of "Nature" we can seem to go away from it, confirm ourselves dumbly in an ecstasy of "unnatural" secular production, lose all

---

3. An emphasis on self-sacrifice (to open to the holy, the *sacre*, by giving up self-interest) in this context appears strange when a person experiences relief from the force of self-sacrificial values. I overhear in these values an ancient sense that gods suffer ill the successes and presumptions of humans, suffer, if not with jealousy, certainly with sacred anger human efforts to make their own worlds without attention to divine interests. I also overhear in them the sense that by getting ourselves out of the way we can find a clearing where "the" divine or something like divinity can manifest itself, i.e., "Nature" in all of its splendor. Perhaps "Nature" has brought with it, in these instances, the power of metaphors to engender mere difference vis-à-vis something missing but addressed in the metaphors, mere absence of connection in the midst of metaphorical connections. And perhaps some people have felt compelled to debase them*selves* in useless efforts to overcome the trope of difference that happens as "Nature" functions metaphorically. A felt imperative toward self-sacrifice in "Nature's" metaphorical displacement of firm, nondiscursive grounds? Let's see if there are other options.

sense of the "natural," and calculate ourselves to death in human fabrications. A sharp distinction can be drawn between "Nature" and fabrication, as though human production were not "Natural," as though human making were fundamentally different from "Natural" growth and movement: "Nature," after all, creates life. People only create things. This turn of mind is also informed by a sense that human effort without a good bit of *self*-sacrifice falls short of something like "Natural" purpose and beauty. In this sensibility people who merely produce often appear to be over and against "Nature" and to be corrupters of what is truly "Natural."

Can you imagine what a "naturalist" would say if people could fabricate continental drifts and cause huge layers of subterranean mass to push up shores, fields, and forests into mounds of dirt and rock half a mile high and hundreds of miles in length? Or if people could cause glaciers to grow and change the climate over entire continents? Unnatural fabrications! Technology most foul! But when such processes happen "Naturally" people often judge them to be awe-inspiring and in some sense appropriate for the earth.

People frequently have created powerful images that at once place them at a focal point of "Nature's" meaning and also displace them from that point. Sometimes, for example, people imagine that their kinds were at one time at peace with "Nature" but somehow, by their own ways of doing things, lost that peace and now must suffer if such a union is to be even momentarily restored. (O the poverty of the modern world! O the destitution of those separated from "Nature"! As though certain meanings in "Nature" did not require the separation, the destitution, and the horrified satisfaction of recognizing them.)

Perhaps the meanings of *phusis* could eventuate without a sense of "Natural" belonging, shared "Nature," fall from "Nature," unified "Nature" or a sacrificial return to "Nature." Perhaps physicality can appear without secret or sacrifice. Perhaps such absence of Natural sacredness is part of what is astonishing in the world's happening. And perhaps an image of unity in "Nature" is part of the problem that I need to address.

The ancient Greek *ta panta* is often translated as "universe." *Pan* can suggest "whole," but the word leans in the direction of "all things," "everything that is." The move is a big one from all things to *uni*—"one," "whole," or "entire"—and verse—from *versus* and *vertere* which mean "turned," "turned toward," and "to turn." For the word "universe" suggests a unified turning movement toward unity, a movement that composes a unified entity of multiple parts. "All things" can certainly be interpreted as a "universe," but like *phusis, ta panta* does not necessarily suggest its dominant Western interpretation and translation. When we talk about all things or even about the being of whatever is, we are not, on the basis of the words, necessarily talking about a whole entity comprised of diversified movements toward unity. The dominance of unity and organic, systematic wholeness occurred as a way of reading *ta panta* and *phusis* and as a way of making sense of the bewildering diversity of movements and things in the world. But it's a way of making sense at the cost of an unfortunate detachment from both things and their bewildering withdrawal from human sense. If a person is not bewildered in his or her familiarity and bearing with the huge variety and dispersion of things, that person is probably not in touch with things in their own irreducible occurrences. I know of nothing more helpful than theories and senses of unity to aid people in getting settled about where they are and who they are. I personally would not want to live without them. But to assume that they have a special truth beyond their pragmatic (and crucial) functions in producing a familiar world is like confusing a map with the mapped things. Maps can guide us for good or ill, but they never compose the things or the terrain that we fall into, bump up against, or turn around in twice and get lost. Our theoretical ability is something like a bat's sonar or a shark's nose: it guides us, sometimes, to where we want to go and helps us to avoid what we find dangerous. But it would be a pitiful bat that concluded that its ability to zero in on mosquitoes and avoid trees showed at the same time that the unified nature of the world is revealed or at least best exemplified in the functions of sonar equipment.[4]

A universalizing move that projects our theoretical inclinations into "Nature," especially our inclination toward unifying perceptions and thoughts, appears to me to be without justification before the severe, nontheoretical differences of lives and multiple organizations that we encounter in our world. There are surely kinships everywhere, but there are also differences, even in kinships, that hold open the limits of both kinship and human engagement to what is other to kin and on the border of engagements. Such differences hold open the limits of images of unity to mere diversity and hold open the limits of meaning to absence of meaning. Such radicality of difference, in its sublimity of holding open, appears to me to characterize physicality and to require in its attunement a kind of discourse that moves away from many of the values that traditionally ascribe unity to "nature."

---

4. I imagine that the convinced naturalists in the bat population would click their tongues over the artificially produced sonar machines on boats and submarines. In the first place, biological sonar is natural and right. In the second place, sonar equipment is supposed to fly and is unnatural for water, especially for movement underneath water—although the bat naturalists might nonetheless approve of whales and dolphins as inferior creatures who naturally lack the ability to fly but who, in their sonar capacities, do point at least indirectly toward the superiority of bats and show a unified movement upward. I will not speculate on what a religious bat might think.

John Sallis' interpretations of Plato's *Timaeus* take a different turn from those controlled by traditional ideas about "nature" and origin.[5] The dialogue composes, he says, first a turn from *phusis* to discourse regarding *phusis*, a new beginning with regard for the natality, the originary quality, of *phusis*. This dialogue begins as a return, a movement back to *phusis*, but a movement that in its beginning and returning seems to have a center, a movement of springing forth that is rather more like a rotation or revolution than like a beeline. *Phusis*, in other words, seems to be at play in the discursive turn to it, but as we shall see, it's not like a fixed center or a defining entity. It's more like *chora*, whatever that will prove to mean. For now I wish to emphasize that originary movement is at the front and center of our attention, and the moving thought of movement is valorized by turning back, in a strategy of beginning, toward the originary enactment of *phusis*. The dialogue's (and now Sallis') return to *phusis* happens as a doubling back of *phusis*, like an originary change in direction as the dialogue (and he) turns in discourse to the origination of things. So the dialogue composes a disciplined process of making, a *poiesis* with *techne* ("skill"), which intends attention to phusis rather than merger with it or an opposition to it—a return and recoil with it, and not primarily a departure from it (46–47).

This return is complicated by a distinction that is alien to a major thought in this book. Timaeus, in his beginning (which turns out to be the first of the four beginnings—when you count this prelude—that he initiates) distinguishes perpetual being (*to on aei*) from things as they are manifest to sense, and by this move he wishes to turn from such things to "*logoi*" in order to "behold (*skopein*) in them the truth of beings" (47–48). In this distinction the image of "selfsame" operates—a timeless continuation of being that is comprehensible "by intellection with discourse" (47). A person makes the turn of this distinction, as Socrates says in the *Phaedo*, by posing a *hypothesis*, "that is, one *begins* by setting something under sensibly manifest things, under them as a basis, their origin, their original" (48, italics mine). "For what is posed over against the sensible manifold is a *one*, and it is posed from *logos*" (48). I wish in my discussion to change this discourse to one in which "selfsame," "one," and "timelessly beyond

---

5. The following remarks compose responses to and interpretations of John Sallis' book *Chorology: On Beginning in Plato's* Timaeus (Bloomington: Indiana University Press, 1999). Page references to this work are given in the main text. My effort is not to render interpretively Sallis' book as a whole but to provide readings and glosses on parts of it in the context of this book. His account of *chora* in *Timaeus* provides the instance of an alternative to many resonances in "nature," and I wish to follow closely that instance. I shall persist in my use of *phusis* instead of its translation as "nature."

the sensible" are not attached. But the point of emphasis now is that we are involved in a turning and a preliminary beginning and that in this originary doubling back, the issue of *phusis* is already implicated. We can follow Timaeus sympathetically at least this far: Whatever is generated is subject to perishing, including, we are to suppose, discourses. As Sallis notes with emphasis, from the very beginning, Timaeus leaves suspended the distinction between *eidos,* what something is, and the seeming of things (48). We are, after all, just beginning the return to the *phusis* of the cosmos, and we will need to see if this beginning can make the turn so that we can begin to see what we are after. The basis at this point in the dialogue is genuinely hypothetical, is tentative, and it might turn out that the way in which a supposition functions as a basis can lead us to see something of *phusis* that is not otherwise apparent: it might be that the way *phusis* necessarily happens, i.e., its self-sameness, its self-enactment, comes to pass in the very making of a *process* of coming to know. If that were the case, *noesis* and *nous* in intelligent dialogues would be *phusic* of *phusis*. In some translations, that says that intellection at its best would be natural, of nature. Timaeus seems to point in that direction when he uses "demiurge" (*demiourgos*) for a maker, a person who crafts, such as one who crafts a dialogue with skill (*techne*), and he uses the word as well for the god who skillfully makes the cosmos (50). There *appears* to be a *phusic* aspect in a certain kind of making that skilled divine and human makers carry out in common. And this appearance is coming about in a discourse that even in translation shows the sincere and struggling intelligence of Timaeus who himself appears as an image of one who makes discourses, an image that is made in a discourse by another craftsman who is struggling to catch sight of the cosmos, which turns out to be, possibly, in the image of something self-same, changelessly perfect in its kind. With all this imaging and shifting about, sighting something changelessly perfect appears like a fairly shaky affair.

There is a lot of language in Timaeus' first speech about the cosmos that sounds familiar in the tradition of "nature," language interpretations of which would seem to have had a major role in forming that tradition. In that speech, Timaeus is predisposed, for example, to think of the maker of the cosmos as having a model like a paradigm that a craftsman follows as she produces her piece of work. A divine maker follows a paradigm in the making of the cosmos. Not only is divinity invoked in thinking of the origin of all things, but divinity appears in the image of a skilled worker (51). Timaeus' thought takes place in a context of perpetual being and generated things, with what is self-same and attached to "perpetual" and with what is attached to time, produced things, and images. (And that means, of course, that the discursive context for this expression of thought about what is self-same and timeless is temporal and imperfect, even if time is not yet determined. So a sense of temporal imperfection often interrupts the talk of what is timeless, self-same, and, in a later terminology, perfect.) And although I think *to pan* would be better served in translation by "all things" rather than by "universe," Timaeus leaves no doubt that he is thinking of a self-enclosed, unified organism when he thinks of the cosmos as the place of everything (53–54). I also find Timaeus in this speech clearly a figure of desire for assurance that harmony and world order finally define the life of the cosmos, that *phusis,* in its selfsameness, be a force of good harmony, and above all that the world be an image of something timelessly good and true. His first speech—a prelude—is thus composed of the stuff dreams are made of.

At this point in his interpretation Sallis emphasizes, not the specificity of Timaeus' assumptions and desires but the part this prelude plays as it comes to an end in his frequently interrupted and discontinuous discourse. He also emphasizes Socrates' statement of wonder when the first speech breaks off and Socrates accepts this hypothetical prelude. It's as though wonder interrupts the hypothesis, or at least arises as the prelusion ceases, as though this break provides something that the assumptions and imagery cannot provide, namely, a new beginning (56). You would be right if you thought that had things been going perfectly well in his speech and were he following with consummate skill the perfect image of the cosmos, were his thought not in some sense broken, he would not need to "fix" it with a new beginning. If, however, what he wanted to see were not some actuality or entity but were elusive and not exactly a "what," then we could expect the appropriateness of an introduction of discontinuity in the midst of theoretical determinations and a degree of astonishment before the actual, wondrous insufficiency of theoretical exactness. "Something" that is not a model and perhaps not exactly a form is at stake in this dialogue about the lives of everything.

The "nature"-making language continues, however, in spite of a new beginning. There are in Timaeus' address a preoccupation with a beginning, a certain complacency regarding a good maker, a prioritizing of goodness and beauty, an infusion into the cosmos of soul and intelligence, an unquestioned value bestowed on all-inclusiveness as well as on number. Animation has a divine origin, and life is submitted to the values of unity and order. And, given the sought timeless self-sameness and the derivative nature of body, Timaeus realizes in the midst of his account that he has made a bad start. He started, not with what properly comes first—soul— or even with the beginning of things, but with bodies, and here he is, going on about "fabricating bodies," about corruptible things when he should be paying attention to what is properly first in the creation and in the order of things. But regardless of this inadvertence, he discourses about orders of interlocking and proportionate orders, showing the cosmos to be quite a beautiful, self-subsisting image of perfection—at the same time that he appears to invoke Hesiod's *Theogony* in which Chaos comes first and next "wide-bosomed earth, the ever-sure foundation of all," thereby suggesting that quite possibly paradigms and soul do not come at the beginning of things, unless, of course, things began with images and discourses. With this break in theoretical uniformity and this confusing hindrance to the expectation of serene certainty, hypothetical trembling continues to make the images of grounding and perfection a shaky affair.

Sallis notes other instances of discontinuity and unpredictability (86ff.), including the humorous and complex scene in which Timaeus speaks about the artisan god who tells the other gods in an address to them that although they are born (i.e., subject to *phusis*) and hence not immortal, they are not to worry, because he will separate birth from death and thereby protect them from the general fate of death for all things that are born. Their deathlessness, in fact, finds surety in his will which binds them deathlessly together—there's no confidence like that of a technically skilled artisan who's proud of his work! For some of these gods have the job of implanting deathless souls in mortal bodies of their making—being, I suppose, soul-farmers who are to carry out their fabrications in accordance with the benign will of the guarantor of their own special gift. At this point readers of the dialogue might well welcome further interruptions, and they will not be disappointed.

But before we shift ground too much we should note that Timaeus is aware of complicating his own speech by giving an account of another speech, that he is not less given to irony than Socrates is, and that he is fully aware that he is a discourse-crafter—thereby giving us to be aware that he is the fabrication of a discourse-crafter, and that in the midst of all this crafting and storytelling—no matter how much fun we're having—something is missing, something untold and, we might begin to think, untellable; and *that's* what we're after. So Timaeus keeps on interrupting himself, retelling stories, and dallying around in a very skilled way as, in his search for origin, he develops a sense of disorder in the midst of the orders *that* he addresses and the orders of his images (88).

What do we look at if we want to have a vision of perfect order? Timaeus picks—unfortunately, given his seeming intent, from the perspectives of modern astronomy—the heavens (among other things such as the "circling years"): the good, the greatest good, of vision is found by the thought that by beholding the *noetic* revolutions in the heavens we might then make the revolutions within ourselves imitate those celestial revolutions. It is a matter of mimesis between the human soul and the cosmos, of imitating within oneself the order beheld in the heaven above, of making order within be like that of the starry heaven above (89).

Order in ourselves like that "above"? A rapidly moving "North" star? Supernovas and galaxy-eating galaxies? Celestial devastation beyond imagination? Sweet *noesis* is in trouble!

Never mind my jest. Timaeus is sincere, and Timaeus' sincerity is having difficulty. "Mimesis" and the heavens seem to remind him of music, and he ends his first discourse (after the prelude) with a little song that celebrates celestial mimesis in a context with "only the slightest dissonance" (89). The note of dissonance has to do with something not paradigmatic, not crafted, not an artisan, not an image, not a discourse, not intelligible in any usual sense of the word. And if telling stories about divine and human orders and harmonies with seemingly minor and often charming incongruities here and there is a genuine pleasure, this other matter is not so much pleasant as it is *difficult.* Because this other matter has to do with something like distortion and dissonance right in the midst of causal connections and image-making—Sallis calls it "*anoetic* causality"—that shakes the foundations of *noesis: ananke,* necessity. So a song about celestial regularity with a little tremolo is not a bad idea at this point.

I recently had a conversation with a man for whom an image of steady, eternally founded human nature is absolutely crucial. He is a passionate man with reddish hair that I have seen blowing in winds from the sea, making him seem like a small-scale cross between Boreas and Poseidon. He said that belief in human nature that is beyond either "natural" or cultural causality is necessary for his and humanity's "security," that without it we are lost to an adequate basis for responsibility and normative choice. He believes that individuals have access to this ground when they approach it with adequate discipline and dedication, that we can each discover this imperative-granting guidance for ourselves by means of morally serious intelligence and courage to buck our often misguided social norms. He is given to dialogue and good humor, loves a good story, and rather enjoys the outrage that his "security" can arouse in more tentative souls. But his is a security without a sense of the necessity of *chora,* a necessity that I believe lies in his own character, and a necessity to which we now turn in a speech by Timaeus that might well play havoc with "nature" in the midst of affirming it, and would certainly play havoc with my friend's insistent security.

Sallis calls Timaeus' turn to *chora* "another beginning" (91).

> Interruption appears doubly at this juncture. It cuts doubly into the discourse, dividing the discourse at the very moment that it becomes the theme of the discourse. For the discourse is interrupted in order to be redirected toward that which can and indeed does interrupt the very workings of *nous* to which Timaeus' discourse has in large part been addressed up to this point of interruption.(90)

In other words, the doubled interruption and re-beginning itself constitute a mimesis of "something" that *nous* cannot reach directly. "Necessity" is posed as a generation that is *anoetic* and that is combined with *noetic* production, "posed" because of *noetic* "persuasion" and placement and yet taking place with implacable difference from *nous* and intelligent determination: an unnerving, ever-present interruption of crafty *noetic* placement *in* that placement.

You cannot produce necessity any more than you can produce *phusis,* and although genuine skill (*techne*) goes with production (*poiesis*) in its most elevated sense, applicable as it is to gods and artists, untechnical and unskilled necessity nonetheless generates. And although good production depends on an intelligent paradigm, we are now looking at, as it were, "something" that is utterly deviational and that generates, "something" closer to prodigious birthing without clear purpose. For Timaeus is not addressing the necessity of law.

> It is rather a necessity that would operate outside of the law, that would even determine this very outside: this necessity would be an outlaw eluding the *noetic* supervision that determines the lawfulness of *poiesis,* resisting the rule of *nous* even if responsive to persuasion. (92)

We might be addressing now a monstrous dimension in "nature," traditionally imagined, but I don't think so. I think that we are honing in on the enactment of *phusis,* whether Timaeus explicitly says so or not, honing in on "nature itself," if someone finds that kind of terminology helpful. "Nature," as I have been speaking of it, is a configuration that has often carried an intention to eliminate unorder and the errancy of excess to order. And here we are, in the midst of a dialogue that has nurtured some of the deepest and most insistent images of universal order and that is about to turn to a kind of generation and nursing that is not exactly what most scholastics and some "natural" scientists have in mind when they think of "nature" or of the universe: generative necessity without intelligible purpose, without a subjective nature, without objectivity, fecundating prolifically, truantly, and ignorantly, right in the middle of orders that are pleasant to the handsome and well-ordered eyes of good and intelligent people.

But I doubtlessly overstate the case from Timaeus' perspective, because he will not let *ananke* separate from *nous.* He seems to be carving out a space of togetherness for errant, generative necessity and serene, well-ordered *nous,* as though they can live together in union, if not in a harmonius unity, at least in a union of differences. We will have to see if this standing together gives the game to *nous* and to "nature" in a more traditional sense of the word.

Timaeus finds his new beginning by means of attention to generating as distinct to producing. And here is where any tremolo that you might have overheard in his song comes to bear. Imaging, telling, narrating, reporting, calculating proportions, establishing orders! None of these stabilizing marvels of *logos* and *muthos* will quite do if we are to get to the beginning of generation. And Sallis says straight out that, "Timaeus' withdrawal from saying the beginning corresponds precisely to the withdrawal of the beginning from being said, its withdrawal from (the) discourse" (97). We are venturing with this strange mimesis, in what I am taking as an effort, among other things, to think *phusis,* to approach no place (*atopos*) that is not "natural" and not *a* part of a universe, although it is utterly *phusic* in its withdrawal from *nous* and in its astonishing fecundity, a no place that requires discursive displacement when people attempt to think in "*its*" regard. We are approaching "beginning" outside of the order of *logos* by taking a "third" way in this interruptive discourse. We are presently working with the hypothesis that a mimesis takes place, as it were, in the recoiling interruptions and beginnings, in this chorology, this language of *chora,* that composes, not a recognition, but a generative beginning. We are exploring the probability that one does not approach generative beginning directly and with straight eyes—something seems to require a deviant crossing, and such cockeyed, compelled starting over, not just again, but again and again and again, has a complex function of dislodging inadequate distinctions (like that of paradigmatic, intelligible *eidos* and sensible, changeable things) and functioning as well to promise, vaguely, a mimetic, performative engagement of beginning. This is mimesis—a doubling—by means of interruptions and a way of speaking that is very different from the previous discourses, so different as to be a deviation that approximates perversity. Instead of protective artists and gods we are going to speak of "the receptacle" and instead of a steadfast paradigm, we will speak of the nurse, as it were. We are headed toward the edge of stabilized sense, unity, and coherence, toward dangerous groundlessness, dangerous, at least, when this movement of thought is experienced within the context of the hypothesis and immanently reasonable steadfastness that defines the expectations expressed in the earlier parts of the dialogue. This is like a movement through intelligibility and its interruptions to the edge of "nature" and a manifest difference—I will call "it" *phusis*—in an effort to approach the occurrence of beginning, "the [as it were] nurse of all generation" (99). In the choralogical movement, likely stories fall away as we undergo the edge of both demonstrable competence and definitive beginnings. And Timaeus has certainly been jarred loose from a fixation on enduring archetypes as he makes his way to *phusis* in its maddening fecundity that is outside the encompassment and limits of cohesive, unified narrative discourse, and knowledge.

At this turning point in the dialogue you can see that we are addressing one of the defining issues of this book: the limits of "nature" before the lives of dynamic things. I have located, as it were, this edge in the eventuation of manifest things, be they sounds or squirrels in trees. "Physicality" is a word I am using, in part, to name the hinging region of discursive sense and wild difference; and in Sallis' account of the *Timaeus* the wildness of beginning fecundity (*phusis*) is emerging as an un-*noetic* frustration at the heart of a dialogue by the philosopher who is often appropriated as the father of the expectation that nature in all of its fluctuations has its truth in non-fluctuating, immanently intelligible archetypes that are called *eidoi* and that are usually recognized in translations as "ideas." Although the expectations of *noetic* intelligence could easily lead to either a compulsive returning, again and again and again, to the uncompromising difference that defines the limit of *noesis* or to an equally compulsive dogmatic closure before it, we are now on the edge of a discourse that attempts to find a welcoming openness to the unwieldy difference of beginning fecundity. This welcoming, perhaps, can be sewn into a discourse, a "third way," that finds in its own disruptions and limits an altered manner of mentation and speech, one that finds something like insight in the manifestation of a difference—*hupodoxa*—that it can not be grasped or otherwise encompassed by meanings or grammar. Sallis notes that "the word *hupodoxa* means not only 'receptacle' but also 'reception,' even a hospitable reception such as was proposed at the beginning of the dialogue, the hospitable reception now being accorded Socrates, the entertainment that Socrates, listening silently, is now receiving from his hosts. The word also means 'support,' 'aid,' 'succor,' hence the connection with the issue of nurse" (99).

The word *hupodoxa,* however, also suggests "a kind of surrogate mother who holds, aids, and succors the newly born child" (99). And that meaning complicates the considerations of this discussion. The word suggests "mother nature" or "Mother Nature" in addition to its sense of "harboring or sheltering something alien and of doing so in a way that conceals" (100). Sorting out those conflicting connotations will continue to be important as we consider *phusis* in a way that gives space for the difference of physicality in connection with human interests. If I am right, there is something important for human interests in resisting language that gives subtle dominance to human interests as people recognize their environments and even themselves. We are not departing from the interests of people. We are finding that these interests are physical and that physical events considerably exceed in their appearances the circumference of human meanings and intelligence. This observation is given a unique emphasis in Sallis' account of the *Timaeus* by his accentuation of the inadequacy of the images and names that are applied to "the receptacle." All references to "it" are undercut by its "definition": its *phusic* enactment has no form by virtue of which it would be itself. "It" seems "to have" no "nature." Since the receptacle "determines" the beginnings of specific things and since these things present "it" by their limits and by the absence of direct access to their origins, the receptacle appears to withdraw in the things that present it and in the images by which it is, as it were, recognized.

The question of necessity is finding an increasing emphasis in this account of the *Timaeus.* The interruptions in the dialogue, we find, compose an integral part of it as they relativize the order of the discourse that they *interrupt.* We find ourselves in a rhythm whereby the necessity of *eidos,* for example, while definitive for one manner of intelligence, is not allowed to define the dialogue's progress or the mimesis and doubling that Sallis discovers in the interruptive processes. Beginnings appear in an eliding of stern definitions, and another, more peculiar necessity seems to appear, a necessity of nondetermination in the birthing of determinate things. Necessity without definition that runs through definitional necessities and escapes, as it were, most truantly—necessity found not in ontology or logic but in duplicity: "it" cannot, must not happen as clear direction or *noetic* visibility. We are approaching "something" for which a traditional image of "natural necessity" does not apply, although we are addressing *phusis* in a way that is relevant for our reflections on physicality. So while I am placing in doubt the image of a sheltering surrogate mother, I will give emphasis to the suggestion of nothing familiar—of "alien" and "fugitive from *logos*" (106)—that is carried by *hupodoxa.*

The image of "fugitive" applies in the dialogue to fire, for example. While fire's generation and passage might be said to be in and from the receptacle, it remains "an almost unspeakable fugitive" (106). Words and discourses in its regard, I would say, virtually bounce off of it, if they reach it at all, and fail to grasp or include it in recognition and saying. Fire is not a this or a that in a discourse. Nor is it a discursive movement. In a contemporary manner of expression we could say that *its* burning, transitional arising, and extinction don't mean a thing and that our good sense with it reaches the very edge of good sense where the richness of fire's meaning is stalled before the flaming combustion: fire withdraws from its images of presentation. A rigor at the edge is required, a "third kind" of discourse in which the burning brightness of fire is called upon, as it were, by fleeting images and with only a minimal disturbance of the nondiscursive alien "that" is so alien that it falls outside of even the grammatical familiarity of a "that."

In the last paragraph I placed emphasis on a resistance to discourse in the happening of fire. In this instance I am going outside of Sallis' attention to beginnings to an attention to happenings that do not valorize origins. Or I could say that as original determination appears, on Sallis' account, duplicitously and without final definition, the issue of origins turns toward happenings in which preoccupation with beginnings changes to a preoccupation with a duplicity in discourse: naming, knowing, and defining the happenings of things seem to have a "re-," a departure from and return to the happenings, a "re-" that wanders around the discursive movement. Discourses of recognition themselves happen. They bring to life bodies of meaning and experience that engender kinds of contact with other happenings, that influence and form communal and personal identities, and that provide cultural events with enormous power. But they do not constitute the happenings, like fires, that they address. These happenings seem to wander off—the fire keeps on burning or burns down and changes to a glow of embers, and the "fire" of experience, the "fire" of passion, the "fire" of "burning" insight are distant doubles of happenings that they are not. It is as though we burn with passion, as though a strange subjunctivity invests our happening like fire, as though we were a fiery event when we experience overwhelming allure, intense merriment, or a consuming feeling. "Fire" happens differently in our sense of kinship with it, indifferently firing and leaving our discourses, not necessarily in ashes but in synapses of other physical and richly meaningful happenings.[6]

My hypothesis is that when people are predisposed to experience events and are relieved of a quest for definitive origins that explain why something occurs and that define its meaning from the beginning, they are more able to pay attention to the often astonishing happenings around them, happenings that never quite fit their duplications in meanings and values. In that sensibility, "nature" fades in its unifying traditional powers, and we begin to find alternative manners of differential expression and recognition before the occurrences of our lives that happen physically and indifferently to the meanings by which we recognize them.

I would push Timaeus too far if I interpreted *chora* as mere void or vacuity. But still, *chora,* for him, does not name something. The word names, as it were, nothing that can be named. The word addresses nonthis-non-that properly insofar as *chora* is an impossible name in its context in this dialogue: it does not mean a thing, and by refusing its seeming function of naming it duplicates "the" non-thing whose name the word cancels. Monstrous errancy, says Sallis. Nomadic, outside of the order of *logos,* amorphous, terribly other, always other to what is generated, occurring in duplicity, vaguely manifest as withdrawal from visibility. But with all of this doubling without resolution, *chora* nonetheless suggests a vague "there" in a movement of withdrawal. With Sallis' interpretation we find a most remarkable moment in early Western thought: determination by nondetermination at the beginning, generation without sufficient definition, doubling exactly where we might expect immobile essence. Instead of

---

6. "Do not come to me with metaphors of love," she said. "Come to me with love."

an ineffable being or way of being, we find in *chora* only a group of references that requires no originary purposiveness. We have the discourses of a receptacle that cannot be anything. It is *like* a nurse, a strange mothering, nurturing generator of offspring that receives forms but is formless, aporetic through and through, a capital frustration to discourse, a contest of form and formlessness, a demand for a rigor of thinking that holds without resolution to doubling and beginning again and that finds in such a process a mimesis of no determinate being, a necessity without definition, a welcoming reception for the *coming* of orders without subjective intent or mathematical proportion. "As chorology," Sallis says, "Timaeus' discourse comes as near as it ever will to the beginning. In becoming chorology its palintropic engagement brings it into a region where it can most nearly, as enjoined, begin at the beginning, even if only in recommencing, in a second beginning. In this discourse Timaeus ventures to call by its proper name that which heretofore has only been counted or else addressed by the names of images. Yet the differentiations that set it apart have such a disruptive force that even the concept of proper name will in the end miss the mark and prove capable only of alluding to the sense—or nonsense—at issue here" (114–15).

Ineffability but not a being. Like mere receptacle. Like nurturance without judgment, like necessity without law. Like spaciousness where beings might shine. Not a place, but perhaps placeability, not a gatherer, but perhaps gathering allowance of beings, not an orderer, but perhaps generational of orders. Perhaps "the" place of being without being a being. But for all the ambiguity and nondetermination, Timaeus in his discourse is able to say quite a lot about non-it. Perhaps here dreaming and awakened awareness are not too different—Timaeus seems to move into a translated state, almost like a seer, as he recounts non-it's qualities: everlasting, perpetual, always, indestructible, without beginning or mortality, in no sense something generated (118–19). Non-it is never fully here, but seems to be plentiful as a transcending, as it were, there. Were non-it dreamlike, Timaeus' hypotheses and seeming sight would be no less powerful as an articulation of a vision, stronger, I believe, than a hope, a vision of ineffability instead of void, promising, if always frustrating for *noesis,* a vision of truth other to *logos,* and, of course, a vision of generation without end. It is the kind of vision that forecasts "nature" in "its" ineffable, strangely reassuring, if faceless presence. If only dreaming were not generative of the dreamed! If only "forever" were not a dream! If only "always" were ungoverned by time! If only forever were!

I have dreamed at times when I preferred not to wake up from the dream and sighed with the return of implacable light. And I have dreamed when I wanted to wake up and to know that I was in a bed in a room in a house that I knew well. Regardless of my mood, when I awaken I find myself in the midst of events that no dream can hold and that allow me to know the limits of dreaming and the danger of subtracting dreaming from the dreamt shades. Shades of eternity, I expect, enjoy the nonnecessity of all other shades: though they move people strongly, they come to pass as fleetingly as fire but without fire's heat and leaping flames. Shades appear, decline, without necessity other than that of their passing moments, bringing to bear in their exile random memories, tickling people's imaginations, inspiring fantasies of insight, and giving spell to the severe circumspection of what bodies know: that there are only the happenings of passing things and beyond them, very likely, other happenings in various shades of palpable light and darkness.

But Timaeus also finds reason for his dream-hypothesis by reference to the distinctions of things in their spaces of occurrence. After his paean to *chora,* he says that "as long as one thing is something and another is something else, neither of the two will ever come to be in the other, so as to become, at once, one (and the same) and two" (119). Each generated thing happens with such singular insistence that it cannot be else than its own happening. It's as though it were harbored in its place, and even when disaster befalls it, *"it"* is befallen. No thing gives itself its singular happening—each thing is as though birthed and held in its own limited and living moment, as though its happening were nursed and beheld by a generator, a mother, of its limited occurrence. No explanation seems to work here, no condition becomes visible to encourage a search for methods of understanding. Timaeus faces the need for a different discipline, one that attends to the preserved singularity of a formed life. In addition to the satisfaction of merely seeing the uniqueness of happenings, he needs—searches for—a more sustaining image that preserves the mystery of such happenings by immanently refusing any form that might hold it—*chora* seems to him to be motherless. For it seems the happening of things, for Timaeus and the discourse that he speaks and that speaks through him, need meaning even if that meaning trembles in passage and requires continuous recommencement. I do not think that for Timaeus the happening of things *has* meaning that is available for discovery. I think that he has come before a certain inscrutability in a discourse that has persisted to its own limits, persisted to the limits of what appears to it and in it, persisted to the limits of appearance and inquiry that define it, and, most important, to the limits of its most formidable and gentle power, *nous,* that sees beyond images, measurements, and calculations and beholds ordered forms—timeless self-same entities—which are most available to the intangible and perceptive power of gifted, trained souls. This persistence exemplifies an honesty most prized in the philosophical traditions that this and other Platonic dialogues spawned—the honesty of persisting to the limits of a discourse's power and agency and to a point where a release takes place and a person tells stories that appear likely within the range of the meanings and values that motivate the dis-course—and then, when storytelling comes to its limit, seek the life of something else that is not a story but that moves in storytelling and beyond, moves in a withdrawing kinship. That lets us know that the lives of stories and discourses count beyond the sum total of their accuracies and intelli-gence. This is the point of limit and narration where people dream, where shades of trusted meaning take over, where ancient and powerful hopes and visions come to power, where submerged anxieties take reasonable forms of grammar, and where shards of other incorporated practices of mind, seldom visible, come to play palingenetically in small creations of images, rhythms, and languages. This is where the force and meaning of "nature" comes most persuasively to life.

For "nature" exceeds more or less meaningfully generated events. Such events are "natural" because they belong in some sense to "nature," and "she," now gendered, never quite betrays her purposes beyond the trajecto-ries of "natural" events that are usually describable by reference to what people know about them at a given time. She hovers or storms or proceeds otherwise without voice in formations and movements that (and the life of which) people know they do not make and frequently cannot harness. She is often like an image of generation that people have long wished to influ-ence and understand in the many wakes of destruction, surprise, with-holding, and overabundance that come with her lack of care for individuals and with her strange gifts of singular happenings. "Nature" succors the events of things with an unconcern for the "who" or the "what" that only infinite, faceless fecundity can afford. And yet, "she," ever mysterious, pro-vides that gift of distinct life-happening without which, nothing. How else might we think of such awesome, anonymous, and spacious perpetuity in that dimension of life that appears to Timaeus to be unconditioned—the very eventuation of individual things?[7]

The direction of discourse taken by Sallis moves decidedly away from a sense of *chora* that sees "it" as a productive subject; but while *chora* is not a synonym for "*nature*," Plato's imagery and language regarding it, I believe, informed a broad sense of what "nature" can mean. And when we follow Sallis' reading we find in the *Timaeus* a manner of thinking of *chora* that carried over in conceptions of "nature" as a generating, purpo-sive being: although *chora* does not make things like "nature" is often said to do, she, in Timaeus' discourse, provides nonetheless site for generation as well as for individuation. *Chora* "grants, furnishes, supplies (*parexo*) an *abode* to all things, to all things inasmuch as they are generated" (119).

7. See the discussion of micro-memories in chapter 4 for an alternative to this interpretation of life's eventuation.

That is, *chora* does not "herself" make generated things; she abides with all generated things. But as "she" changes in "her" own withdrawing, sustaining eventuation, she betrays nothing. This is a discursive perception that is wayward and on the very edge of a specific, disciplined thinking. The issue addresses the context and the discursive motivation that predispose people's thinking toward what we might call resolutions at the borders of meaning and sense. Why does a person need to say more when good sense is exhausted? Why might people look for meaning when they come to implacable difference vis-à-vis what things and processes can mean? This area of predisposition—an area composed in part by the power of the *Timaeus* in our traditions—is the site where telling transformations might occur that would lessen the force of "nature." In Sallis' account we find the force of "nature" outstripped by chorology. We find a site that dissolves resolutions of final meaning. And we find a site that provides nonetheless an ungrounding ground that is, as it were, hospitable to generated things.

I have no doubt that people perceive in part thanks to the beliefs and values that extend provable claims and verifiable experiences to wider ranges of meaning and affirmation. The discursive move to a name that unnames itself in its proper usage and that in such movement composes an intimation of ineffable eventuation is not quite a perception in any usual sense of that word. But the move does happen in a discourse of proper names and grammatical requirements of reference—the move weirdly outlines a limit, a border of reference, signification, and imaging. It composes a discursive puzzlement that gives this particular discourse its motivation and aporetic collapse. And it tells a story in a way that dissolves its own likelihood into a different discourse that Sallis calls a third way. A chorology. In it there are no gods behind the scenes. Even the projection of a mother's image, almost Gaia-like, suggests neither personality nor will nor purpose. It is a story that dissolves its own imagery and leaves us to begin again with only a trace in the dissolution of recognizable agency. In Sallis' persuasive interpretation, *chora* in "her withdrawal is *almost* like an absence that traverses and preserves generated events." And yet everything that happens takes place in "her" abode, in her abiding and withdrawn grant of moment, place, and time. "She" is never exhausted, is perpetually excessive to the totality of occurrences. "She" is like a virtual sameness of happening that lacks identity, an ungenerated clearing for generation, a trace of ground that lacks presence. In this discourse Sallis describes "her" as monstrous in the sense that "she" fits in no context and is perpetually outside in the midst of occurrences that "she" succors. "She" means "that necessity that determines or underlies necessity as such" (120). The phrase that occurs to me at this point is "ungrounding ground," i.e., in Sallis' language, "origin and abyss at the same time" (123).

This discourse has taken *chora* away from all standard explanations, from any proper knowledge, and has placed *chora* in the context of dream and divination (123–24). It is as though we come to the boundary of good sense in a dream and, if we are fortunate, awaken transformed so that we speak hesitantly from the dream, knowing that the dream is a dream but finding through it something to be said—something disclosed—that is beyond the powers of wakeful alertness to establish and designate with the clarity of good sense. In other times "it" might be called "the Unconscious" or "God" or "the Ground of Being" or "Being itself" or "Nature"—in all instances called, named, but missed too and known to be missed by virtue of being named.

The "matter" here—as in the question, what is the matter with "nature"?—is found in an envisionment of necessity, outside of all determinations, an envisionment that manifests a predisposition toward the value of "unconditioned" as a qualification of "necessity." Timaeus expresses this predisposition beautifully as he thinks about nonreducible events of singularity, events that can be only themselves in their spatial and temporal happening. Surely there is in his discourse a necessity for the identities, images, and connections that he can know with reasonable certainty. Perhaps now, however, for us there is no such necessity. Perhaps the necessities of concrete events are found in their temporal concreteness and in considerable excess to form. Perhaps such necessities have no other necessity at all. Perhaps "nature," as well as *chora,* manifests the border dreams of a discourse and the absence of anything else.

Those last four sentences are dominated by "perhaps." The issue is whether we can think in such transitional "perhapses" without even a hint of transcending necessity, outside of specific contexts. Can we think without "nature"?

Overtones of universal cohesiveness, continuity, meaning, and necessity seem to accompany "nature," I have said. Such universality and hence transcendence draw people away from the palpable and unencompassable specificity of occurring things and place emphasis on meanings that turn things toward posited movements in the direction of overarching unification. Even Timaeus' story of impersonal, ineffable, abiding necessity for necessities has that effect. I have said that even if discourses of "nature" have force now, there are options to those discourses, that people can recognize things without that kind of likely story. I am presently engaged in such a discourse. In it, for example, experiences of astonishment do not require universal necessity or something transcendent beyond our worlds of meaning. In other chapters I will indicate manners of recognizing gravity and physical compositions that operate without such a requirement. Presently I will emphasize the meaning of limit in order to show one way in which a transition beyond the force of "nature" can take place.

To begin again. One of the most forceful aspects in Sallis' account of the *Timaeus* is found in his emphasis on re-beginning. *Chora* presents no firm origin in which or before which a thinker might pause. "She" provides no substantive "there," no *point* of beginning. Naming "her," even giving "her" pronominal reference, figures *chora's* withdrawal. But in that withdrawal a spectral trace of *chora* remains. This ungrounding ground requires a discourse that is uncircumscribed by its own designation, formal definition, or sensuous perception and that brings out with awareness the occurrence of this trace. Such a discourse would loosen the hold of all definitions and methods for establishing certainty. To begin *again,* for example, is a strategy for this other way of thinking when definitive origins are the issue. As though beginning again and again breaks any dominance that one might give to form and definition and maintains alertness to the happening of "other to form."

"Other to form"—*chora* in the present context—however, does carry the meanings of ungenerated, undying, nurturing, necessity, giving, hospitality, and other good things, in addition to monstrosity and alien. "To begin again" can also mean examination of dominant and subordinate values in our patterns of recognition and perception. I suppose that a person could call this the *chora* aspect of recognitions, but Timaeus was interested in eternity—not the eternal-seeming aspect of a compulsion that always starts over when a resolution might be reached, but in eternal generation, deathless realities, and unchanging qualities, ever in *chora's* trace. If *chora* were not *a* unity, at least "she" happens like gathering-unity-in-generation. And "she" apparently is like an invariant nurse—the birthing, ever-giving necessity of all necessities. *Chora* is like undying, generative limitlessness at the border of all limits, like nurturant space that gives place in determinate occurrences.

One of the major problems with this imagery in the context of this discussion is that the meanings of "receptacle"—of *hypodoxé*—carries such powerful overtones of a kind of place. *Hypodoxé* can mean reception and receiving, entertainment, harboring, and admission, as we have seen, as well as a quarter for troops, a reservoir, the stomach. It suggests stewardship and acceptance of responsibility for something. *Hypodoxeion* can name a storage place, a reservoir for fish or wine, perhaps a barn or storehouse, a host, and, interestingly, a socket for a hinge. It is a word for holding within limits. Even when Timaeus' language is pushed to its limit, one can reasonably understand him to have in mind, if not exactly a container, certainly a dimension of hospitable wombishness. His language gives considerable force to suggestions of superlative hospitality as well as, in the indetermination of definitive origins, to monstrous difference from all determinate things. He appears to be thinking of a dimension of ultimate generation—far from chaos—in the meanings of hosting, the creation, if not of a safe harbor, of a harbor nonetheless for all things in their living, strife-filled differences and identities.

So why not think in terms of chaos, of sheer void, of mere absence? Because, I think, Timaeus is given to want something like "Nature," something like a hospice for coming-passing lives. On Sallis' interpretation, Timaeus pushes the meaning about as far as it can go. Sallis will not allow us to fix the meaning of *chora,* and he requires us to begin again (and again) if we are to think such generation appropriately. He is certainly outside the bounds of any image of "Nature" that establishes its character in subjective terms. But *chora* does appear to happen generationally. And if *chora* lacks purpose, "she" certainly and with fecundity does set herself apart from mere emptiness. By that setting apart she inevitably becomes unspeakably plenteous and immeasurably rich in generosity, no matter how intensely one doubles the discourse and begins again. Of course, *chora* is not subject to definition. Of course *chora* is all-bountiful. Of course *chora* is not mere void. I think that Eckhart would not be entirely unhappy with this thought.

What is so bad about mere void? For one thing, the words will not allow any positive attribution: the words can mean empty and vacant, having no incumbent, being without, not producing any effect, useless, and entire lack. Their antonym is "full." In our mythologies, usually when a god comes on the scene, void, if "it" were ever "there," is seriously compromised if not evacuated by the god's fullness and radiance. And "Nature," too, is usually intolerant of void. Perhaps—I am not sure—a strategy of return is contained in the "re" of this intolerance. "Nature" comprises implicit strategies to avoid void. This virtually unapproachable master word is designed to allow a sense of presence so commanding that all direct contact is deferred, side-tracked, and rendered incomplete. Surely the Surround that pervades all determinations is not completely empty! Surely origination means originator even if "originator" is aporetic for our best intelligence! Surely determinate things happen in surpassing richness of Being!

When I confront the enormous draw of "Nature," I feel the force that moves in the deepest recesses of theism, regardless of the form that a theism takes. It is the force of resistance to void and emptiness, to inattributable and unworshipful no-thing, to total and complete silence before the most profound instincts of living things to hear in their living a resonance to Life as such. To say that such resistance is resistance to death understates the issue. People can accept the observation that all things die. But acceptance of the likelihood that no-life, no-being at all, infests life and lives, that void is not and yet insanely pervades non-provisionally the providing of being is another matter. There must be "more." Why?

Are not the lives of things and the meanings that things have for us in our ordinary lives enough? Are not the specific, minute, and huge differences of things in their occurrences sufficient for our hopes and tragedies? Do the specific events that shape us not give us plenty for concern and meaning? Are the totalities of things not sufficient if they lack Being or Ground of Being? Do we not live in a time when ancient preoccupations with Life beyond lives is optional? When the question of Ultimate Source can pass to nothing of concern to us? When capitalizations for overarching unity are not needed for our sense of meaning as we live?

THREE

Phusis *and Its Generations*

... out of nowhere,
nothing answered yes.
— *"Five Tzu-Yeh Songs"*

When I began to work on this book I thought that the primary issue in it would be termed "body." As the process developed, however, "physicality" replaced "body." I was surprised at first by the growing realization that what I had in mind did not quite fit with the remarkable range of meanings in the word "body." I had thought that by setting some of those meanings and the experiences that they suggest over against other suggestions and experiences in the word's lineage, by means of the struggles and conflicts among the suggestions and experiences, that I could reasonably enlarge their often restricted usage. I hoped to connect "body" with "nature" in such a way that I could make apparent a pervasive reciprocity in all appearances of corporeality, intangibility, flesh, meaning, and resistance to meaning that seemed to me common in the two words' intentions. I thought too that by valorizing body I could bring together a greater reciprocity between accounts of appearances and our present knowledge of bodies.

Complex fleshly bodies are defined in their division from their environments by membranes that locate their organized parts and maintain their structures, by their capacities for self-replication, reception and use of energy, and their manners of integrated and more or less open connections with the world around them. They certainly have "natures" in the sense that they have dynamic and integral limits and self-defining regularities. From a scientific point of view they are describable by the work of physicists and chemists that make explicitly experimental assumptions whose validity is shown in realizable predictability and other methodologically based forms of verification. In bodies we also find organizational continuities, processes of transitions such as those of growth and decline.

They occur with density and in withdrawal from conscious grasp with astonishing difference from meanings and values in their regard, often in a silence that defies language and with an intractable metamorphic and contingent there-quality that frustrates management and usage. If bodies are not infinitely complex, they are certainly enough beyond our reach toward sufficient accounts to be like an infinite complexity.

Work in both physical and behavioral sciences has made, if not obslete, at least highly optional the ideas that mind and body are two completely different kinds of entities, that there is a pre-established law of universal harmony, that "mind" and "body" are identical, or that local trajectories in bodies require for their understanding a universal purposiveness. It's not that these powerful and often beautiful ideas have lost all of their force regarding bodies or that they do not contain within them elements that strongly influenced the development of contemporary science and thought. It's rather that very different ways of developing knowledge, when compared to ways that dominated previous centuries, can now form our language, concepts, and imaginations. We are able to recognize bodies as highly organized and vulnerable cellular entities that are to a degree self-contained and to a degree quite dependent, that are open and porous in their environments. Twentieth-century thought in several traditions, including those of phenomenology and Anglo-American philosophy, has subjected both dualism and reductive materialism to withering critique and set directions for other manners of conception, imagery, and engagement. We can easily think of bodies as constituted by all manner of "worldly," historical, and "natural" forces, elements and influences that are not possessed or begun by other individual bodies but nonetheless inhere in bodies. So why not follow the developing lives of conceptualization that move away from mind-body dualism and reductive materialism, but have a disciplined appreciation for random, mutational events, historical and social formations, and systematic as well as chaotic dynamics in the development and lives of bodies? Why not stick with "bodies" and participate in the transformations that impact the word's meaning in understandings that characterize many parts of contemporary knowledge?

I want to address meanings, experiences, and appearances of physical things as well as resistance to meaning in their occurrences and not to address primarily "our" *knowledge* of the composition and formation of bodies. I want to address also the collapse of meanings in meaningful experiences and appearances. While I do not think that the "sciences" are *the* enemy or *an* enemy to understanding physical appearances or to our experiences of "bodies," I do think that they are not designed to elaborate fully meanings and experiences and their limits. The danger is not that the sciences will objectify everything they touch; the danger is that other manners of approach will not address persistently enough the meanings, experiences, and values and their limits that define purpose and perspective in our lives. While scientific knowledge and other disciplines of knowledge are like other physical events in their porosity and ability to influence each other by their patent differences—cross-fertilize, if you will, and thereby engender some unpredictable surprises—nonetheless there are in the occurrence of physical events dimensions that appear and are experienced and that are other to knowledge and meaning regarding them. In addressing experiences, appearances, and meanings I found that "bodies" could not do enough work in helping to describe physical events. The word "body" is strong in its suggestion of mass and substance, but it does not lend itself as well to lightness, porosity, and intangible occurrence. It is stronger in its suggestion of fullness and viscosity than it is in suggesting absence of content in the happening of things. The word also carries at this level of description a heavily dualistic lineage, and that by itself, and despite efforts to overcome it, is reason enough to let the word have a rest in this kind of study. I believe that "physicality" can do a better job than "body" in this work in addressing physical events, their appearing densities, histories, masses, inherent regularities, and truancies. At least that is a hypothesis in this book.

RECAPITULATION

I have placed emphasis on the everyday availability of things in their astonishing eventuations in order to draw attention to a severity of non-meaning in their meaningful appearances. In this emphasis I have pointed out the difference between what happens and the happening of what happens and emphasized the singularity of happenings. My intention is to include nonvoluntary and nonsubjective physical aspects in considerations of both what happens and the happening and to indicate that "physicality" can well elaborate "happening" without severing it from what happens. One motivation for this intention is found through the observation that "spirit" and "nature" in their emphases on ordered continuity, transcendence of bodies' lives, meaningful universality, and present plenitude have functioned in our lineage—often contrary to purposes in their employment—to distance people from the concrete specificity of things in their dynamic interconnections. Close attentiveness to specific things in their physicality, however, includes attentiveness to absence of definitive origins in natality, non-order with order, non-meaning with meaning, mere instrumentality with human experience, chemical and historical compositions with ecstasies, no continuity with continuities, and void with lively plenitude. And even the possibility of those eventuations with a lack of definitive origins, non-presence, and unorder often has an unnerving effect on people who are predisposed to find a plenitude of presence and purpose by means of spiritual insight and universal order in "nature." I am expressing a way of engaging with events in which such predispositions and their consequent detachment from things are neutralized and sensibilities with other predispositions come to definitive expressions.

In John Sallis' interpretation of Plato's *Timaeus,* I found an impressive account of an overlooked aspect in the lineage of "nature," one in which the meaning of origin on a cosmic scale includes such monstrous ambiguity that its like can only be thought in the movement of continuous recapitulation and renewed beginning: the thought of origin happens as beginning again and again with the question of cosmic beginning. Now I would like to take a turn away from the issue of origin by linking *phusis* and physicality on the one hand to a sense of void in the interest of drawing primary attention to the occurrences of things and on the other hand to the density of things that vastly limits intelligibility and meaning in our engagements with them. In this way I expect to eliminate a certain obsessiveness that seems to appear with efforts to bring thorough and far-reaching intelligibility and meaning together with the occurrences of things.

A NICE TRY: HEIDEGGER AND *PHUSIS*

In chapter 1, I said that astonishment with things can consist in a perception of a surprising strangeness in familiar occurrences. This strangeness is ordinary in the sense that people may experience it in the everyday course of worldly events and that astonishment shows a dimension of ordinary life. It's not that a special or separate world breaks through the haze of everyday experiences and knowledge. Rather, astonishment composes experiences of things in their specific differences and concreteness. Astonishment comprises an attunement to a dimension of occurrences that shows things at once in their meanings and their mere there-ness as they are— their blunt excess to their meanings. Such attunement encourages in people a certain reticence in their inclinations to see things only in terms of the uses and identifications by which they recognize what is happening. The occurrences of things exceed those uses, identifications, and recognitions, occur in a normal excess to what we make of the happenings in our world. Astonishment gives us to pause, to listen, to wonder and to puzzle, not to solve or to resolve or to conclude—or, if we are anxious, often to react to it by qualifying it with explanations or with stories of other worlds that have transcendent purposes and overarching continuity. A significant measure of meanings found in "nature" bear the marks of that kind of anxious response.

Martin Heidegger's approach to *phusis* offers a strong challenge to the approach that I have taken. On the one hand, he finds in *phusis* a primal meaning in our tradition that has formed a nearly forgotten basis for interpretations of "nature." Its meanings include an unresolvable tension, a "strife" of difference that I will discuss. On the other hand, *phusis* is terribly misshapen in the representational thought of modern science and philosophy and also requires an approach that tacitly opposes a large measure of this book's conceptuality, style, and language. I would like now to confront his account of *phusis* and in the engagement to show both its force and its limits for the account of physicality that I wish to develop.

Husserl wrote in *The Crisis of European Sciences*, "If we pay attention to the bodily aspect of the things, this obviously exhibits itself perceptively *only* in seeing, in touching, in hearing, etc., i.e., in visual, tactical, acoustical, and other such aspects."[1] In physical, sensuous experiences people would find their world in hopeless disarray were it not for a nonphysical egological unity in those experiences. The unity and possibility for the sensuous meaning resides in "the ego's active functioning" as a living, sensuous body (*Leib*, as distinct from *Körper*, physical body). That is, sensuous unity resides in nonphysical consciousness. The "I" holds sway as the unity of a sensuous diversity that a mere physical body (*Körper*), one without "the ego of affection to actions," could not experience.[2] "In my perceptual field I find myself holding sway as ego through my organs and generally through everything belonging to me in my ego-acts and faculties."[3] We do indeed, Husserl says, sense merely physical bodies but always with a living, ego-unified body: "we are perceptually in the field."[4] The world comes "passively" in its availability, but we are "active" in its perception. This world of sensuous life thus requires egological unity and through its phenomena, as we pay attention to how they are given, we are able to find the transcendental unity that can ground and give meaning to all knowledge.

Without giving adequate credit to the range and power of Husserl's description of "the life world," I note his predisposition to transcendental and highly ordered unity in all experience. Scientific knowledge, but only when it is properly grounded in the universal unity of subjectivity, can provide a crucial, connective cultural force for our understanding of the world. But even though perceiving consciousness is in the world that appears, and even though Husserl is favorable toward properly grounded and limited sciences, meaning can be found in its origins only by a strictly designed

1. Edmund Husserl, *The Crisis of European Sciences,* trans. David Carr (Evanston, Ill.: Northwestern University Press, 1970), p. 106, emphasis added.
2. Ibid., p. 107.
3. Ibid.
4. Ibid.

philosophical and transcendental work. Such expectations as we find in *The Crisis* are those from which Heidegger's account of *phusis* takes its departure. Body and bodiliness, he said, compose the most difficult question and one that he was not sure how to pose.[5] He lacks Husserl's transcendental certainty. He lacks confidence in traditional conceptions of body. He does not believe that consciousness is a proper starting point. He does want, however, a descriptive approach to the appearing of phenomena. He wants to get behind the assumptions that form the meanings of body, to begin again with the thought in our tradition that preceded concepts of body, nature, and subjectivity and that suggest other ways of thinking in occurrences of beings.[6]

"Nature" comes from the Latin word *natura,* which, as I noted in the last chapter, comes from *nasci,* to be born, to originate.[7] Heidegger's departure from that word is defined in large part by its function in naming the systematic representation of the truth about beings. It prescribes metaphysical meaning and order for all relations and for all beings without carrying with it either the manner of thinking or the meaning proper to *phusis.* Like Husserl, Heidegger wants to shift the emphasis of thought from *what* occurs to its *occurring*—to the *how*—but unlike Husserl, he, in his descriptive efforts, returns to this primal word *phusis* with the sense that the way the word is to be thought is not at all clear and with the further sense that the meanings of *natura* developed in an absence of awareness in and for the occurrence of *phusis* according to early Greek thought. The meaning of *phusis,* however, is basic for metaphysical concepts of nature but is honored primarily in the breach of proper attention that the word is due. The very distinction that Husserl uses between *Körper* and *Leib* in fact carries the greatest loss in our tradition regarding *phusis:* it indicates that consciousness is the seat of formation and order, of the how of phenomena. *Phusis,* on the other hand, and as we shall see in greater detail, requires a manner of thinking that does not give priority to consciousness of any kind and does not turn the occurrences of things and their fundamental

5. See, for example, *Zollikoner Seminare,* ed. Medard Boss (Frankfurt a. M.: V. Klostermann, 1987), p. 292.

6. In the following account I will not give a history of the development of Heidegger's accounts of *phusis.* His interpretations of the ancient Greek word and experience come in a variety of contexts with considerable repetition, and although the contexts are different and range from discussions of metaphysical thought and technology to direct readings of Heraclitus and Aristotle, his understanding of *phusis* revolves around a group of interpretations that remain fairly constant in a variety of works by him.

7. The following observations are based on Heidegger's "Vom Wesen und Begriff der *Phusis:* Aristoteles *Physik,* B, 1" in the *Gesamtausgabe* (Frankfurt a. M.: V. Klostermann), vol. 9. Henceforth, GA followed by volume number. "On the Being and Conception of *Phusis* in Aristotle's *Physics* B, 1," trans. Thomas Sheehan, in *Pathmarks,* ed. W. McNeil (Cambridge: Cambridge University Press, 1998). See especially pp. 239–42 in the German and pp. 183–85 in the English text.

connections into states of affairs that are best accounted as objects within a subjective order. In a phrase, *phusis,* for Heidegger, indicates primordial eventuation of disclosure and hiddenness, an ungrounding ground, with all things and without objectivity or consciousness. *Phusis* names no being—nothing specific—and means the same as two other basic and traditionally ill-considered words, *aletheia* and being.[8]

And yet the issue is nonetheless one of generation, the Greek *gen-,* "that which lets something come of (*entstammen*) itself."[9] That which lets something come of itself is not something that produces something else or that stands in opposition to something else: the issue of generation addresses *phusis,* not efficient causation, and "*phusis*" names, as Heidegger finds it in early Greek thinking, the eventuation of beings in their disclosive coming forth with accompanying concealment. This is the account that I will address in this section.

Origin does not mean point of origin or suggest any manner of subjectivity. "*Phusis*" does not mean anything that our dominant traditions would recognize as "nature," or "Nature," or natural order. *Phusis* as *aletheic,* as concealing-revealing occurrence, comprises unresolveable difference— "strife"—and astonishment can be a most appropriate companion with *phusis.* So far so good. But, as we shall also see, in addition to the remarkable and constructive force of his account of *phusis,* the way in which Heidegger prioritizes being, his judgments about technology and science, his overriding seriousness, and the way he prioritizes the history of thought leave out of consideration a dimension of occurrence that composes the happenings of specific things and give to his thought crucial aspects of abstraction and alienation before the lives of things.

"*Phusis*" names for Heidegger the primordial occurrence of appearing. In his *Introduction to Metaphysics*[10] he emphasizes the importance of making a "leap" of thought from contemporary conceptions to another way of perceiving, a leap that is necessary if we are to find the meaning of this word in our classical and pre-classical Greek heritage. This leap is crucial because *phusis* names the appearing of what appears in thought and

8. "For the earth in its worldly meaning (*Erdkreis*) goes out of joint—if indeed it were ever fittingly joined—and the question arises whether modern humanity's planning, even if it be planetary in its reach, can ever create a world fitting (*Weltgefüge*) for earth." Ibid., p. 242 (German), p. 185 (English), trans. altered. Sheehan translates *Weltgefüge* as "ordering of the world." *Gefüge* may be correctly translated as order, but Heidegger places in question in this essay the concept of order, and as I understand this sentence, he is addressing the way earth and world join in planetary planning. The issue of *Fug, Fuge,* and *fügen* is one of fit and fittingness in his thought, and order in connection with nature and *phusis* in our tradition composes a highly questionable interpretation of fit and fittingness.

9. Ibid., p. 239 (German), 183 (English), trans. altered.

10. Martin Heidegger, *Introduction to Metaphysics* (New Haven: Yale University Press, forthcoming). *Einführung in die Metaphysik* (GA 40); henceforth *EM.*

language as well as in all experience, and the way thinking and language happen comprises the specific ways in which attunements and presentations of *phusis* take place. If people persist in manners of thought and language that are not alert to *phusis,* those manners of thought and language will obscure their own disclosive lives. They will find their best fit with things by means of systematic orders that are insensitive to their own non-systematizeable, appearing occurrences. So we have a double opportunity as thinkers according to Heidegger. We find strategies, always problematic, to release ourselves from the grip of traditional preconceptions about order, generation, and origin, and we must experiment with ways to find fitting engagements with the difference of sensibility that is found in early encounters with the being of lives. The stakes are high for Heidegger in this effort. What has been lost regarding *phusis* figures a culture-depleting loss of sensitivity to the unusable, astonishing, un-orderable, ever-rising dimension of life. So we need to learn to think differently, to begin again, to bring our arising perceptions into accord with their own *phusic* dimension, and to become attuned with the *phusic* dimensions of all occurrences.

Consider what he says about *phusis.* Heraclitus uses the word to name "the ever and always-enduring rising" of things.[11] It names the rising and opening up of whatever is at the same time that it suggests an unreachable dimension of hiddenness in the eventuation of things. *Phusis* suggests disclosive upsurgence and self-concealing. It does not suggest presence but rather presencing.[12] For Heraclitus it does not mean primarily the sprouting of seeds, the rising up of growing things, the rising of the sun, or what we could recognize as "natural processes." It names, rather, the dimension in which "earth and sky, sea and mountain ranges, tree and animal, humans and God arise, and arise in such a manner that they show themselves and are available for naming in their arising as [specific] beings (*Seiendes*)."[13] It names the occurrence of appearing and the availability by virtue of which we can recognize the various connections and processes that some people call natural. In this sense, *phusis* occurs before nature can be thought.[14]

---

11. Martin Heidegger, *Early Greek Thinking,* trans. D. F. Krell and F. A. Capuzzi (New York: Harper and Row, 1975), p. 112. Henceforth *EGT.* See also *EM,* pp. 15ff.

12. *EGT,* p. 113.

13. Martin Heidegger, *Heraklit* (GA 55), p. 88, translation mine.

14. Or, "*phusis* the first sighted," ("*das anfänglich Gesichtete*") but overlooked, as when people walk into a room and immediately see its space but ignore this sighting and notice only what is in the room." *Heraklit,* 144. In *Besinnung,* p. 370, Heidegger cautions that *phusis* is not something to be gazed, that sighting of *phusis* is in no sense a gazing. I will address this below when I consider the *phusis* of thinking. See also *Beiträge zur Philosophie* (GA 65), pp. 189–90: nature is *phusis* taken as an objective field of objects.

Modern science, Heidegger says, sees in the growth of things only mechanical relations of efficient causes and effects. Scientists often find in growth only chemical discharges and plays of forces that they understand in mechanical terms. Science, he states, produces knowledge by techniques, calculations, methods, not by thought. *Phusis* appears in such an orientation as closer to a feat of "natural" engineering than to the disclosive uprising of things. Indeed, in such a context *phusis* can appear only as anachronistic, irrelevant for knowledge, at best merely poetic.[15] As "originary opening," however, as unconcealing, *phusis* is another word for *aletheia*—truth—the disclosive happening of things with no pretense of correctness. *Phusis* "is" that without which nothing at all would be. It names continuous, opening eventuation of all things.[16]

Phusis thus means the *coming* to presence of things, not an activity of *bringing* things into presence. In presencing, things are not concealed. They stand out and draw attention. In fact, people mostly pay attention to things, including themselves, at all levels in their lives in their need for shelter, sustenance, endurance, etc. The necessary draw of things in their presence draws away from their coming to presence, away from their happening, their full *phusic* dimensionality. It is as though *phusis* withdraws in the draw of things, and people become so rapt and wrapped up with things that they find little motivation to notice that life is happening, that things, no matter how fine or terrible, come to shine, to appear, to be. Concealment of *phusis* thus happens in the appearing and presencing of things, due not only to *phusis*' being no thing but due as well to the draw of things. And consequently people usually live in the dominance of things as though there were nothing astonishing in their happening. Or they treat the happening of life as though it were primarily a matter of one thing causing another. Or they look for a dominant thing that explains and gives meaning to everything else. For Heidegger that means not only that life loses its intrinsically sacred quality but also loses a spirit-engendering sense of marvel and mystery before life's happening with no apparent necessity outside of its own groundless eventuation.

"What does *phusis* mean? It means that which arises on its own, that which shows itself from itself."[17] In its occurrence, "clearing (*Lichtung*) and

15. Ibid. See also Martin Heidegger, *Aus der Erfahrung des Denkens* (GA 13), p. 146, and *Besinnung*, 366ff, for an account of *phusis*, truth, and the formation of a concept of nature. Heidegger brings this aspect of his thought to sharp focus on p. 380 with the statement: " . . . unhiddenness (*Unverborgenheit*) is an essential naming of *phusis* itself, the name for the being of beings." For further elaboration, see *Beiträge*, p. 191.
16. See *Besinnung*, pp. 366ff, for elaboration of *phusis* and unconcealment; also *Beiträge*, p. 330.
17. *EM*, p. 11. See also *EGT*, p. 15; *Beiträge*, p. 190; *Heraklit*, p. 157.

rising up reign."[18] The design[19] of this reign does not figure an original, definitive beginning or a purposive process. It—the design—is not a figure of anything but is rather the passing inevitability of *phusis.* I say "passing" because although Heidegger elaborates appreciatively Heraclitus' phrase, ever-rising, in his account of *phusis,* there is never an indication that "ever" means an unending line of time. It suggests, rather, no end of beginning in sight, unlimited occurrence at the moment. And while *phusis* is, for Heidegger, the meaning of time and in that sense is not under temporal control, the primary thought is that time happens thanks to *phusis* but enjoys no guarantee of never disappearing. No pre-temporal domain of timeless presence happens. Time happens with *phusis* and *phusis* with time, and neither gives lasting presence to the other.

Heidegger is addressing a casting forth—*Entwurf*—of life, its coming forth to be, its coming to pass, its occurrence as presencing: a design without substance or necessary figuration, a design with no purpose other than to be, a design that is not even subject to the temporal structure that Heidegger outlines in *Being and Time.* It is design as disclosure and concealment in things' coming to pass, design that, when attended properly, can provide a release for people from those affections and concepts that lead us to think that things, in the specificity of their designs, could provide a definitive structure for the way life must be.

Heidegger thus transformed the question of origin, of a definitive beginning or source of life, into the thought of the eventuation of what happens. He traced this transformation to early Greek experience and perceptiveness that has itself in our lineage been transformed into traditional conceptions of nature, objectivity, and subjectivity. He uncovered in the early Greek perceptions of life and *phusis* an initiating thought that finds its satisfaction not in scientific verification or quests for certainty but in a kind of mindfulness that lives without metaphysical or scientific resolutions. It is a mindfulness that maintains a sense of mystery and human limitation before the lives of things. It encourages awareness of the unmasterable and utterly nonhuman dimensions of all lives and awareness of the struggle that maintaining ourselves consonant with such mystery and limitation requires.

These are untimely thoughts on Heidegger's part in the sense that they do not fit with most assumptions that function silently in "our" best

18. *Heraklit,* p. 142.

19. Heidegger uses the word "*Entwurf*" which I will also translate as casting forth. There is this double sense in his use of a word that means, in this context, not order but a figuration of concealing-unconcealing, a figuration not unlike *chora* in the sense that its meaning disassembles any definitive form that might be assigned to it.

knowledge. They call a halt to contemporary, robust pursuit of frontiers of conquest by information, technique, and learning. They suggest with considerable power a defining connection between traditional metaphysical thought and present-day science and technology. Metaphysical efforts to discover meaning in all regions of life, a "discovery" that comes to manners of intellect that install such meaning, eventuates in present-day efforts to master methodically our environments by means of construction, prediction, and control: traditional thought and knowledge, "metaphysics" by Heidegger's account, exercises control, even a kind of manipulation, in its accounts of being-and-nature-with-meaning, and this controlling aspect grows into the more obvious technological and methodological efforts to control lives. Being (*phusis*) eventuates with many lively meanings and things, but none of them define or have sway over the occurring of what occurs. The transformation of the early experience of *phusis* into meaningful objectivity has participated powerfully in the rising up of cultures that expect to be able to direct themselves according to the nature of things—once the appropriate structures, methods, authorities, and funding are in place.

Even were Heidegger's interpretations to compose no more than a likely story with far more projective, imaginative texture than he recognized, still his accounts of *phusis* bring to the foreground what I take to be an important fact: operative concepts and images about order, origination, meaning in life, and nature compose a forceful predisposition in the ways we collectively and individually conduct our lives. Or, to speak in a manner closer to Heidegger's thought, *phusis* occurs in obscurity as the eventuation of thought and language, even when thought and language fail to recognize their own phusic dimension. When the lineage of *phusis* operates in our cultural predisposition as "nature" or as a determined, overarching presence, thought and language give rise to a world that is recognized as subject to control by humans and that is determined by definitive kinds of things rather than by ungraspable presencing. In this case, the eventuation of thought and language is pretty much overlaid by the priority of causes, initiatives, and authoritative meanings that derive from definitive states of affairs. In a word, human mentation is experienced primarily in terms of subjectivity and its correlate, objectivity. In that experience a lot about lively occurrences is not appreciated, especially a dimension of singularity that appears as unorderable by meanings as well as an unorderable dimension of no specific necessity for occurrence as such.

People might read Heidegger's thoughts on *phusis* as suggesting that capital "B" "Being" enjoys a priority so massive that "beings" have at best a secondary importance. He is certainly persuaded that a fundamental error occurs when any way of being is given priority over being (*phusis*). But that interpretation by Heidegger can be held only at the cost of seeing that for him being occurs as the eventuation of beings, that *phusis* has no status other than beings' eventuation, and that Heidegger is not addressing a deep ground of being that can be accessed by mystical experiences. In this aspect of his thought, Heidegger is attempting to show that we can fully appreciate beings' singularities only when we give marked and persistent emphasis to their eventuation. Eventuations give beings to be their own events, their own singularities. That emphasis means that no being or group of beings have complete jurisdiction over the life of another being—no Source, no Origin, no Order. Hence Heidegger's word *Ereignis* that I am translating as "eventuation" can also be translated legitimately as "enownment"—being enowns beings in the sense that "being" names each being's arising into its own event.

That is a forceful and creative aspect in Heidegger's consideration of *phusis* that I would like to keep in view. Another aspect is consequent to his persuasion that *phusis* must be thought in its withdrawal from the singularities of all events. He has good reason for this persuasion: many limited events have formed the basis in our tradition for making cosmic universal judgments about the essential nature of all things. People might project their religious or moral beliefs and meanings onto the entire world and contend that those beliefs and meanings essentially define everything. Or they might take a form of causation to define essentially all connections. Or they might privilege the way some kinds of recognitions occur, such as perceptions of objects, and require such recognition for any "true" knowledge. And the meanings of nature have so firmly built into them a notion of universal Source as to render the word at best questionable. But in his sharp differentiation of *phusis* from things, even granting their inseparability, Heidegger presents *phusis* as though it were not definitively and finally worldly.

We do not, however, find *phusis* in an unworldly place. Its appearances happen only in temporal and earthly contexts. But the concealment, the *lethe,* that comes with its appearance not only indicates that *phusis* can be thought solely in continuous and performative presentations of things—artistic and thoughtful presentations that are attuned to the things' eventuation. Concealment also functions to hold *phusis* at a distance from the very things that eventuate. It functions to give *phusis* a strange kind of status in Heidegger's language, not the status of a being but the status of an undetermined and wholly privileged word, a conception of ever-rising life that escapes circumscription, that occurs indirectly in the *ways* all things are conceived, and that enjoys the privileges—the authoritative status—of a master that cannot be touched, one that requires people to return to it endlessly as though "it" were an intangible pearl of immeasurable value to which we are drawn but which we can never quite perceive. Upon this intangibility depend, for Heidegger, the truest hopes of our culture, a possible resurgence of profound religious sensibility, and, indeed, the destiny of human life.

This apocalyptic side of Heidegger's thought bears consequences. Consider what he says about human life in the context of sidereal expanse in his *Introduction to Metaphysics:* "If we properly pursue the question, 'why are there beings at all and not rather nothing?' in its sense as a question," he tells his students in this lecture,

> we must avoid emphasizing any particular, individual being, not even focusing on the human being. For what is this being, after all! Let us consider the earth within the dark immeasurability of space in the universe. By way of comparison it is a tiny grain of sand; between it and the next grain of its size there extends over a kilometer of emptiness; on the surface of this tiny grain of sand lives a stupefied swarm of ostensibly clever animals, crawling over each other, who for a brief moment have invented knowledge. And what is a life span amid millions of years? Hardly a move of the second hand, a breath. Within beings as a whole there is no justification to be found for emphasizing precisely the being which is called human being and among which we happen to belong.[20]

But, he says, when beings as a whole receive focused attention in the question of why there is anything and not just nothing, they provide human beings with quite a distinct and significant relation to mortal life. In contrast to human beings' seeming insignificance in the universe when people consider human beings and the universe in objective and theoretical terms, the questionableness of lives' happening at all gives moment and meaning to each happening and to human life most especially. This cosmically insignificant "grain of sand" becomes *the* site of all that matters.

Heidegger is pointing out that there is no objective basis for the assumption of human value in the universe. So far, so good. The priority of objective presence that formed a major metamorphosis of *phusis* in our tradition has led, however, according to Heidegger, to a sense of things, including vast space, in which human life is degraded to insignificance. People can recover a sense of significance and meaning when they follow the still living, if faint intimations of *phusis'* meaning: although all things come to pass, although being itself is always in question and never supported by an everlasting Presence, people can find their meaning in the non-objective eventuation of *phusis* (i.e., being, *aletheia*). Contingent life comes into its own in its unresolvable, ever-rising questionableness. In that experience, people do not expect resolution. They find what life means as they struggle to live appropriately with its questionable eventuation.

20. *EM,* p. 6.

And yet, Heidegger apparently does not experience astonishment in the "fact" of human insignificance in the midst of vast things—in which vastness even the primacy of *phusis* blinks and sputters to nothing. I doubt that we need the matter-splattered space of the sky in order to meet with the obliterating denseness of physicality. We meet such denseness in the most everyday things—in the space of you and me, in the disclosive word that will not be what it discloses, in this body or that window, in the transpiration of ideas, in the slosh of liquid in our inner ears. The eventuation of things—physicality as I see it—happens with things in density, meanings, lineages, connections, and mere nothing at all, as I shall elaborate. But Heidegger holds *phusis* apart from its situated context of historically determined meaning, and in this privileging he weakens the emphasis on specific events that we also find in his thought. Rather, he lets *phusis* appear as though protected by infinite transcendence and with a sense of purity and priority attached to it that make facts and daily life seem "merely" mundane and spiritually inferior to disciplined concentration on being, its question and its thought.

AN INTERLUDE WITH MR. DEWEY ON EXPERIENCE AND NATURE

John Dewey developed a "method" of thought that he names empirical naturalism and that "inspires the mind with courage and vitality to create new ideals and values in the face of the perplexities of a new world."[21] As I move from Heidegger's account of *phusis* I would like to pause with some of Dewey's reflections as helpful points of departure—way stations—in the work of this chapter. He is alert to the importance of contemporary knowledge (including scientific knowledge) in orienting philosophical thought to changes of sensibility regarding our physical world, changes that are profound when compared to the sensibilities of earlier times. Like Heidegger, he finds in metaphysical transcendental thought a pathological loss of direct engagements with things. In contrast to Heidegger he does not regret many of the changes effected by scientific knowledge, although he certainly sees danger in an exclusive emphasis on science and scientific instrumentalism. He finds, rather, that we need to find ways of thought and recognitions that inspire respect for concrete experiences, interest in human potential, hope, courage—inspire vitality in our interpretive interactions with things. The dangers of technology and science compose opportunities for cultural development and enhancement, not a need for

---

21. John Dewey, *Experience and Nature* (New York: Dover, 1958), p. x. In this section I will include page references to this book within the text.

retreat to earlier conventions and habits of mind. Although one would be stretched to find two more contrasting styles of thought, Dewey shares with Nietzsche a conviction that future-oriented vitality initiates the creativity and dynamism that a healthy society requires (although he does not share Nietzsche's or Heidegger's passion for antiquity and philology in their approach to future time).

Dewey is clear that our world is composed of events with histories, not substances, and that regularities among events are not governed by substantial guarantees of regularity. When we approach "nature" on his terms we are approaching a group of interconnecting events that are contingent in all of their dimensions. "Experience" names our contingent means of access to other contingent events; it is our most "natural" means of "penetrating continually further into the heart of nature," into "a growing progressive self-disclosure of nature itself" (x).

This is language that is hard to swallow for those of us who find "nature" a construct, who hear unconscious echoes of the idea of substance in "nature itself," and who doubt that "nature" has a heart, that "its" disclosure is best conceived in terms of progress, and that "penetration" is a happy word for what people do when they experience things with intense and attentive awareness. But my purposes in this engagement with Dewey are not primarily critical (just as my engagement with Heidegger does not have the primary intention of conceptual critique). It's rather his way of connecting feeling, experience, and "nature" that appears to me vital for this discussion, for in that connection, as far as I can tell, we find a prioritizing of physical eventuation without transcendent spiritualization or materialistic reduction.

"The *intrinsic* nature of events is revealed in experience as the immediate felt qualities of things" (xii). Not in language. Not in an intentional a priori structure of subjectivity. Not in objectivity. Not in disciplined thought. The immediate felt qualities of things in experience reveal the *intrinsic* (that's Dewey's underscoring) "nature" of events. I would like to add to the emphasis by underscoring "of things": the immediate felt qualities *of things* reveal—I interpolate—the *intrinsic* aspects of events. This means that the occurrences of events and the affective experiences that reveal them enjoy a basic, if often interrupted, continuity. In Dewey's language that also means that events and feelings are both "natural." I would prefer to say that events and feelings, while different, are worldly and accessible to each other.[22] But experience, for Dewey, can name a direct engagement

22. I place the word "worldly" in this context since I wish to emphasize the extensive and worldly dimensions of physical occurrences. I take this emphasis to be compatible with Dewey's emphasis on the sociality of experience, although I doubt that "experience" can carry the full meaning of "worldly," as we shall see.

with things in which the image of "nature" there, and I here, will not work.[23] This initial and persistent emphasis on things in nature is one part of the vitality that Dewey feels and incites. It composes an emphasis, not on "reality" that is abstractly conceived, but on events in their specificity, on things in their interactive dynamism without other, higher justifications or reasons. Dewey is looking to understand *things* in their "nature," in their occurrences, and he finds in this sensibility a liveliness that seems to come with things in their full and un-metaphysical range of engagements. The point is: the vitality of engagements with things needs no justification and no grounding in addition to their own physical and social events.

In their specificity and concreteness, however, events take place in environments that are unstable and precarious—in "an aleatory world." "The world is a scene of risk" and the whole of experience comprises a flow of often unpredictable episodes and irregular eras with fortune and disaster. The perilous world in combination with human interest in survival and flourishing produces a fearful nature, an unreliable whole of things: human action is forever trespassing upon the domain of the unknown, upon the anxious borders of unpredictability where dire consequences "haunt" the best laid plans (43). Humans transpire in given circumstances that make their efforts closer to a wager than to a region of artful control and regulation. Human stabilities are *by nature* dangerous instances of unstable constructions. The "dire" dimension of life is, according to Dewey, a fact.[24]

This fact is peculiar when it is compared to the facts of, say, mathematics or the measurement of weight. It refers to an incalculable and immeasurable situation, to, we could say, the contingency of things in a social environment. Presumably it applies to all other facts, to all constructions of certainty, and does not name a thing but names the invisible "nature" of things, their very occurrence: "in the end what is unseen decides what happens in the seen" (43). But no one is there to make a decision that produces contingency. "The tangible rests precariously upon the untouched and ungrasped," and they "are indestructible features of

23. Dewey and Husserl share much in common in the primary importance they give to ordinary experience for advanced, disciplined knowledge as well as for everyday life. Dewey says that the scientist "sees to it that ventures of this theoretical sort start from and terminate in directly experienced subject-matter. . . . And this experienced material is the same for the scientific man and for the man in the street. The latter cannot follow the intervening reasoning [of science] without special preparation. But stars, rocks, trees, and creeping things are the same material of experience for both" (p. 2a). And experience is, for him, at once in nature as well as of nature. In his often noted words, "it is not experience which is experienced, but nature--stones, plants, animals, diseases, health, temperature, electricity, and so on. Things interacting in certain ways are experience; they are what is experienced" (4a). In experience we are with things in *their* occurring before we know anything about them.

24. You can see that, in this context, facts are not necessarily completed events, and that they can compose observations that are based on methods of investigation and established regularities of experience. But they are open, not because being withdraws from them or from experience but because they always express fluid contexts of experience and knowledge.

any and every experience" (43–44). That is a primary and "natural" "datum in any experience" (44).

The natural tendency in human experience is to "safeguard against the uncertain character of the world . . . to deny the existence of chance, to mumble universal and necessary law, the ubiquity of cause and effect, the uniformity of nature, universal progress, and the inherent rationality of the universe" (44). These efforts to assure regularity are "magic formulae" that arise naturally from feelings of fundamental insecurity and threat. For Dewey, our techniques of control, from machinery to universal laws, constitute natural responses to nature's experienced hazardous course of events. But "our attainments are only devices for blurring the disagreeable recognition of *a fact,* instead of means of altering the fact itself" (44–45, emphasis mine). The "nature of the existential world" does not support *meta*-physical constructions for the relief of the ungrounded, chancy, and natural turns of events.

This mundane and natural situation of contingency is found through feelings of thorough insecurity in the midst of experiences in an indeterminately large surround that is euphemistically and euhemeristically called a whole. In this instance "natural" feelings reveal a fact of nature, reveal something intrinsic in natural events in a human world. And from such disclosive feelings arise all manner of ideas and beliefs that function to produce the image of a well-organized and purposive universe. Such images are as natural in their origins as they are inept in eliminating the fact that they indirectly express and directly attempt to overcome the insecurity of contingent intentions (45ff). The bottom line? All images of lasting continuities, be they relativisitic or absolute in their conclusions, betray what people naturally know by their affective and disclosive constitution. They function as instruments of attempted control that in fact distance people from the specific events in their lives.

There is nothing wrong with people's interests in avoiding disaster. That comes with the territory, and their inclinations toward flourishing show another fact of human life. Nor is there anything wrong, in Dewey's view, with people constructing artistic, philosophical, and social environments that maximize what they find beneficial for their lives. But when such "natural" constructions of interest, desire, and apprehension betray and obscure their own fragility—their own natural dependence on uncertain developments—and when they distance people's recognitions from uncertain eventuations of things and inspire people to expect Order where none exists, these constructions are "violent" and displace people in their relations with things (65). They naturally produce mindsets that are at odds with their own nature; but empirically we have just what we started with: "a mixture of the precarious and problematic with the assured and complete" (54). We have, still, the fact of contingency in all events.

So "nature" names for Dewey a collage of events, not a unified entity. It is a word to collect together the progressions and transformations in the ways things themselves happen in occurrences of various figurations of interaction. It is indeed a master word: nothing escapes its governance in Dewey's thought. I am not sure of the extent to which it falls under its own jurisdiction for him as a dispensable part of the collage of this thought. But I am reasonably clear that he intends for it to eventuate in his thought for the enhancement of experimental and empirical thinking and recognition, to give attention to each event's complex but singular, social occurrences, to encourage attention to transformational consequences, and to indicate that all stabilities (including its own?) have no governing Stability to support them (does his use of "contingency" suggest a peculiar stability?). "Nature" names an absence of universals, be they purposes or principles. It names continuous lack of completion. It suggests a continuous arising of unfamiliarity. Dewey certainly thought that his thinking—his "naturalistic metaphysics"—occurred within nature (68). And in this conviction he considered nature "something" in which we find ourselves and our world, in which and by which we are formed and governed. Not a god, certainly, but godlike in some of its seemingly absolute functions. But never mind such tension between "nature's" status and non-status in Dewey's thought. Sympathetic interlocutors will have no doubts that they are led away in Dewey's work from any sense that nature is like a subject or a particular being. Nor will such people be inclined to think of bodies in atomistic terms; they too are inactive events, and human bodies have an affective immediacy with other events that exposes them to what is own-most—to what is intrinsic—in those events. When reflective people and trained scientists are attentive to affective interactions with other events, the knowledge that such reflection and science produce will be appropriate in its measure as it develops and transforms into ever-rising contemporary forms.

PHYSICAL EVENTS

I have been so unkind to the little word, nature! I have singled it out with special and uncomplimentary marks—"nature." I have put its usefulness in doubt repeatedly. I have made accusations about its bad effects in people's ways of connecting with things. And now we have seen Dewey using the word with the purpose of bringing people back to the singularities of events in a context that respects organizational systems and social, historical influences, while valiantly resisting reified universals and metaphysical grounds. At best, for Dewey, "nature" indicates eventuating situations and the regularities that happen to characterize them. His emphasis on feeling, for all the subjective suggestions that the word carries, gives an opening for further considerations of the physical constitution of human beings' most basic perceptiveness. I begin this discussion of physical events with an appreciation for Dewey's accomplishment, as well as for Heidegger's, and with an interest in shadings, shifted emphases, and altered vocabulary that will allow for an understanding of our encounters with things that in the main do not fit, quite, with Dewey's or Heidegger's understandings and in some particulars do not fit at all with either of their ways of thinking.

I note especially "ways of thinking." I wish to present a reflective orientation and attitude that enjoys a lighter mood than Heidegger's, and one that is not turned by an epistemological preoccupation like Dewey's. It is a manner of thinking that does not always begin with or return to the question of being. It expresses the persuasion that too much weighty seriousness in thought corrupts our perceptiveness by nonvoluntarily giving priority to seemingly static dimensions in events and often to a sluggish energy and motility. An overbearing seriousness often comes sooner rather than later in our tradition, a tradition that often associates seriousness with profundity and lightness of mind with frivolity. Weighty seriousness gravitates by centering, by fixing a center. It often seems either to engender or to arise from an obsessive interest in a stable center for things in their variations and mobile borders; it seems unable to free itself for its own dispersions and vicissitudes.[25] This is not a question of being frivolous or without seriousness. It is one of the ways seriousness of intent occurs. It is a question of whether thought's concentration and commitment insist always on the trajectory and values of their points of departure, on their own colloidal identity, or whether they give themselves to change and unpredictability. It is a question of whether knowledge, thought, and belief grow and develop by mutation so that their identities seem to lighten and often to break into other forms of affirmation and expression. This can be a matter of people's releasing themselves to transformations of mind in the midst of strong intention and direction. Lightness of mind usually figures, I believe, a lively expectation of transformation within the dynamics of its identifying values and meanings.

Traditions are, of course, bearers of habits of mind as well as being progenitors of them. Dewey provides a good instance of departure from many traditional habits by his emphasis on new developments in knowledge as well as in social practice. Departures from aspects of Western

---

25. "Artists," Thomas Mann reported, "have become ailing eagles because art has become solemn." His observation was connected directly to the unhappy, weighty and pathetic solitude of the contemporary artist, a solitude that would connect with that sense of isolation that comes with solemn efforts to establish firm, if artistic, centers in our recognitions of things. "Voyage with Don Quixote," in *Essays* (New York: Vintage, 1957).

European politics and culture, departures that have helped to form American democracy, are active in his thought, especially in his accounts of transformational knowledge and the nonauthoritative instabilities of "nature." Heidegger, on the other hand, finds his radical departure from the Western mainstream of traditional metaphysics only within that traditional stream and, outside of phenomenology, not from the contemporary formation of new knowledges or from the creations of a democratic society. His close work on canonized texts composes the sites of his most decisive transformations of Western thinking—and all the while, he thinks of his project as one that returns to original and largely lost meanings *in* the texts that he reads, as one that returns the tradition to its forgotten radicality.

When people address direct experiences they will invoke epistemological and traditional discourses as well as find the marks of those discourses in experiences. In the address I use, however, we find that there are aspects of direct experience that defy the very intelligence that perceives and helps to form them. I wish to put emphasis on those aspects by means of "physicality," aspects that appear in their address not to justify metaphysical or ethical responses, but the recognition of which can have a valuable bearing on our ways of being with each other and things in our world.

BEGINNINGS

Throughout this book I use "physicality" and "physical" to include the occurrence of such things as DNA, cellular clocks, and the sounding equipment in ears as well as psychological formations, traditions and their constancies and conflicts, and social environments. I do this in part because the events that I am paying most attention to are appearances—the coming to appear of things and their durations in people's worlds. Included in this emphasis is a second one: in their appearing, the lives of things show a considerable excess to meaning and sense. I have indicated two sites of such excess. One is in the eventuation—the physicality—of such things as sense organs, brains, blood, cellular organizations, etc. All things, I believe, appear to people in the niche—the environment—of people's intra-communicative cellular and social lives. That's about the same as saying that people have to be there for something to be with them. (And the idea that people's brains, i.e., their consciousness, can operate in some areas—"pure regions"—where there are appearances untainted by histories, psychologies, and all the other "cellular organizations" of social, personal, historical lives strikes me as absurd.) Our appearing physiology happens in the formative generations of minerals, patterns of gene expression, the spaces of mutational randomness as well as in the shapes and rhythms of people's life-forming events that are carried in practices, languages, regulations, and a lot more. (I will say more about these things in the following chapters.) The very site of appearing is physical, and "physical" here means cellular and organically functional as well as individual and socio-historical—indeed, while distinguishable, in events these regions are inseparable. So: in the physicality of appearances and also in people's perceptions and thoughts—in the social-multicellular events of people's worldly niches—what we broadly call evolutionary and social history happen. That's one complex dimension in the physicality of appearing.

A second dimension is found in the appearencial impacts on people, on their communicative cellular, social systems. Just as there are unencompassable aspects in the happening of cells and languages as people live them, aspects whose happening appears in excess to what recognizably appears—"something" within our identities that is at once constitutive and foreign to *who* we are, "something" at once within us and without us—so what impacts us as appearing brings with it its own outside-us, other-with-us, otherness-to-us that comes with appearing presence.

When we consider beginnings we are at the edges of appearing. A maddening thing about the origin of a fetus' *life*, for example, if you're trying to figure out when or where its life begins, is that the initial cells involved in gestation are already alive. The cellular systems of sperm and egg are alive, and their DNA give rise to a much more complicated, growing, palingenetic life. The *life* of the fetus does not begin as its system forms. The origin of its life goes much further "back" in biological development. I expect that the biochemists are right in saying that the origins of biological lives arose from no life and are found in the syntheses of bio-molecules and the development of self-replicating systems of DNA. The beginnings that I have in mind, however, are those by virtue of which there is something for people to refer to, something "there," an appearance. The physicality of such beginnings does not suggest a unified origin, as appearances emerge. Things impact us, are there to name or enjoy or avoid or blow up or not notice. Things emerge with the impacts of taking and making spaces. They make differences. They appear with and without, both, at once, social and personal histories with cellular developments and limitations. In the emerging of things we find people, worlds of meanings, vast generations of development, intelligences, no intelligence at all, much commotion, meaning and no meaning, and impenetrable silence. When I speak of physicality I would like to draw attention to the emerging of things without suggesting the necessity of authorship ("Nature gives . . . allows . . . requires . . . ," etc.), of Necessary continuity among operations, of Laws governing laws, or of Origins with definitive purposes for the "whole" of things. When such emphases become habitual, I expect that the question of definitive origins will have less significance than it has had in our mythological and philosophical past.

Phusis, as a basic meaning in "physical," as we have seen, connotes beginnings and births but not necessarily a definitive event in a series of events. Nor does it necessarily suggest the overarching presence of an initiator or of an efficient cause. It can name the emerging of appearances, their nascent happenings, their coming to be there and transformatively persisting for a time. When I pay attention to this *phusis*-dimension of things, I find nothing that guarantees their happening. They simply occur with all of the conditions that play in their lineages and interconnections.

Events happen—come to be, emerge—with a shocking lack of meaning in the midst of their meanings, I have said. They bring in their appearances a deterioration of meaning, something like a demarcation of meaning's limit. Not only do they not tell their stories. They also limit the reach of narration. They can, by doing nothing but happening, draw us to silence, a perceptive silence in the sense of composing no recognition in the midst of recognizing them. In chapter 1, I figured this silence by means of astonishment, but we might also think of it as no word in the borders of meaning, no complete presence, just eventuation—*that* dimension of physicality. I suppose that most people have experienced such silence in relatively dramatic ways, while in foreign circumstances, alone on a mountain, in deep water, or in a room or a personal relationship that becomes strange in its familiarity. Silence becomes apparent in many situations and with many feelings. However a silence might become apparent to individuals, its own happening offers nothing but what people make of it, and usually it is obscured by our "making of it." I find that the silence of events often does not mean a thing. "It" happens without—without plenum, without purpose, without reason, without even a shade of humanity or divinity. Events in their specific eventuations happen in silence without meaning as they make their sounds and meaningful differences in their appearances.

As people undergo silence they find nothing in it that authorizes their lives, nothing by which they can evaluate themselves or know who they are, nothing other than their historical experiences of themselves. We are usually held hostage by lineages of identity and interpreted experiences, but the eventuations of the lineages that play so many roles in our physicality, even those eventuations, in their silence, leave our lineages alone to their specificities and multiple, mutational conflicts. The eventuations of our experiences in the silence of physicality mark limits to our practices and voices. They cut across our claims of authority with their dimension of no authorship. Nothing overarching and "natural" gives our practices and voices to be as they specifically occur in their fecund lineages, in their texts, cellular communications, dictionaries, genes, codes of law and order, grammars, hormones, methods of discovery, manners of educating and cultivating, upright postures, neuroses, passions, diets, social catastrophes, diseases, ligaments, muscles, hemisphered brains, and comet-carried minerals from exploded stars.

In our physical world things come to be and we with them with an unencompassable complexity of lineages of narration, come to be with stories and habits, with silence and with such starkness as to leave us feeling alone in the company of our accounts and ways of living, alone in a "universe" or, depending on our attitude, in an awe-inspiring richness of environments where we might thrive for a time and at best tell stories that comfort and enliven us and orient us toward the lives of things.[26]

I have blurred the lines between things and appearances in order to indicate that our appearing world is not one solely of appearances, that things that appear usually bring in their appearances an "already here" quality that constitutes another dimension of the silence of emergence and eventuation. With the rising up of an appearance comes also something like a discontinuity of appearing, an eventuation of not appearing, bringing with it a "where" in which appearing was not happening. There is nothing strange in that if a person is alert to the appearing limits in appearing events, and people could well feel good about events in their independence of appearance, feel a certain comfort in reasonable certainty that the world is persisting, quite without regard for whether it appears, that we are in a site that is not completed or exhausted by appearances. Only a very strangely turned mind could miss the excess to appearing that comes with appearing things, a turn of mind, perhaps, that expects events to be like dreams or to be thoroughly meaningful or a mind that requires a world that is permeated through and through with the sounds of purpose and order and nothing else.

Beginnings—the multiple arising of multiple things bearing with them no unity of generation, bearing silences among differences that are in and out of continuities, non-appearing with appearing, and strangeness with all familiar things.

RESONATING LIVES

"Physicality" can suggest a complexity of elements with varying degrees of organic organization inclusive of mentational happenings, social and institutional histories, spaces, times, flesh and sand, genetic memories, energies with their attractions and repulsions, and much more. The word

---

26. I have an image of an expanded brain that could hear all of the sounds as something—whether a social experience or the arrival of a light—emerges: the crunching of worms in the ground, water sounds, the sounds of turning pages, of computer operations, doors closing, birds' wings, conversations, bodily organs at work, insects, solar winds—all of the sounds as something rises up to appear. But I have no idea what stories such a brain might tell.

here intends to say that the arising, persisting, and cessation of lives happen with resonance in interconnections with whatever makes up the environmental niche of their happening. They are constituted by interactions with other lives that happen there, whether those lives come with vibrations, particles of dust, small chunks of denser things, air and light, genes, habits, or groups of social formations. Singular lives happen in the investments and impacts of other lives. They are intrinsically relational, including the strings of cells that hold memories or register an itch on my toe. Lives and living moments are not necessarily like texts or images, as you know when something hits you on the back of your head or you need to breathe and can't or, at night, when you are barefoot and step on something before you know it's a very large frog. Lives engage us and we engage lives, usually at a level that the more enlightened among us might call primitive and that those who think of consciousness as referring only to human, rational reflection might call (ill-advisedly, in my opinion) unconscious.[27] It's the lives of things that draw and repel us, often at a level of corporeality where our conscious identities are minimally operative and there is no designated "them." Relation upon relation upon relation, in knowledge, beyond knowledge, in feelings and beyond them too, always coming and going, always transforming, usually there long enough to make a difference. Lives in their interconnections are so much *there* in their events, so rampant and fugitive in their dispersions, so often ill suited to the orders we inflict upon them, so likely to inflict their unregarding wildness on our orders. (By "lives" here I do not mean only vines and elephants. I mean the viruses in our blood as much as the deer in our gardens, the cells in our brains as much as the mouse in my cabinet. I mean economic systems and rational beliefs. I mean all physical events.)

I expect that one of the reasons many people are drawn, even awed by big and complex things like mountains, cities, oceans, storms, and also by the immensity of extraordinary accomplishment is that "something" uncultural and untextual resonates in such events, "something" of the extensiveness of lives that is hard to ignore, "something" unreachable and yet operative in our physicality—inside and outside, beyond art and thought, yet appearing, dumbly, inchoately, "something" quite physical, reverberating without a care and yet strangely familiar in a dimension of our lives that is without intelligence and needs no words.

You can see the sensibility that operates as I speak of the lives of things. I will address in the following chapters some of the dense and light elements

27. Unconscious in relation to what? To self-reflexive consciousness. But a string of cells in an operating neuron is certainly an event of awareness, and self-reflexive consciousness is certainly a neurological event.

that compose varieties of resonance and kinship among many different lives. Such kinships are, to my ears at least, no less astonishing than the kinships of sounded meanings and vibrations in ears and winds. The kinships of lives are physically and elementally resonant. They have to do with gravity and light, minerals and proteins, variations of movements and rhythms and other compositional likenesses. Physical kinships—commonalities in physical events, as I hope to show in the following chapters—can play out among sentient creatures as feelings and senses, subliminal awarenesses, draws and repulsions, something like a preverbal understanding—not particularly a bonding but a capacity for responsiveness, occasionally for sympathy, at times for a quiet yes or no that wells up, or so it seems, from nowhere.

My children found the lifeless and cold body of a day-old kitten that had been left by dogs that had killed its mother. The kids were young and insisted that I doctor the kitten and bring it back to life. With a reluctance and foreboding of disappointment that you can appreciate, I dutifully counseled them about the odds as they cuddled the body and heated a towel to wrap it. I began to rub the area of its heart, and my daughter did a tiny version of camp-learned mouth-to-mouth resuscitation. And suddenly! The little body inhaled in three tiny, consecutive gasps—its heart began to vibrate like a disturbed clock, it moved, and was alive. We all had tears in our eyes as we laughed. In addition to the cultural aspects, I think that there was also operative in our feelings something like primordial kinship as we perceived inhaling, heart beating, and the (re)beginning of a life.

The kitten venture was better than any discourse, but it didn't last very long. The little one breathed, ate from an eyedropper, snuggled up to a well-tended hot-water bottle or a breathing child's tummy, and died two days later. There is also, I believe, a primordial resonance when a warm-blooded creature perceives another such creature as it dies. That resonance may be accompanied by indifference or relief or terror or shock or sorrow, but whatever the response, I expect resonance to occur that composes physical awareness of death. Consider, for example, death tremors: when a body is shutting down, some part of the brain often sends out signals to activate all those hormonal events that have resisted the dangers of life-threatening shock or wounding. People having death tremors become agitated and shake, will not sleep, as their bodies react to a precipitous slide toward death. The name of this response—death tremor—suggests the degree of its effectiveness. But this enactment also indicates a kind of physical awareness, a resonant antipathy in impending disaster.

Such homey, ordinary, un-heroic examples of physical resonance as these could be multiplied, I believe, on a massive scale without a person's needing, in narrating them, to deviate toward exceptional accomplishments, foreign environments, or mystical judgments. My suggestion is that lives often have physical attunements with each other that appear to arise in compositional and organizational likenesses, that when alertness occurs, it happens physically and environmentally, and that when we pay attention to lives and their resonances we are, at best, directed to other, interconnected lives.[28] A conviction that arises for me out of this emphasis on resonant lives can be stated this way: it's mortal lives that count, whether negatively or positively. What else matters but lives? I wonder at times why that is so hard to understand in many parts of both Eastern and Western philosophical and religious traditions. Is it because people know that they are in a very big place that holds uncountable dangers and they want most to survive, that the place itself is not especially friendly, that maybe Something with interests and plans that could help is there, Something that counts for much more than any of the weaker lives, and that Something is the One or Ones that need primary attention? Everything else seems at best secondary? Is it that individuals usually want most to be their own events and this desire often fires a mood of unconcern regarding lives that are not relevant to this desire? Is it a question of sympathetic resonance in conflict with another kind of resonance, an organic interest in persisting, one that inclines organisms to ignore what does not directly aid or threaten them?

ORDERS AND SYSTEMS

Capital "L" Law, as far as I can tell, has its only justification as a site for departure to more invigorating environments. The lives of things are certainly regular in many of their aspects, and some of those regularities are definitive of groups of lives. Lives enact orders and organizations, and people enact orders and organizations that apparently carry back to elementary systems of cellular communication and replication. We enact these primordial, physical systems of organizations as we go about ordering and organizing ourselves in sophisticated ways. Organic lives and deaths comprise orders in all of their physical dimensions. But when the meanings of final unity, ultimate order and authority, and universal harmony are added to those of order and system, then repression and conquest in the name of "higher" authority seem likely to result.

Perhaps people usually move toward growth and reproduction. Perhaps the meanings of Law compose a version of growth and reproduction insofar as they provide bases for incorporation, control, and conquest of other lives.

But even if the orders of movement are law-like, the meanings inscribed in capitalization and the authority and universalization that the

---

28. This suggestion is developed further in chapters 4 and 5.

grammar suggests add another dimension to inevitability, often a dimension of domination and mastery and, rather sooner than later, one of interpretive privilege—and all of that frequently within motivations toward greater peace, stability, and decency among people.

The issues we are facing as we confront orders of "nature" are, of course, those of interpretation—orders of interpretation, in the present instance, concerning what is traditionally interpreted as orders of nature. I have said that lives (including the lives of interpretations) happen outside of the circumference of interpretations as well as outside the circumference of art and habits of mind. I have modified "lives" by variations of *phusis*—e.g., "physical lives"—in order to check uses of "nature" that have slipped into the sway of such interpretive meanings as universal, harmony, purpose, and definitive origin. The strategic use of "physicality" encourages hesitation and uncertainty with "nature" and suggests further that this word that is supposed to emphasize the nontheoretical concreteness of things and orders has in fact often placed lives and things at a considerable remove from their physical events. Most people in this culture do not experience the heavens as filled with bodies that affect human orders and that might, as it were, clap their hands in joy over their creator's law-abiding majesty. But many of us are not much less anthropocentric than that image is in our images of Laws, Purpose, and Unified Origin, or as we use "itself" in reference to nature. One consequence that we have seen is a frequent tendency to recognize things in terms of "nature," to give "nature" a value-laden priority over lively events, and to look for a unified meaning for everything. In another time, such disinheritance of things from their own eventuations might have been called nihilistic. I would prefer to speak of devaluations of things by reference to "nature" and "its" requirements. Although things have orders in their organizations, I doubt that there are atemporal, universal things that are found by insight, higher vision, or revelation—Laws, for example—of which living things are exemplary. And the mischief in the atemporal images seems clear enough in their roles in peoples' many efforts toward moral and cultural domination as well as in predispositions to engage things by reference to Something other to their own eventuations in their environmental niches.

DIMENSIONS

The following chapters will address in several contexts cultural, social, and psychological dimensions in physical eventuations. With the emphases that I have given to organic functions, cellular organizations, and nonreflective awareness, however, I would like to note at this transitional moment another emphasis that has arisen at crucial moments in the previous chapters: cultural and individual memories and circumstances compose physical, appearing events. Appearances arise in social environments that carry with them histories of cultural formation. "Laws of Nature," for example, express institutional, existential, and religious histories, histories that carry over palingenetically in meanings and hence in the appearing of things. The lives of things happen historically as they appear with their identities and significances—as they mean some thing. Things bear histories in their appearing lives, in their placements, meanings, and relative values, in the movements and awarenesses that compose them in their worldly happenings.

These claims apply as well to the appearing of thoughts and interpretations. I doubt that a person can understand Husserl's thought well without an appreciation for a history of anxiety regarding finite time that figures the value of transcendental subjectivity in modern Western thought. A careful engagement with Dewey's thought requires recognition of a history of passion for individual freedom and independence that composes his mentation—composes the life of his mentation. As you read these words you might consider the histories of literacy, printing, books, education, and philosophy that comprise the life of your and my minds. Living, appearing mutations, like other things, happen physically, i.e., nascently, meaningfully, memorially, culturally, corporeally, and personally. They are organizations of mutually impacting, temporal factors, extremely complex, that emerge with capacities for recognition, endurance, and transformation.

"Physicality" and its derivatives are not, of course, one whit less historical and physical than "nature." Their advantages are found as they lighten the weight of prescriptions that are interpreted as "natural" and allow conceptualizations and images in their sway to stop sooner in their applications and references than do most discourses of "nature" as they function to describe how things happen with ordered organizations. The discourse of physicality also encourages people to give way to dimensions in theoretical and interpretive events that are beyond the range of theoretical and interpretive grasp, such as the happening of neurological firings and cellular communications as people think. When things happen with commonalities they often "communicate" physically, and only some aspects of such communication are adaptable to the senses people make of them. Senses and meanings, too, are physical through and through. Human lives, as well as nonhuman ones, happen in the impact of meanings and the difference to meaning that comprises appearing living events. Recognition of this impact and difference in the context of physicality might grant priority to the singularities of lives, and "nature" might become more friendly to singular lives in "its" own appearing, historical, and mortal dimensions. Then we might well speak of orders and their eventful, corporeal, and historical inevitabilities without suggesting a "natural" drift to Unity (uni-verse) or to cosmic purposes overarching systems of lives.

Part II

TOPICS AT "NATURE'S" EDGE

FOUR

Physical Memories

> To live—and this means to see the light of the sun.
> —Homer

> The event of lighting is the world.
> —Heidegger

TO SEE THE LIGHT OF THE SUN

Heidegger gives the quotation from Homer with which I begin this chapter in his account of Heraclitus' Fragment B 16.[1] The context in this essay for Homer's line is Heidegger's description of the Greek word for life, *zao*, which has *za* for its root. *Za* intensifies that to which it is added. *Zatheos*, for example, means "very holy" or "most divine," *zapuros* means "most fiery," and *zamenes* means "very forceful." These are words that Heidegger uses here to describe the forceful and fiery *phusic* in-breaking of what Homer metaphorizes as the light of the sun and that Heidegger takes as meaning the shining of whatever appears. Heidegger's interpretation is that *za* means the pure letting-rise and letting-dissolve within and for the sake of the ways in which appearing, shining in, breaking in upon, and arrival occur.[2] Heidegger translates *zein* with an emphasis on its verbal meaning, as rising into the light, and the context suggests that life is an unmistakable, emphatic occurrence of shining, of beings' dehiscence, of their

---

1. Martin Heidegger, *Vorträge und Aufsätze* (Stuttgart: Neske, 1975) p. 266; *EGT,* p. 116 (see chapter 3, note 11). In Greek, Homer's sentence reads: *Zein kai horan phaos helioio.*

2. Ibid., tr. mine. The German reads, "Za *bedeutet das reine Aufgehen-lassen innerhalb der und für die Weisen des Erscheinens, Hereinblickens, Ankommenes.*" I have translated *Hereinblickens* as "shining in." I take that liberty in order to underscore Heidegger's observation that, in the context of a passage from Pindar, the gods let themselves occur, shining, and thus let themselves be seen in appearances that burst forth with such power that the locales of their shining appearances are most holy. Their gazing into the world composes their shining forth in appearances: when a god looks in, the god shines forth.

arising into the light and coming to appear. Life brings appearing with it; indeed, to appear in the light composes life.

We can elaborate in this context Homer's metaphor of the sun by the phrase "the appearing of the shining one," and we can expand the meaning of "to live" by the words *Erscheinenlassen des Scheinenden*—to let happen the appearing of the one who appears, to let shine the shining one.[3] Genuine life—really to live—means that a person's life is utterly given to the shining of what comes to light and, in that givenness, to let the shining be strikingly apparent. This interpretation puts considerable strain on Homer's words "to see the light of the sun," but it has the advantage of stressing the kinship of the eye that sees the light, the medium of light, and the sun that is the origin of light. Heidegger's interpretation suggests the lightness of life, its difference from all material and organic conditions, not only its appearing quality but also its fiery dehiscence as things rise up out of darkness, utterly absorbed in their mortal flame as they are given occasion for their times of light and energy.

Human lives are intensified when people live in close, alert dedication to their kinship with the elemental occurrence of living. To see the light of the sun does not suggest, in this context, a passing glance upward or even happy attention to the sun's rising. Nor does it suggest an everyday sight of things in the sun's light. Heidegger has in mind, rather, the shining occurrence of being as well as attentiveness to the shining of the sun. In such attentiveness a person finds the sun's shining, as it were, in and with the appearing of things. One is attuned to shining as things come to light in their appearing. When that attentiveness happens a person is able to confirm the beauty and value of life even if what appears is quite unwelcome.

The situation is different with animals, Heidegger says. Animals do not speak as we do, and consequently their own events are closed to us. He means that they are essentially different from us and that we are best advised to avoid anthropomorphic and mechanistic interpretations of them out of respect for their difference from our occurrence and ways of recognizing them. Language is the marker of this difference. The arising of human life is closely associated with language, that most elusive and enlightening human quality, and because of language and its disclosive power we are utterly different from animals in the way our lives occur. In our linguistic occurrence our appearing is unshared by other creatures. Heidegger thinks that by virtue of language we are not animals, not like animals, and are not privy to other creatures in their lives. The shining of what shines is manifest only in the phenomenal events of human beings.

3. Ibid.

Heidegger's approach to language is usually oriented by verbs, by, in German, *Zeitwörter* (time words). I note that he gives emphasis to the verbal meaning of *zein,* and in that emphasis he speaks of life as the appearing of what appears, the shining of what shines. In speaking of shining in terms of *Zeitwörter,* he brings together shining, living, language, and time, and the site of this unique gathering is nothing that we can identify or describe by biological words or, we may assume, by words attached to traditional notions of humanity. By turning to the pre-Platonic use of the Greek word *zein,* he finds a word that he believes might hold remembrance of the utter uniqueness of our lives, a word that precedes our later Western experiences and interpretations of human beings, and one in the context of Heraclitus' thought that might allow the vivification of another beginning for thought and language.

Such a re-beginning might constitute a rejoining of us with a lost sensibility and alertness, with a lost, struggling effort to find attunement in our living with . . . and here words fail us because the memory of "what" enticed, engendered, and measured the thought of Heraclitus or Anaxamander or Parmenides is so faded and diluted and encrusted—*so* imperceptible—in our ways of thought and speech that when people find themselves in the strange draw of these early Greek ways of thinking, they are left only with words that do not suffice, in the impact of their strangeness, to clarify the shining of what shines. Our language, and theirs, cloud the sun's light. Or rather, the words we have miss "what" we sense and "what" the words seem to struggle in vain to say. This sense of forgetfulness and loss, however, on Heidegger's account composes our access to a sense of being that exceeds our recollective grasp. This sense of forgetfulness seems to carry memory. In a continuous loss of speech that arises in encounters with the shining of what shines, we undergo a dim and fractured memory of what it might mean to live, as it were, in the light of the sun. Here is the place where I wish to engage Heidegger on memory in a context of physicality.

"Here" means the intersection of thoughts regarding human being outside of animality, living alertly with the shining of what shines, forgetfulness as an avenue of memory, and memory in occurrences of appearing. While I have affirmatively in mind Heidegger's emphasis on living as an event that is not reducible to any of its conditions, I will say that living is composed of events that are defined by memories, that memories are inclusive of what we vaguely call animality, and that memories are definitive of the occurrences of time. That means that time is determined in a way that Heidegger did not appreciate. And while I will agree with him that we really do not know how "animals" occur, at least in *their* feelings, awareness, and perceptions, in their utter differences from us, our ability to commu-nicate with them and our projections onto them show an unexpected memory of something that Heidegger usually leaves out of his thought. Time, I also wish to say, belongs to memory in the sense that time happens with and in memory. Without memory time does not occur as far as humans are concerned. Nor does memory happen without time. "The memory of time," when one maximizes the ambiguity of the "of," means that each belongs to the other and although we might find time passing through memory like an intangible but forceful ray, moving us and through us without our grasp, we will also find memory marking time like banks mark a river or trees a clearing. Without memory time is not "here," and without time memory does not occur.

THE ANIMAL WITH US

I need to address the issue of animality before I can develop this last thought in a way that seems to me most persuasive. I pointed out that Heidegger's perception of animals' essential distance from our lives has the beneficial effect of deferring our frequent inclination to see them through our own projections, whether those projections be poetic, scientific, or simply routine ways of perceiving them as they impact our lives. There are, however, also experiences of kinship with animals that exceed the projections that accompany them. We can find such kinship not only when we draw close and undefensively to an animal's pain or pleasure. We can also find it in moments of intuition or communication in which people sense deep and nonrational attunement with an animal. Sometimes that experience happens by means of eye contact. It can also happen in broader, affective ways in which an animal is apparent in its present difference with a feeling of kinship or relationship that I do not know how to describe other than by the phrase "intuitive recognition." I do not mean that in such recognition people are free of anthropomorphizing or other psychological projections. I doubt that any recognition is totally free of those forming impositions. But I do mean that more than projection happens, and that "more" is more on the order of disclosive appearance of "other-than-subject," "other-than-I," than it is of subjective appropriation. I agree with Heidegger's observation that "animality" is as much a question as "human" is and that the questionableness of both notions leaves their relation in a conceptual limbo. But on the other hand, those creatures in their singularity with people and in their own singularity can give rise to encounters of deep familiarity that give people an occasion to face qualities in themselves that they share with the creatures that they nonetheless recognize as quite different. I wish to appeal to those experiences and not to scientific discoveries that indicate our evolutionary development from animals. Although such references could be helpful for this account, the experiences and appearances of animals constitute sufficient basis to support the observation that we encounter animals with a sense of recognized kinship that does not leave them in as great a darkness as that in which Heidegger abandons them. In that abandonment he overlooks an important dimension of our lives.

My larger point is a modest one: our memories appear not in a complete and essential distance from animals but in a recognizable affiliation with them—appear as genetic or cellular memories. And that means that in our memories we are not absolutely apart from creatures that we generally think of as so different as to define, by their difference, our utter uniqueness in the world. With the passage of utter uniqueness passes also a certain ethereal and almost mystic quality that can be attached to a sense of human difference from animals. Part of our worldliness and ways of being, rather, are found in our kinship with animals, and that aspect suggests that all things that appear in memories—in their appearing—enjoy a dimension of what we vaguely call animality. It suggests that in the memorial occurrences of our lives something that Heidegger brackets out comes to shine. And perhaps this dimension means that the appearing of what appears—the sun's light in Homer's poetic metaphor—is suffused by a dimension of immemorial animal life that is as strange to our selves as silent gravity is as it draws particles together and gives the sun's fiery light to be.

That observation is important in coming to a second point: memories, and hence time, as I will show in a moment, while providing the occasion for all manner of recognitions, are not necessarily accidental aspects of something like a "pure" subjectivity or disclosive event. Far from pure, when "pure" means uncontaminated not only by what we share with animals but also by indelible, contingent determinations, memories compose worldly events that are completely contingent and are determined by and connected with animality. And if my descriptive claim holds, we may expect to say the same thing about time: time happens with us only as determined memories.

A third observation: when memories happen, time happens. In memorial events time is re-membered. My interest is in a departure from an idea of time as something in which we participate or which flows through us or is in any sense something present. Time composes memorial occurrences and memorial occurrences compose time.

MEMORIES WITHOUT A SUBJECT: CULTURAL EMBODIMENTS

In order to support this last thought, I turn to what I shall call memories without a subject. I have in mind the memories that constitute institutions, manners of life, and the ways whereby separate events are connected and given interdependence. Within a Heideggerean orientation, for example, we could say that formations of technologically oriented societies compose lineages in which the priority of controllable objects is established within a scene of anxiety over the passing and ungraspable quality of every appearing thing. Technological practices embody memories in and of complex processes, and those are memories that are presented outside of the limits and possibilities of enactment by a subject. We also know from Foucault's work that hospitals, mental institutions, and prisons each figure forceful memories of needs, configurations of power, and contingencies beyond anyone's subjective memory. The formations of moralities and faiths also embody memories of the events and passions that motivated them. As we live in and through institutions, mores, and established ways of recognizing and interpreting things, we are engaged in memories that, in spite of their often hidden and inchoate quality, are formative of who we can be, our ways of perceiving, and our capacities to feel as we do. Memories are not only subjective events. They compose the cultures that give our various worlds to be as they are. We not only have memories. We also live within them.

These are ontic claims when we consider them in the terms of Heidegger's early way of thinking.[4] Even if our minds and thoughts are far more informed by social and psychological factors then Heidegger found them to be, in what way am I addressing the issues of the *appearing* of what appears and time as such when I make the claims that I have made? What is the relevance for appearing and time when I say that animality and memory beyond subjectivity play definitive roles in our experiences and recognitions of things? The first and most obvious relevance is found by noting that these elements, animality and memory, compose our ability to recognize and address such questions as those of appearing and time. Neither I nor Heidegger can even perceive the question of time outside of an extremely complex weave of memorial influences. Heidegger recognizes this inevitability in his emphasis on de-structuring our axiomatic ways of thinking. Nor can we speak critically or constructively except within the impact of both personal and nonpersonal memories. The very thought of the appearing of what appears or of time's insubstantial occurrence bears a crosshatch of memories that only the intense and extended work of de-structuring and description could begin to uncover. In our thinking and speaking we give expression to memories only some of which are generated by our own singular experiences. Ontological thinking itself figures multiple ontic and re-membered elements.

---

4. Although Heidegger drops the language of ontic and ontological in the 1930s and in the rest of his work, something like that distinction operates in the division that characterizes his thoughts on appearing and what appears. Appearing, shining, and the coming to pass of things are not themselves historically originated by the ways in which beings appear, shine, and come to be.

So the distinction between ontic and ontological is itself suspect if that distinction is used in order to say that we can achieve thoughtful perception that is free of memories specific to a given body of lineages. Things come to appear nonsubjectively, in memorial events.

MICROMEMORIES: CELLS

A cell: a group of self-replicating biomolecules that are enclosed by a membrane. It has memory by means of chains of DNA proteins that are able to compose an active code, construct another cell with its own likeness and ability for self-replication. It also has an ability to extract energy from other molecules and to transfer that energy into chemical bonds.[5] The earliest cells apparently were alive by virtue of a chemistry that was initiated by mineral-rich dust, by sunlight, volcanic heat, and sea-cooling: they arose from molecular syntheses of tiny specks of matter and processes of heating and cooling and slowly developed from no cellular life. Cells formed a new event—new, at least, on this planet—that had a very rudimentary knowledge of self-nurturance and reproduction.

Consider what cells do and have been able to do for millions of years: locate sources of energy, identify and discriminate among different vibrations, pick out compatible shapes and ignore others, distinguish levels of molecular motion, identify prey (and pursue it), and predators (and avoid them). Cells pick out other cells for mating. They may seek out light or avoid it, regulate their rates of reproduction, and set in motion systems to transport other cells or to translate them into useable shapes or energies. By the intricately correlated actions of millions of cells, I can identify an itch on my big toe and scratch it and worry if it persists. By the memories of cells and their actions I recall the phrase, "cellular action," write it, and then read it. And, of course, by organizations of proteins, cells remembered how to form my brain. Cells and cellular organizations are living, aware events.

Cells are perceptively predisposed toward and in their environments in the sense that their various chemical formations are sized, assembled, and shaped to fit other formations, motions, and temperatures. The outer membranes of cells in our noses, for example, are shaped to fit specific molecules or odorants. When a contacting molecule fits, the outer part of the cell recognizes it and takes it in (bonds with it), shifts its internal shape to pass the molecule through the cellular middle and on to the inside cell wall where it

---

5. See Lewis Thomas, *The Lives of Cells: Notes of a Biology Watcher* (New York: Penguin, 1974); Boyce Rensberger, *Life Itself: Exploring the Realm of the Living Cell* (New York: Oxford University Press, 1996); Bruce Alberts et al., *Molecular Biology of the Cell*, 3rd ed. (New York: Garland, 1994); Ursula Goodenough, *The Sacred Depths of Nature* (New York: Oxford University Press, 1998).

changes the molecule's shape to fit the next receptor cell. This "cascade" of shape changes and passing-of-the-molecule continues to the brain. That's something like my being predisposed to fit with certain personalities and events and not with others. The predisposition allows me to understand some people and occurrences intuitively, without thinking about them, and also gives me to "draw a blank" or to be repelled in other circumstances. Sentient shapes and forms of assemblies of various elements figure awarenesses. From one angle of interpretation we could say that our bodies figure an enormous number of dynamic cellular shapes that are alert and coordinated and that make up many dimensions of aware predispositions with genetically informed memories.

There are in our organism physical memories of the ways to build this body, to form this heart and keep it beating, to recognize and kill organisms that are injurious to this organism—billions of memories that inhabit and constitute cells, groups of cells, and organizations of those groups—physical memories that keep this physical organization alive and moving in large and microscopic ways. Most of these memories are pretty much the same in mammals—in camels, cats, and humans—and comprise commonalities of aware predispositions in our most rudimentary and most sophisticated activities. The cells and their organizations that compose us know of nurturance, affiliation, repulsion, fear, and death—of being alive—long before as well as while "we" form objects of specific recognition through words and concepts. I expect that "we" already know of light, water, and air, of distance and proximity, of speed, torpidity, and tempo, of solidity, space, and time in common with millions of other creatures, as such things happen in distinctly human ways. As meanings take place, cellular memory and alertness are already there.

Cellular memory has a high degree of homology. There are likenesses in structure as well as in dynamics, likenesses in "families" of activators, signal transductions, metabolic pathways, manners of division and connection, and domains of proteins. Our cells carry traits like those of other types of cells that have persisted since long before Homo sapiens (or mammals or complex plants). Our lives in their cellular level are connected to all earthly lives even in the ways mutations happen and in processes of "decisions" that cells make to accommodate environmental changes. We are bound together by cellular memory, by awarenesses that are preserved from common ancestor genomes by chains of DNA, that are both affective and effective in "higher" organisms like us, and that constitute our *phusis*—our coming to be, persisting, and ceasing. We might refer to internal clocks, instincts, nonvoluntary processes, but by whatever name, we live subliminal memories in common with amoebas, reptiles, and birds as we sleep, digest, adjust to circumstances, and think. Homologous, memorial awareness is integral to organic life.

My emphasis falls on the inseparability of physicality, awareness, and a kinship with living things that seems odd if we give our attention only to cultural, linguistic, and self-reflective events.

IN MEMORY WITH ANIMALS: MEMORIES OF FLESH

When I see the rising of the first light of day something quite nonvoluntary rises in me. Were I to attempt to describe this experience fully, I would be moved toward poetry, and I shall spare you that turn not only because my poetry would not be up to the rising of first light but also because that experience would be so much mine. I also know the experience of disgust over first light, especially first bright light—I remember the first line in a poem a friend of mine wrote: "Oh foul sun who preys upon my darkness," and I have another friend who sees his first light around noon and is not too happy about that. Rather than incorporate you into a universal claim that arises out of my own experience, I wish to appeal to your own singular experiences by beginning with my experience of rising light. It is an experience that shows me an animal dimension in my life that greets the light without thought or morality. In addition to other factors, it is, I believe, a physical experience. I am quite sure that this greeting is informed by the happy early morning mood in my family when I was a child, a mood of quiet beginning, new anticipation, and centered energy. It was the time when I most felt my parents' enjoyment of life. That fortunate experience, I say, and many others inform the way in which the morning's light comes to appear for me, and I find in that experience something that I also find in a young dog's or colt's or kitten's boundless energy in their play, their frolicking like beams of light dancing on a water's surface. I rediscover the experience when I feel a rush of quiet excitement before streams of light flowing in patchworks of shades among trees, as well as in westering light in the evening, or the light of the moon, particularly when in its fullness it casts shadows, or the clarity of daylight when, in the light, I see things without obstruction, or in the warmth of the sun's light, its brightness, its letting me see, its power to give things to grow. And I find myself blinking in the sun's brightness, turning from its glare, looking for shade, avoiding its searing heat, and feeling at night relief from its energy. By such experiences I feel something shared with Homer *and* with animals—with cows in the shade at noon, with a cat's energy in the moonlight, with the blinking of a crow in bright light, with the gaze of a lion surveying a savanna from an elevation, or with a bird's enjoyment in bathing in a fountain on a hot day.

My emphasis falls on elements by which something can occur with me and which I find in common with animals. Those elements can also show themselves in terror, sleepiness, sexual passion, deep sorrow, anger, exhaustion, pleasure, birth, curiosity, affection, and silence. I am sure that you can name others. When we give attention to and in sensations and sensuality, our likenesses with animals are not very difficult to appreciate. I imagine that animal aspects in people also arise in dreams, that animal images in dreams express our likeness with sea creatures, birds, and most things that creep, walk, and climb. To the extent that our awareness is attuned by affective spontaneity, we find an immediacy with animals through immediacies in our own lives.

My thought is this: the experiential milieu of Homer's image of the sun's light is intimately involved with sensuous life, and the elemental dimension of his metaphor can associate us with dimensions of physical awareness in which our kind and animal kinds appear in common with the appearing of what appears. In this region of experience we find commonalities by our eyes, our skin, our passions, our enjoyments, our sorrows; by our needs for water, air, nurturance, movement, shelter, and a hundred other ways whereby we live together in earthly commonality.

Things appear in this commonality. Not only animals appear. *We* are in common with much that moves on the earth as we touch and feel and attempt to continue living. In that commonality—in that "light"—things appear as opportunities, feelings, sensations, as dangerous, drawing, strange, or familiar. I do not want to override the enormous differences that define the commonalities. But it is not only in the unique dimension of language and thought (in Heidegger's original and rich interpretation of them) that appearing happens, nor do language and thought happen apart from fleshly memories and experiences: to separate thought and language from our commonality with animals constitutes a great injustice to all three.

Rather than separation, a commonality of us and animals appears to me to be integral not only to the ways things come to light but also to the *appearing* of what appears. To live—to see the light of the sun—means at once enactment of animal commonality. Homer's words "to live" might suggest a radical difference between the sun's light and what is illumined, and that view might figure significantly in the lineage of Heidegger's thought of the ontological difference of being and beings. But I expect that blind Homer's words to arise from an elemental and sensual alertness that shares more with cells and animals than Homer could have appreciated or, certainly, more than Heidegger appreciated.[6] There is as much "animality"

---

6. On the assumption that Homer was blind and that he was the author of these words, are we to take them as suggesting that he thought of himself as dead since he cannot see the light of the sun? Are they meant ironically? I do not expect to know the answers with certainty, but I believe that "the light of the sun" has as much to do with the skin, warmth of body, and life-orientations that arise from more or less light as it does with eyes and brightness. Perhaps the words also mean that shining can happen in words and images, that they are not meant literally. Perhaps they compose a preliminary

in the appearing of a glass of red wine that is illuminated in gentle light as there is in a flash of blinding terror before a growl in the dark.

Sensual alertness also composes both a region of memories and a region for memories. My suggestions have been that in communication with animals and in sensual experiences fleshly memories occur that do not have their origins in language or thought, and although my ways of experiencing the sun's light might be quite different from yours, they exemplify nonetheless a kind of kinship with animals that allows you to find your own experiences of such kinship. I have also suggested that our kinship with animals—our sensual fleshliness—is operative in our linguistic and mindful enactments. Sounds and signs belong to flesh as well as to reflection, whether the sounds arise by singing, an infant's wail, or a dog's bark. And hearing is a fleshly enactment that can turn a cat's ears, raise a deer's head, or put a person to sleep. Our concentration on an idea or a beautiful thing finds kinship with a hawk's focus on a chipmunk or a leopard's attention to a herd of antelopes. As we speak and think, we are involved in activities that have primordial accompaniments with highly sophisticated meanings and perceptions. And as words and images arise in our minds, ancient, animal capacities for association, interest, and mental perception accompany our most refined subtlety. Communicating and thinking enact kinships with animals that are evident as we find them calling each other or us, stalking their prey, following the customs of a herd or a pack, associating places with experiences, foreseeing movements, tracking, dreaming, holding affections and grudges, and teaching their young. Our animal dimensions are operative as we occur in language and thought, as we stalk an idea, give signs and signals, give expression to perceptions, or feel our lives threatened by powerful and strange thoughts.

This kinship means that unfathomably rich sensuous memories— physical memories—are included in our human experiences, that as we undergo the memorial dimensions of any linguistic or thoughtful experience, we undergo an animality that vastly exceeds human sophistication. It means that as things come to shine in language and thought, animality is part of the shining, that "the sun's light" comes with elements that are not restricted to human uniqueness, that human appearing and disappearing—our being—is rich with memories of the flesh. We are kin to animals even in events when we are stunned by astonishment before such "facts" as that life happens and that we are.

---

understanding of being as the shining of what shines. Or perhaps they articulate closeness to an elemental, earthly sensibility that opens us to our being-with-animals. I hear in these words a sensuality that gives things to shine in a dimension that can occur without language or thought.

We can understand the associations of nonvoluntary cultural memories and the memories of animality by considering the earlier example I gave of a glass of red wine in soft light. When I mentioned that example I wanted to illustrate the conjunction of light and sensuous pleasure. Now I would like to expand it by showing the joint occurrence of nonsubjective, nonvoluntary cultural memory and nonvoluntary memory that inhabits our flesh. Let the glass of wine be on an informally set table that is illuminated by the filtered light of an evening's setting sun. Much is figured by this occurrence. A history of wine-making, an enormous body of symbols and associations that help to present red wine in a glass—memories of blood, sacrifice, worship, refined taste, earth and bread, the value of life, perhaps a combination of Dionysius, luxury, cruelty, and unmindfulness. There is manifest also another sense of luxury that is not figured, for example, by soapy water in a dishpan, a sense of occasion, relaxed propriety and friendship. (Such associations might move a person to set his single place at a table with a glass of red wine for a moment of partial relief from his loneliness.) A person might have had personal experiences that reinforce or counteract these memories, but they—the impersonal memories—are already there, available for multiple responses, in the wine's Western cultural lineage.

There is also a fleshly dimension that is not only a cultural formation. There are the draws of remembered taste and release from inhibition, the mere pleasure that comes with a vision of the illuminated redness and filtered light in a secure environment, release of stress in relaxing muscles, salivation, a quietness that seems to come often in this environment. One is not wary or defensive, not poised for action in this particular place. There are instances of awareness of flesh, awareness in which animal memories play a contextualizing part, memories, I speculate, that were seared into the genes of survivors by dangers, pain, and urges to live and find safety, by discovery of conditions fitting for security and by the life-promoting quality of pleasure and relaxation. And yet there is also for animals and for us a silent preparedness for threat should the conditions change. Perhaps the distance is not so great between an animal's grazing in a field in twilight or eating a nut in its own den and our having a civilized glass of evening wine.

My point is that inherited memories in cultures and physical organizations play roles in the appearing of things—that in appearing, memories in our kinship with animals and our lineages compose nonvoluntary dimensions of the disclosiveness of beings. The appearing of what appears belongs to our communal traditions as well as to our flesh. In early Heideggerian terms I could say that the self-appearing of *dasein* occurs as an event of cultural and fleshly memory, or that truth as disclosure includes the memories of both flesh and lineage. Or I could say that *Gelassenheit* happens in part by virtue of our cells' nonvoluntary memories.

THE COMING OF TIME

We have no difficulty understanding memories as temporal occurrences that form a dynamic intersection of past, present, and future events. They are clearly temporal; they belong to time. But to say that time belongs to them—that time happens memorially—is a different matter. When I say that time is dependent on memory for its occurring, I mean that time only appears with the happening of memories. I do not mean that the word "time" names only a mental phenomenon—I have said that memory is not exclusively mental, that it is also cellular and cultural; and time seems to appear as sequences of events, not all of which are mental, as well as nonlinear enactments of past presence, extremely complex physical "information" and finite situations, as forecasting as well as foregoing and presencing; and it happens at once as all of these elements in forecasting, foregoing, and presencing. Time seems to appear only as temporal events and their interconnections, and in that context I wish to say that time seems only to appear with memories.

Consider only some aspects of Heidegger's accounts of time in this context. In *Being and Time* he finds time to occur as *dasein's* mortal eventfulness. In *On Time and Being* he suggests that the site of time's happening is found in the coming of being, in the "there is," the *es gibt*. Common to both descriptions is time's happening as presentative: time eventuates in the *happening* of things. It gives the *appearing* of what appears. And time is not properly identified as a being, not as a substance, a creature, or a synthesis of elements. Throughout the course of his thinking, Heidegger finds that he is not able to think time properly in its gifting occurrence. He finds that language and thought fail in their attempts to say their own temporal events. Time thus remains for him a presenting uncertainty, a mystery in the midst of a self-presentation. But it does seem to appear, as Heidegger describes it, *in its self-disclosiveness,* as distinct to its ontic setting, without physical density and without the specificity of a complex physical lineage that is expressed in institutions and practices. It thus discloses itself without an inherent cultural, memorial dimension. We can say on Heideggerian terms that temporal appearances are always situated, but we cannot say that the coming of time is "itself" a physical event of inherited memories.

I, on the other hand, know of no events or dimensions of time that occur without memories. When time appears as a measure, it comes as lineages of cellular activity and organization, recognition and calculation.

When it appears as mysterious, time comes in and as lineages of physical formation and of ways of speaking and thinking. When time appears in association with measurement or mystery or eternity, it also appears indissolubly in association with the animality of our flesh and the institutions of our lives. Appearing composes events as inherently memorial. Appearing, time, and memory happen at once as the site of interconnection among physical forecasting, foregoing, and presenting as well as the site for linear movements and mortal events of beginning and ending. Memories compose the eventuation. Without them no appearing happens. There are things only in memories' sitings. To occur in time seems to mean that appearances come to appear in memories. Time belongs to memories.

To live thus seems to mean "to be borne by memories," and "to be borne by memories" seems to mean that living is borne by time. In the context of this chapter's leading metaphor, to be borne by both memories and time means to see the light of the sun. Perhaps the memories that were necessary for blind Homer's poetry figure the time of the sun's light.

FIVE

Starlight in the Face of the Other

Indeed, just as our life is embedded in the ecological cycles of
the biosphere, our whole planet [and we] exist as a part of a
much older cycle of material and energy that forms the galaxy.
—Lee Smolin, *The Life of the Cosmos*

> THE HEAVENS
>
> From mind to mind
> I am acquainted with the
> struggles
> of these stars. The very same
> chemistry wages itself minutely
> in my person.
> It is all one intolerable war.
> I don't care if we're fugitives,
> we are ceaselessly exalted,
> rising
> like the drowned out of their
> shirts. . . .
>
> —Dennis Johnson, "The Veil"

THERE, OPEN, WITHOUT INTIMACY

Emmanuel Levinas makes the broad, descriptive claim that the other's
utterly singular subjectivity is lost to another's consciousness, that, as
individuals appear in consciousness, their own event is lost to conscious
appropriation. Consciousness, by virtue of which appearance happens, de-
composes the other and recomposes an image of the other by providing a
present moment of presentation. The other is refigured by presentation.
The other becomes a part of a definitive structure of presentation, a vast
and subjectively founded region of essence in which all elements, aspects,
and appearances happen in a fundamental coherence: radical differences

are converted into the tame differences of beings who follow the laws of a subjective, temporal, spatial presentation. Nothing otherwise than being occurs in being's estate, and for Levinas, being's estate is defined in terms of this subjective region of appropriation. He thinks of this refiguration as more akin to killing than to either positive creativity or intersubjective encounter.

If you are not persuaded that being is found as the cohesion and coherence of transcendental subjectivity, you will have a basic problem with Levinas' descriptive claims even if you are sympathetic with his emphasis on the alterity of persons. If you think of human occurrences as Nietzsche or Jean-Luc Nancy do, for example—as extensive and intrinsically worldly and not at all circumscribed by subjectivity—you will also feel reserved when you encounter Levinas' accounts of responsibility and substitution. Or if you are not sympathetic with those aspects of the Jewish theological traditions in which God is viewed as totally ungraspable and yet as the sacred, withdrawn giver of alterity, obligation, and goodness, you will take pause before the rabbinical and Talmudic motivations in Levinas' thought. I believe that we must recognize the idealist's understanding of consciousness that underlies aspects of Levinas' account of alterity if we are to do justice to his thought, although I do not think that that recognition is adequate cause to dismiss his writings. Rather than engage what is most questionable in his descriptions of subjectivity and presentation, I would like to valorize Levinas' metaphor of the face and to intensify a sense of radical difference in the occurrence of faces by focusing for a moment on our eyes. I want to avoid Levinas' word, alterity, in reference to faces because I would like to work with the observation that it is not so much faces that de-present themselves in experiences of consciousness as it is that radical differences from persona and subjectivities happen with faces, happen in the very occurrences of countenances. *In faces subjectivity comes to vanish.*

In working with this observation I have been impressed with the vast differences that compose faces. Noses, skin, ears, mouths, teeth, lips, hair, bumps and blemishes, and, especially for my purposes here, eyes carry with their singular and coordinated occurrences protracted events that are too far beyond civilization to be called histories. As our faces occur we are in touch—most weirdly in touch—with a vastness of distance and time that in merely quantitative terms makes our usual sense of distance and time seem terribly inadequate for what we want to express. I have no expectation that we can capture what I am talking about or that a system of signs will do for the expressions we want to make. They always fall short of something vastly superficial and extensive. I shall say that we are dwarfed by what we know, that the differences from persons that are enacted in faces constitute a region of reference that makes any sense of subjective, conscious encompassment seem absurd. Although all bodies on earth are constructed of the same kinds of atoms that make up rocks and stars, I shall limit my field of observation to one aspect of our eyes which I think moves our images of time and space outside of a problematic that is governed by most traditional ideas about consciousness. In this process I hope to begin to refigure some senses of difference in our culture, senses that Levinas seems to radicalize but which he in fact has tamed by his stress on personal alterity within a context of thought that is governed by a very specific history and by relatively tame traditional images of subjectivity.

I do not doubt that when a visual image is fully formed in a perception, all manner of social influences and histories have come into play, that perceiving is a communal event. I want to address, however, aspects of the visual occurrence that appear to be socially and historically blind, that bear no witness, and that bear histories only by what we say of them. I realize how strange and ill advised you might find the phrase "appear to be socially and historically blind." Appearing, after all, happens as a social and historical event, and we never understand appearing well if we cast it in transcendental and timeless terms. Such speaking would constitute a termination of the lives of appearances from the beginning of the conversation. Appearances are perceptive and happen in orders of meaning. I do not want to forget that I am speaking of the appearing of something that, I wish to say, is not formed by appearance. But I also do not wish to think of starlight, for example, as sufficiently accounted and appreciated when it is addressed only in terms of the light of appearing. From some angles of interpretive vision, "starlight" is so different from its perceptive recognitions that it terminates with its name. I wish to say something like that now with regard to vision and then say more about starlight later. I shall avoid the word "perception" for what I am talking about when I say "vision" and speak rather of an organic process that, while it appears meaningfully, seems to precede and to recede from meaningful appearances. I will call it a pre-perceptive dimension of vision and in vision that composes an enactment of our bodies and indicates severe limits to the personal and so-called human aspects of our lives. By means of the function of light in vision I would like to indicate something so other to the human person as to place in jeopardy the idea that the other is best or most radically conceived in terms of a conscious being. I am interested in the limits of personal occurrences that happen *with* personal occurrences and thus in the limits of ethics as we think of what has come to have the name of alterity. I will suggest that a prioritization of ethics in an interpretation of alterity and difference encloses too much that is too different to merit such closure and that we should feel uncomfortable with such a loss. In some ways, we belong as much to starlight as we do with each other, and that weird difference to our lives in our lives outstrips Levinas' account of the other as far as his thought of the Other outstrips an identity-based idealism. In fact, since I will be speaking of ratios at some points in the discussion, I will say here at the beginning that the ratio of difference in Levinas' notion of alterity in its connection to the idea of the experiencing subject is considerably exceeded by the ratio of difference between vision and person as I will describe them. Levinas' thought is dependent on an idealistic account of human experience—an account that I find descriptively mistaken—and on a sensibility of sacrifice that arises from a sense of rather too much human kinship in a context of passivity and activity in his description of alterity.

I wish now to present a few observations about light and eyes that are based on facts that are themselves subject to alteration, based, in other words, on "our" knowledge that "we" know to be in transformation. We will see that eyes are quite different from the light they see, and yet they see by virtue of elements that were produced by stars in the generation of blinding light. My purpose is to give an account of one small aspect of bodily functions that does not reflect light so much as it refracts it and does so by means of elements that were produced in the formation of lights. Then I will turn to some of Levinas' observations about differences and others.

UNGRASPABLE DISTANCES IN OUR EYES

We are stardust. . . .
—Joni Mitchell

War nicht das Auge sonnenhaft,
Wie können wir das Licht erblicken?
—Goethe

Starlight does not seem to shine in daylight. What we see of the universe are lights in darkness, and what we see of each other is also pretty much lights and darks and their shapes. After that, interpretations. Interpretations upon interpretations of lights and shadows and their behaviors, of absences of light and sites of darkness. And the organs of sight are themselves, in their structure and formation, indirectly indebted to some of the events that produce rays of light and energy and give a strange visibility to darkness. I do not want to say that our agency is made of starlight, but I do want to say that many of the elements of seeing use products of star-events, of supernovas, and in those elements and their occurrences we find far more alterity than Levinas was able to dream of. Many of us probably share some of the limits of Levinas' range of interpretive vision, and attention to those limits will allow us to see other limits that operate in our values and the ways in which we experience time and space.

Our eyes do not generate light. This realization sets us over-against our Greek ancestors' interpretations of their eyes. Like the early Egyptians, our classical forebears thought of eyes as seeing and shining at the same time. The eyes were, by them, understood not only to reflect light and shine in that way, but to generate a fiery element and cast forth their own light. Euclid and Ptolemy, for example, thought of eyes as emitting oracular beams that touched what an individual sees. Plato, in the *Timaeus,* speaks of light-bearing eyes characterized by a fire that does not consume but that shines with a mild light. This light is kin to daylight, a light that also illuminates but does not consume. Eye-light flows like a pure and dense stream from "the pure fire within us" and meets in a shining union with its like in daylight. This shining element touches things in sight and carries the touch as motion to the individual's body and soul. Eye-light, however, must find its kindred light in the world or it vanishes into the vanquishing alterity of night (who, in Greek myths, is the mother of day), its inner fire refused and quenched by its other and by an absence of its like. In this thought, seeing is shining and is dependent on finding its like in the element of its perceiving. Radical difference from light means blindness. It means quenching the firelight of the eyes.

In this classical Greek view of seeing, objects appear instantly—one sees, for example, the sun or stars immediately—because the sense of distance that is built into the interpretation is a minimal one. In contemporary terms, if eye-light directed to the sun were to travel at 186,273 miles per second, it would take eight minutes just to glance at the sun. And if sight were immediate and did not take even a few seconds, eye-light seeing a star would need to travel fast enough to make the speed of light seem like a snail's pace, and presumably the cataclysm of explosions that would accompany this transformation of matter, time, and space in the speeding light of the eyes, in eye-light's faster-than-the-speed-of-light traversal, would dissolve the solar system and make a considerable dent in our galaxy: a glance at the sun in which the sun was instantly present to eye-light might be enough to start another big bang. So, from a pro-world point of view, it's just as well that the classical Greek and ancient Egyptian observations are inaccurate.

Already we find a sense of distance important in our sense of visual perception and what shines, and the way in which we interpret eyesight now eliminates the idea of eye-light and inner fire, replacing them with theories of interpretation, with flesh, muscles, lenses, rods, cones and neurological structures. Eyes are not even reliable gauges for the occurrence of light, because there are dimensions of light and its speed and density—for example, light rays—that are invisible to an unaided eye. Even the elements of light by which it is defined in contemporary interpretations—the frequency of rays, the wavelength of the rays, their speed, and the medium of their refraction—are not visible. We do not naturally see the energy and energy transfer of light.

Not only is light a carrier of energy that arises in outer space, it is seen by us by means of the functions of complex mineral structures that were themselves produced in outer space and that form living tissues of transfer, stability, and excitation in the events of vision. Light proceeds from matter, is generated by matter and, being absorbed by an eye, disappears in matter. And when we see the light of stars, we see by means of elements that had their origins in stars and that now help to absorb and transmit their light.

I note that the minerals necessary for eyesight were all formed in the implosion of stars that were trillions of miles and millions of years from where we see, that calcium, potassium, sodium, iodine, and phosphorus—all the primary and trace minerals in our eyes—were formed in the unspeakable heat and pressure of stars that collapsed upon themselves and then exploded, sending both light energy and mineral components in an unspeakable tumult throughout the universe.

Consider an imploding star and the consequent explosion that produces the minerals which function in our sight:

> [A] gamma-ray burst was detected in 1979 from the direction of a Large Magellanic Cloud, our nearest galactic neighbor. In one tenth of one second the gamma-ray-generated blast unleashed more energy than our sun will generate in the next 10,000 years . . . on a scale of energy against which the term *vast* fades as an understatement.

In the implosion of such a star,

> the nuclear structure of [the star is] rammed down to solid spheres of pure neutrons. Each is unimaginably dense, where an object the size of a child's marble weighs billions of tons. Were such a tiny sphere dropped from just several feet above the ground on earth, in a flash it would penetrate the entire 8,000 mile diameter of our planet and hurtle on past at thousands of miles per second.[1]

In such implosions, gases formed into minerals and in the following explosion those minerals were thrown into space where they dispersed and some formed what we know as earth, where, with their indispensable aid, our eyes came to be.

Here is one way we can find our eyes both obscure and arresting in their kinship with stars and hence with the sun. And this kinship is not one of disclosure or illumination but is one of densities and organic ele-

---

1. Jay Barbree and Martin Caidin, *A Journey through Time* (New York: Penguin, 1995), pp. 190–91.

ments, of distances without histories, unnarratable things so vast and with such magnitude that we are dwarfed even by our images and stories of them. Only now, I believe, do we begin to approach something like otherness, now as we consider, still within the usage of the idea of kinship, star-elements in our eyes, elements without light, without the ability to give fire spontaneously, and yet elements that are indispensable in their expenditure for light's perception in the eye's function.

The distances suggested by our eyes are not only metric ones. I do not want to minimize the importance of distances that we measure by timing light's spatial travel. Those measures and their capacity to explode our anthropomorphic images, to explode even our senses of vastness, size, and scope, are irreplaceable in our culture's release from many forms of mythological and theological interpretations that bind human beings to blindingly limited corners of perception. These measurements figure distinctly contemporary experiences of awe, and they so revolutionize our senses of distances and spaces that we can no longer measure ourselves by only the sun's presence or feel defined within earthly dimensions. They explode the past boundaries of what is knowable and give us to gasp at the sheer extent of light's spatial traversal. Indeed, one of my efforts is to invoke this cultural explosion occasioned in our metaphors by quantitative measurement when I note our visual kinship with stars in the functions and lives of mineral components in our eyes. But the distance I wish to note is not only the one that is measured by light's speed. It is a distance from ourselves and our consciousness and our communities of endeavor and knowledge that I also want to note, a distance that is figured by the radical otherness of stars that I am presenting by reference to star-formed minerals in our eyes. We seem to belong to this difference of distance in our eyes' formations and enactments in the sense that something that does not belong to anything vaguely human, in our usual understanding of "human," happens in our experiences of light, darkness, and visible form, something more of stars' deathly implosions and explosions than of our meanings and longings. This is a distance from meaning that links us to other creatures of vision, that silently figures mere otherness in our eyes, that never shines or discloses, that marks a disaster of sight within sight's happening, something we do not see as we see and to which we belong as we experience light. I do not mean that sight is reducible to imperceptive minerals or that matter explains immaterial experiences. Such reductions are too human, too explanatory, too controlling, too blindly incorporative of such elements into a manageable structure of meaning, too violating of what is not subject to ownership or public declaration. These minerals seem to me to escape the light of declaration. And yet they do not seem to be like empty space or a chasm of mere passage or utter darkness. They are too dense for such metaphors, too atomic and organic we might say, too "there," too other. Our recognition of the minerals of sight qualifies even the metaphors that cluster around death and the possibility of no possibility at all. They seem to fall outside of experiences of dying and death. They occur in the eye's visioning and give the "I" of agency and being to falter and our sense of human dominance to fail. Far from an inner and pure fire, we find no fire at all in our kinship with stars. In our eyes' refractions, convergences, focusing, inversions, bleaching, and transformations to neurological patterns, the mineral functions do not radiate light but help to absorb it in a strange process of transfer and recording that gives darkness to most of the light-energy that reaches the cornea—less than a quarter of the light that enters the eye goes beyond the retina. The rest is reflected or absorbed. Darkening accompanies the light of our eyes, and in that darkening we can find some of the functions of our inheritance from stars.

You can see that my purposes are literary and philosophical and not scientific. I want to shift some of the images, metaphors, and concepts by which we think of otherness, to emphasize an externality that is not governed by images of consciousness or self or the mysterious withdrawal of an other; I would like to begin with images of origin that have nothing to do with spirit or history or subjectivity or value, to own my metaphors with a background of surface events that reveal nothing akin to our *images* of them, and to define kinship in terms of radical difference from what we usually recognize as our being. This means that I would like to place the metaphor of other within a history of metaphorizing and to find histories *in* metaphors and their functions but not in the "deeds" of an other or in the beginning of histories or in the withdrawal of Something transcendental. In thinking of other, I would like to step outside of the power of an image of a thing in itself or to itself, step outside of the "I" of obligation and responsibility, outside of the problematic of agency and relationship, and to think of other as other to the worlds in which we provide "I," images, responsibilities, and metaphors for all things. If we can begin to think of our eyes—our "windows to our souls"—in terms that refer to things prior to agency and disclosure, in terms that do not follow a lineage of spiritual fire but in terms that engender images of implosion, forces that are subject only to quantitative description, and a radicality of distance that leaves in shambles the delicacy of *our* losses, we might have a way to think of other in surface terms that are not limited to contexts of writing, texts, human relationships, or inwardness. We might find such other in our eyes—I am sure we can also find it anywhere in our bodies—by means of minerals whose images of origin now implode other images of meaningful agency. You can see that the issue is not one of denying the importance of agency. It is a function of limiting the power of agency to dominate our senses of other bodies. It is a matter of shifting to images, metaphors, and concepts that move away from the lineages that have given us to see things primarily from a perspective dominated by such ideas as inner, outer, subject, object, passive, active, and the relationships that we imagine in that context to define our ability to respond.

OUTSIDE OF BOOKS AND WRITING

When our systems of metaphors and images encounter other systems of metaphors and images, we may experience anger and confusion, if not trauma. And such encounters can move us to think, to think differently and with hesitation.

When Philippe Nemo asked Levinas how one begins thinking, the rabbi said that it probably begins by means of traumas or "gropings to which one does not even know how to give a verbal form, a separation, a violent scene, a sudden consciousness of the monotony of time."[2] But instead of turning to war experiences, psychological trauma, or political crises, Levinas turned immediately to the reading of books and to his reading of his people's book, the Bible, in particular. This compendium of diverse texts, compiled largely by priests, presents an "extraordinary presence" of characters, an "ethical plenitude" and "mysterious possibilities of exegesis," all of which signify "transcendence" for him. The Bible composes a "founding experience"—a pre-philosophical *experience*—in its "holy story," a place of the first meaning of beings, the place where meaning begins (23–25). In it one finds the imagery of holiness not through a holy Presence but in people's declaring in word and action "Here I am" before the Infinite, the Most High, "the invisible God." Although I am not sure that the word "trauma" would help us much at this point, his phrase, "gropings to which one does not know how to give a verbal form" certainly addresses the subject, because the invisible God is not, he says, invisible to the senses (106). Rather, God is not thematizable in thought or language without massive betrayal of God's Goodness and Highness and total Otherness. God continuously dis-appears in infinite transcendence as people find themselves here—before-the-other, find themselves as here-I-am in a passivity that composes testimony to the Other whose palpable withdrawal leaves our consciousness stunned and obsessed by striations of we know not what, striations and cuts and fissures and besettings in a consciousness that becomes blind when faced with the non-shadow, the non-appearance of the other-in-proximity.

The Bible in this view bears testimony to the sensible, unthematizable withdrawal of God in His Glorious Transcendence. It speaks of the stunning command of the Other who is never finished in "his" invisible

---

2. Emmanuel Levinas, *Ethics and Infinity* (Pittsburgh: Duquesne University Press, 1985), p. 56.

non-presence with consciousness and good sense. The Bible gives the testimony of those who found themselves with a meaning of goodness and responsibility that totally escaped the realm of finite reference and human self-formation. In *this* context we can indeed invoke the word "trauma" in the way I think that Levinas meant it. The Bible gives tortured expression to a people's experiences as they find themselves connected with the Most High God in complete passivity, without the possibility of explanation or the possibility of completing the obligation that is bestowed upon them in the name of Goodness.

The book. Levinas had a lifetime of intense encounters with books but with none so much as the Bible and its Talmudic lineage. In it he found a language bearing witness to a perceived proximity of the Other, of God, a "relationship" that language cannot grasp or hold syntactically or narratively and one that never finishes, one in which, as he says, God, addressed as Thou, continuously transcends into One who is referred to as He. In the Bible, God, though never revealed, announces Himself by the testimony of the people. He—and Levinas' God is spoken of in the uninnocent pronominal masculine—is found in the Bible's testimonies as people meet each other and find *themselves* announced in the other's approach. They find themselves hostage to God and to His contract with them over which they exercised no originary choice, no equality of partnership, no creative spontaneity. When they ignore their responsibility, they suffer, and when they attend to it, it—their responsibility—offers nothing that they can presume or intend or complete or schematize. The Bible composes testimonies to such struggle that is carried out and signified in their sense of a living bondage to God's command. Levinas finds the meaning of his thought in the Bible's testimony to the Infinite's commanding "Here I Am."

Levinas' trauma—"the gropings to which [he] does not know how to give a verbal form," the "separation," "the violent scene" that occasioned his thinking—is not separable from his encounter with Jewish theism and scripture. In this tradition, on his reading, such trauma and violence happen in God's absence to the people "He" chooses, happens in a break from presence and revelation that leaves a chasm for perpetual decision and failure. In this tradition Levinas finds himself responsible before he can act or experience anything. And while for him human consciousness, which he calls in *Otherwise Than Being* the for-itself, is quite alone with itself in its acts of appropriation, human existence is not alone. Like the Hebrew people found themselves with each other under a covenant with the Most High to which they were not consenting parties, but in accordance with which and in violation of which they were guilty sufferers, so Levinas finds all of us, whether or not we want it or like it, to be with each other in obligation to each other and under requirements remarkably like those that can be found in scriptural law. With each other, our autonomy is always violated by the other's ungraspable and present existence and violated as well by an insurmountable guilt of inadequacy in our responses to the other. The "here I am" of the other is no more disclosive of an essence or a stateably present being than the Most High is, and the chasm of nonpresence that marks the other's palpability is no more overcomeable than the chasm that holds people and God apart from recognizable appearance. "Nameless singularity" is one term that Levinas uses for the withdrawn presence of the other. This seems to be a radical image for presence that describes presencing by valorizing a palpable distance that neither appearance nor disclosure can overcome.

In such distance we are left with the positive option of witnessing, not in the sense of telling what we saw of the Most High but in the sense of telling, in an absence of objective certainty, what happened to us and what we underwent. And this undergoing is a matter of flesh and blood, of sensuous bodies by which the utter singularity of a fleshly movement occurs with us in its very life, happens with us outside of any meaning we might ascribe to it. An individual's life, whether Most High or not, is to itself and outside of all perceptive engagements.

As sensuous body meets sensuous body, each finds itself under the demand of the other's singularity, and it is here that a tradition of subtle and delicate morality, of powerful images and sensibilities, of suffering devoutness comes pouring into the absence of disclosive appearance. A life meets a life in a remarkable people's remarkable self-understanding, and the rabbinical philosopher speaks with the authority of one who knows that there is no completion and no essence before the face of a living God or before the face of the existing individual. This is a region that requires trusting faith, for infinity of life takes place in the broken, withdrawn presence of the Other. In Levinas' image, when a face countenances another face an irreparable distance of alterity occurs, one fraught with ethical meaning and one defined by another person's own living event. In Levinas' thought we find reference not to an essential presence, but to the incomparable singularity of another person. The distance is defined by a specific and personal "between" that nothing abstract or belonging to one's self can bridge. As he says, "the locus of support for the mind is a personal pronoun" that is founded on nothing the experiencing subject owns or can own (*Otherwise Than Being*, 106). It is "a point already identified from the outside, not having to identify itself in the present nor to state its identity, already older than the time of consciousness" (*OB*, 107).

"The" book and a corpus of writing have given Levinas a space for testimony that seems as radical as Blanchot's when Blanchot writes of seeing the light of now exploded and dead stars with the words, "Shining solitude, the void of the day, a deferred death: disaster" (*The Writing of the*

Disaster, 2). Perhaps it is as radical as when astronomers speak of space and time swirling and tottering around a black hole, when in the speed and pressure of unspeakable gravitational draw, space and time merge, change, and dissolve. We cannot pretend to know what that means, and we know that our knowledge has been brought to a halt before something totally outside of our reach. But Levinas' images are those of a distance defined by a solipsistic consciousness in relation to what it cannot avoid and cannot be, and his is a testimony that is occasioned by a people's written history. It is liberated from "our" knowledge of the universe, and it is anchored by a sense of personal presence that bears the trace of oppression, exile, and uncertainty before a God so alive that no knowledge can reach Him.

But the stardust in our eyes? The elements from colliding bodies so massive, so violent, so absent in the traces that remain of them? Our bodies in their galactic dimensions? Our bodies so removed from the persons that they enact? So beyond the metaphors of relationships? So unwritable and so outside of a people's history? So akin to nothing that could be Most High and to nothing that could make covenants? That is so other as to defy the noun "alterity"? This is a kinship—and I grow weary of this failing word—that interrupts inclusive nouns such as nature and cosmos and universe, one that requires metaphors and images other than those of a calling deity and one that allows our sense of goodness to assume a shape of mortality without divine anchorage and without universal aspirations. The minerals of our eyes allow us to think again, to re-image our senses of destiny, to reconsider the scope of our values, and to look again at the *solus ipse* of our "ipseity." Our faces seem to bear much more than relational distance. They seem to bear an anonymity that sees without fire or spirit, and that brings us closer to the simplest fungi and protozoa that have receptors that respond to the presence of light. We are creatures of gravity, star-elements, and forces that neither know nor call, and in the knowledge of that impersonal lineage we might find reason not to make values the final arbiters of our existence. Otherwise, the elements of our evaluative vision might function blindly toward the violence of comprehensive judgments in which we take our historical experiences to exceed their placed limitations as we collide with each other in implosions of normative absolutes and goodness.

The elements of our eyes seem only to function, not to wait for anything in particular. I think that we need to be careful when we look behind and beneath what we perceive. It seems that when we start to look for meanings behind appearances our imaginations take off like rockets, and we talk ceaselessly and confuse everything our imaginations produce with non-imaginative things. That is as true, I believe, of scientists as it is of prophets and ordinary people. So we might proceed with care when we look behind appearances, not so that we do not imagine but so that we can enjoy imagining, not getting seriously hooked by its products, and so that we can keep distances among our images, among the shadows they cast, distances with darkness from which they arise, and distances untraversed by meanings among things that we imagine are there. To be able during a day to find nothing but images behind appearances, to enjoy the efforts to provide for the day's dwelling places, to avoid feelings of catastrophe or of absolute responsibility and to come back home refreshed and enjoy a dinner with people we love—that would compose, I think, a good day's work.

To what point have we come in this rift of departing metaphors? My last paragraph embodies attitudes considerably different from the feelings of mourning, exile, and persecution that so powerfully determine Levinas' writing. It resists the option of continuous guilt that forms Levinas' thought. It places human alterity within a context of nonhuman differences and suggests that an overdetermination of human alterity, especially in the context of the Most High, is not good for humans. That last paragraph and the lines that precede it suggest indirectly that the obsession that Levinas' writing embodies needs to be problematized, that the heavy obsession and the fixated seriousness that it engenders might well be considered pathogenic no matter how justifiable we find the ethics on which it fixates. Such obsession has the power to so overdetermine even the body's life that such life becomes tied to relations that place it in bondage in a process that promises a measure of freedom—we should beware, I think, of gifts from the obsessed; they usually constitute hooks.

But how much do you want to be unhooked from the mourning, sadness, guilt, and sense of suffering that pervade Levinas' thought and pervade as well much of our religio-ethical tradition? Is there too much satisfaction in my words? Too little anguish? Do guilt and anguish constitute our hope of escape from complacency and pride of place and from the injustices that such satisfactions can bring? What perceptions of danger occur when we hear a silence when our lineages customarily speak of self-sacrifice, senses of oppression, and imperatives to participate in and with the suffering of others? And what kinds of threat to *our* sense of community do we hear when self-sacrifice is detached from our sense of proper connection?

I am suggesting that we might turn to things like dust from stars that are neither high nor low, that do not call for pity or grief or guilt—that call for nothing—and that leave us open to see how we might best enjoy the light and darkness in our world. These mineral-organic things, within some metaphorical concepts, might provide us a measure of freedom from histories of suffering and oppression that leave their scars in tortured lives of ethical responsibility. It might be that our *departures* from these histories, and their monumental perpetuation, can give us options preferable to those envisioned by people who have been wounded by the terrible injustice of oppression. There is something in the cold, distant, explosive shining of stars that we might take as an opportunity to look away from ourselves, not with the meanings of obsessional self-sacrifice but with a lightened perspective toward our griefs and engagements.

SIX

Physical Weight on the Edge of Appearing

Philosophy distinguishes itself by the unique way it profits
from death.
                    —Jean-Luc Nancy, *The Birth to Presence*

A friend of mine said in a conversation that Nancy's work on community
lacks an adequate, historical account of the concepts of community
that he addresses. He pointed out that the lineage in which Nancy thinks
has made the valuable contribution in contemporary philosophy of insist-
ing that we situate our thought by careful work in the texts that have helped
to form the problems and concepts that we use, modify, define, or take
apart. Nancy, he said, presents too little of the historical homework, and
that omission leaves his writings often a little thin and rather more like occasional aesthetic reflections of fairly abstract ideas. When such a light
approach has to do with weighty matters like human connections and their
implications for people's suffering and well-being, it—this manner of lightness—approaches perversity in addition to irrelevance in its lack of direct,
historically grounded, and engaged concreteness. At the very least Nancy
might have provided a careful genealogy of the formation of the concept of
human community in whose exhaustion he thinks.

In contrast to my friend, I am more worried about the pathogenic
force in most forms of weighty seriousness than I am about aesthetic approaches to political and social issues, although I agree that most of what
we philosophers do in ethics and social and political philosophy does not
have much practical effect in the halls and councils of governmental
power. When we think, we generally have more effect on the slow transformation of concepts and conceptual movements than on current policy
formations and political practice. And usually concepts and conceptual
movements invoke certain aesthetic things like vague, pre-reflective images

and metaphors, associations of certain values, and a range of perception and forceful feelings. If, for example, people most like and value weighty methodical studies, well stitched and comprehensive systems of thought, and thorough presentations of historical engagements with the problems and questions at hand, Nancy's works will indeed seem occasional and limited in their rigor—they will seem like moments of interesting, if dense, insight but not like major works. They will feel light in their density, too light to be philosophically weighty. But if lightness is valued and if weighty seriousness is an object of suspicion, Nancy's essays will seem all the more valuable because of their occasional manner. A person will then feel differently about their limited range and will appreciate in them a different rigor from that of monumental works, a discipline of constraint that is presented in his style and in what happens in his thought to the affect, imagery, and content of many of the most powerful concepts and meanings in our tradition. In this instance, with immersion in his work, people will find themselves able to perceive Nancy's lineage and their own loyalties differently in comparison to the way they perceived them before their engagement with him. His kind of density and lightness changes the entire atmosphere of thought when compared, for example, to that of Heidegger or Hegel.

In Nancy's thought manners of affirmation and feeling change—there is, for example, no predisposition in his work toward heroes or toward nationalistic or religious mythology. He has learned how to think without the force of the values of ontological reconciliation, immanent universals, or defining grounds, and he has learned this with unusual and persistent discipline, enough discipline to make people uncomfortable when they find or at least sense that they are far more controlled than they thought they were by such meanings as those of reconciliation, immanent universals, and defining grounds.

Nancy's thought spawns different hopes from those of many other thinkers. Hopes, for example, bred of historical or national teleologies do not arise in his thought. It spawns different values that turn decisively and rigorously away from many of those that move definitively in the core of Hegel's or Schelling's or Heidegger's thought, and while thoroughly indebted to his engagements with them, he finds no obligation to retrace either his odyssey with them or their genealogical heritage as he engenders a different hierarchy of images, feelings, metaphors, and values in comparison to theirs.

But the rigor of his thought of finitude does undermine some of the strongest motivations of the thought of these others, not by historical confrontations but by transformations of conceptual knowledge in the light of what I will valorize by the term "hard things" and by descriptive accounts, not of lineages of meaning but of the existence of meanings

and their occurrences in thought and practice. Nancy is developing an experience of thinking and physical interconnection in his thought that
provides a way of perceiving that is quite distinct from that of most of his
predecessors. In this process he finds that at least some of the traditional
ideas and uses of power that appear to be destructive of people's differences and needs wane and that some of our inherited dread before death
and dying shifts decidedly from the dominance of anxious escape and in
the direction of communal, differential affirmation. It is thinking *in* these
transformations and expressing the transformations in his thinking that
give Nancy's work originality and moment. His approach need not replace
explicitly historical studies. They have their own importance. But it does
provide an occasion to think with changed images and values. Nancy's approach gives occasion to think with a certain lightness that challenges a
predisposition toward weighty thought that I find in myself regarding
heavily grounded rigor and monumental intellectual figurations of intellectual accomplishment. It might be that one of Nancy's most significant
contributions is found in a lightness of mind that challenges the *weight*
of meaning, truth, wisdom, and ethical soberness in our tradition. His
thought might bring to light an occasional dimension in our contemporary experience in which meanings are qualified by a continuous draw of
nonmeaning at our places of confrontation with living things. Within the
force of his thought we might find motivation to think again and differently and with less historical weight than we previously thought possible.
And we might discover that weighty seriousness can be a progenitor of
states of mind that seek unity, wholeness, and purpose to the considerable
disadvantage of physical things.

In the interests of conceptual transformation regarding the idea and
sense of physicality, I would like to bring together occurrences of luminosity, density, lightness, and weight in thought in such a way that we
might think of physical events in reference to such occurrences. In this
context I will engage Nancy, who is attempting to think at the edge of
contemporary interpretations of human community and who is wonderfully perceptive before the collapse of the forces of "universality" and the
slightly less powerful image of horizon. For Nancy sees that "the availability of the singular," as he puts it, now requires that we experience
"finitude" in its "endless ending."[1] And such availability suggests the
events of bodies and thinking, their palpability, their escape from phrasing, and their weighty, opaque composition with things that we have a
lot of trouble finding words for—trouble now because *matter* and *spirit*

---

1. Jean-Luc Nancy, *The Gravity of Thought,* trans. F. Raffoul and G. Recco (Atlantic Highlands,
N.J.: Humanities Press, 1997; hereafter *GT*), pp. 78, 79.

dissatisfy us for good reasons and material reductions just do not tell us what we would like to know. We would like to know what our physical events mean as they happen, not what they mean because of universal categories or because of enumerable organs and parts of organs or because of a horizon of meaningfulness within which they are said to take place.

This effort to think of physical events in reference to luminosity, density, lightness, and weight is, I hope, compatible with your own efforts to affirm physical events in sole reference to themselves and their complex histories and not by reference to something that they are not. I would like for these remarks to support your desire to find meaning in the physicality of events and to think of them in the ways *their* meanings happen. I hope that we come to find our thoughts themselves as physical events without reducing or elevating our thoughts to something that they are not. Nancy's convictions that appear so helpfully in this context are that physical events, inclusive of thinking, are thoroughly, intrinsically interrelational. "Interrelational" means for him worldly and thus "absolutely" finite and hence not universalizable without disastrous totalizations and refusal of their singularity (*GT,* 78). So, we begin with the expectation that luminosity, density, lightness, and weight might tell us something about physical events, that physical events will tell us something about bodies as well as something about our thinking of them. And before we are finished we will need to find out how to use these words as well as "singularity" or "the singular" in the lightness of "universality's" demise. The image of light density without horizon is also going to cause problems. So I will attempt to get all the help I can from Nancy and to consider not only the gravity of thought but also our common physical gravities wherever they are found. There will be something light about all this gravity.

Scientists apparently do not know what gravity is outside of a force exerted among bodies in mathematically calculable ratios, among bodies whose own composition requires the force of gravity. They can see an operation but they have no idea "where" it comes from or where it is going or how it came to have the status of law that they give to it. To call gravity an "it" is awkward, and to say that "it" has a nature is extremely awkward since it does not appear to have come from anywhere or to "have" anything or to be any one thing in particular. All gatherings and condensations, no matter how minute, depend on "it," were "it" an "it," and the very happening of the waves or particles of force, if force is composed of waves or particles, themselves seem to depend on the force of gravity that they enact. So we may begin with the image of physical events that happen in a force whose operations are detectable but whose composition not only escapes our understanding but also puts in question the very idea of composition. I do not mean to suggest that we should think of bodies as essentially mysterious because of the operation of gravity. Rather, they are, in their density, very lightly composed, so lightly that their weight seems to come down to an other, to something that is virtually weightless.

I am beginning with gravity as a metaphor in part because I do not know what I could mean by saying that gravity is a real thing, partly because when I write of it I seem to make it a literal thing, partly because a metaphor dissipates that kind of literalness and introduces the subject matter with a light touch, a sense of losing the very thing the words present, and partly because we have difficulty believing that "gravity" is not in some sense very real. Gravity strikes me as naming something or other that is necessary and operative for everything, not subject to weighty measurement, and yet responsible for weight in all cases. It is like a force of collocation, like the very force of location, place, and, I expect, time.

So Nancy has my attention when he speaks of the gravity of thought. When he considers the weight of a thought, images of suspension hover in his prose. You can see part of what he means if you recall ancient scales, like those of blind justice, that weigh by the balance or imbalance of the contents of two equally weighted saucers on the ends of a suspended chain that is held by a central fulcrum. The lighter contents are suspended—hung higher—by virtue of the weightier contents in the other dish. The weighing composes an appraisal, an evaluation, an exchange of weight by a figure that does not see the process. To weigh and to be weighed suggest a blind suspension from which consequences can follow. One aspect of this image weighs in on the side of judgment and the forces of criteria that, due to the weighing, bring results from the comparative exchange, and *that* can be a grave matter in the sense of being very serious. Here the weight of evaluation, which is a manner of thinking that does not see much concerning itself, counterbalances all the other contingencies of exchange and often moves toward fixations in placement, a model for which we will find to be universalization.

But is the very "materiality" of weighing itself in the balance? Nancy "confesses" in a manner that can be taken as an elaboration of a certain blindness, that "thinking can never grasp weighing; it can offer a measure for it, but it cannot itself weigh up the weight" (*GT,* 75–76). I take this confession to mean that Nancy knows that what he is doing as he thinks about thinking is both evaluative and representational but that what really counts is lost to the balancing act. There is a draw here, not measurable by "a few ounces of fiber and neurons" that is like gravity in the sense that it is both operative and so light as to fall outside the reach of possible measure. Something happens like a "leap" from the regions of just propriety and from even such indirect evaluation as that provided by language. Is this leap from weighty materials to the weight of weighing (evaluating, appropriating) like an escape from gravity (*GT,* 76)? Or does another kind of gravity come into play?

If there were something like an escape from gravity in thinking, it would be in addition to the force of weighing that happens in thinking. Nancy names this force of weighing "appropriation," and the conduct of such force is found in bestowal and discovery of meanings. Thinking does indeed weigh the world when "the real" happens "as meaning" (ibid.). That is, thinking happens as a palpable occurrence with palpable effects; it weighs in on things and affairs, provides directions and recognitions, directly affects people's behavior, gives more weight to some things than to others, and above all, finds and bestows the power of meanings in and on things. If we pay attention primarily to fields of meaning we could well decide that thinking happens completely within a horizon of meaning, although by that decision we would give "horizon" the meaning of a limiting metaphor—which is a weighty thing to do to horizon. We would have considerable difficulty in thinking of "horizon" as a metaphor of infinite openness—that is, as a metaphor for finitude—because it would suggest that thought is limited by meaningfulness. That would be something like what Nietzsche described as the ascetic ideal, by which existence is so dominated by meaning that its dimension of open meaninglessness is sacrificed to an anxious evaluation that insists exclusively on meaningful unities.

Nancy, by contrast, finds that the gravity of thought comes with things, "hard things," that "are there" but that resist thought (*GT,* 2). "Hard things . . . are mute, yet they call you to a *logos* that does not gather, but to a *logos* that maintains the heterogeneous and discreetly guarantees that these things reveal no secret but that of being there" (ibid.). In thinking we find, instead of a horizon of meaning, things in their resistant difference to thought and meaning. Thinking appears to be drawn out by such things, and this force has the sense of gravity. Thinking seems to end, to be buried by unthinkable things, and this coming to its end has the sense of "grave." It's a weighty matter that invokes thought and carries thinkers vastly beyond themselves into places where thoughts and meanings implode.

In this dimension thinking ceases to weigh or to be able to weigh. The weight of appropriation and meaning is lifted. We could say that we have come to a blind point in thinking. Thinking does indeed make sense. But as it makes sense it is drawn disastrously by the sheer density of things in their mute alienation from a horizoned region of meaningfulness. There is no essence to be found here (*GT,* 76). Thinking, as it is drawn out by the weight of hard things, exists without essences. The "dissonance" between thinking and what is here to be thought composes both a fundamental attunement in thinking to its continuous mortality and "the whole weight of thought" (ibid.). "Bodies are heavy," and that means that bodies constitute the materiality of thought and come to thought with this drawing mortality, this weight of attraction to disaster (*GT,* 77). Thought is weighed down by the density of what it is not, a little like a string of stars drawn into the orbit of a heavier mass, except in the instance of thinking, "reason" brings this draw and density into itself, becomes a site of vast, material excess to itself, and composes its own ending in the draw of what is not thinkable. In Nancy's phrasing, reason becomes present to itself in becoming distant to itself. In this sense "gravity" composes the very element, the physicality, of thinking without ever becoming something quite specific, quite material, or quite universal—almost, perhaps, but not quite. Thinking is already incompleting itself when it comes to the meaning and image of universality.

All meaning, indeed, is composed of this presencing and distancing that belongs to thought's gravity. In meaning thought is distant to itself by virtue of the hard things that it confronts and brings to itself in its happening. *Its* weight is "the weight of an extremity," the weight of what it is with, cannot be, cannot depart from, cannot get within its grasp, can neither encompass nor penetrate, cannot be within or be without. That is thought's gravity *and* the (blind) weight of meaning. "It is the weight of an extremity on which an irresistible force is being applied at the place of a possible eruption of meaning (that is to say, in every place) causing at once shattering and compaction, concentration and explosion, pain and joy, meaning and absence of meaning" (*GT,* 77). We may say in this context that such gravity composes the events of flesh and blood, the happenings of neurological firings, the postures and structures—the physicality—of thinking.

And as this body in its dehiscence is unspeakably weighty, it is also light. "This is intolerable, unbearable (one bends, collapses under the weight of what is to be thought, that is, of what just *is*), and yet this has no heaviness, it is lightness itself (one can think whatever one wishes). This is grave, the existence of the world is grave, but this gravity has the lightness of that which exists without any other justification than existing" (*GT,* 3). There is a weightlessness in this weight, "without bottom or center," a suspension by which meaning hangs in the balance, a draw that will not be measured in the midst of thought's weighty bestowal and discovery of meaning (ibid.). By this lightness of suspension, without horizon, "we are repeatedly taught that there is no sense in trying to totalize meaning (even if by a minor or temporary totalization)—in trying to adjust to a completed knowledge of the event of an existence that, precisely, exists only in the disjunction of the presence-to, in unconnected tremors, and in the halting quality of its events. Meaning is an event, not an ending (*finition*). Or, rather, its ending is itself endless (*sans fin*)" (*GT,* 77–78). Death, in other words, completes a meaning by incompletion.

We are thus able to see in Nancy's description that meaning has a quality of light endlessness in its ending: it opens out as it closes down. "Meaning does not have the sense of an answer"—it is always "non-completed," "nonfinished," "yet to come"—and "not even of a question; in this sense, it has no meaning" (*GT,* 78). But it is an event of an opening. Meaning is endless in the sense that it is always possible in its grave disaster. "It brings no salvation, but greets (calls) the to-come and the end-less" (ibid.). Meaning moves as mortal temporality, always answering without an answer. It is, in the language of another of Nancy's books, "inoperative." "It does not gather a community or bring about intimacy, but relentlessly exposes a common exteriority, a spacing, a co-appearance of strangers. (This is why there is no primary or final place, no capital, no Rome, Athens, Mecca, or Jerusalem. There is only the gap between places, which constitutes place, and the weight of each place, of each landing or meeting place)" (ibid.). We can say on these terms that the lightness of the grave event of thinking's ending, its continuous opening out, happens as a dimension of gravity, not an escape from it, but as opaque non-presence in the nonfinality of thought's collapse in weighty meaning. Gravity draws thought endlessly through incompletion before hard things.

Such physicality, this coming to be in ceasing to be in thought's existence, enjoys what Nancy terms "commonality." Commonality is not composed of anything for which the word "nature" would be appropriate. Thought's commonality is found in its gravity, its draw and expiration with hard things, its grave aspect as it appropriates to itself what is in it and yet exterior to it, and finds in meaningful appropriations an endless ending of meaning and hence of itself in its life of appropriation. And thought's commonality is not found in a law of ending, not in a categorical necessity that thought die before its other. Rather, thought's commonality happens as grave events, events in which thought is lost to itself in its coming to presence. No law appears—only appearing, collapsing events in which people find themselves together. "Community is calibrated [i.e., given its commonality] on death as on that of which it is precisely impossible to *make a work . . . ,*" Nancy says in *The Inoperative Community.*[2] The descriptive emphasis falls on exhaustion in the meanings of law, category, necessity, and universality, on the exhaustion of those means by which we make big sense of things and collect them within a stated horizon of commonality. It is the still point of blindness in thought's perceptiveness that Nancy allows to show obliquely in this written perception. And this is an obliqueness that I think we can appropriately call dense. As in the case of

2. Jean-Luc Nancy, *The Inoperative Community,* ed. P. Connor, trans. P. Connor, L. Garbus, M. Holland, and S. Sawhney (Minneapolis: University of Minnesota Press, 1991; hereafter *IC*), p. 15.

gravity, there is no "it" here to see as we perceive commonality. If there is any positive use for the meaning of horizon in this context, it would be found in phrases such as "the loss of horizon" or "the trauma of no horizon"—it seems to be the case that gravity has no horizon and is no horizon, that gravity happens rather more like a drawing event through horizons and beyond than it happens like a force composed of a horizon's luminous density. That a horizon is shot through with gravity is more to the point; it is subject to gravity, and gravity happens as weighty condensation and light dissolution and is finally encompassed by neither condensation nor dissolution. It is simply not a thing.

But it works, and with this statement—"it works"—I wish to take a direction distinct from Nancy's. But first I would like to pay attention to what Nancy says about "inoperative," because I would like to note an inoperative dimension in physicality, and I would like to consider the option that our physical commonality is calibrated by events of difference to our perceptiveness, events that nonetheless compose our perceptiveness and ones that Nancy describes by the words grave and death. In this way we will have access to an aspect of physical density that is quite worldly, or, we might say, access to an aspect of our very being, one that is outside of our grasp, common, useless, vital, and filled with implications for the ways we might intend to relate with each other.

"[B]eing-in-common is not a common being" (*IC,* 29). When we address commonality we are not addressing anything pervasively immanent. With being-in-common, we do not begin or end with anything that requires bracketing to get to or anything that haunts our subjectivity, that cloaks itself in mystery, that properly inclines us to deep and perceptive communion with a few or a many, that promises merger or the tribal inspirations of The People, Sacred Soil, and The Blood of Our Fathers and The Sacrifices of Our Mothers. Being-in-common has a grave aspect in that singular people's dissolutions and continuous losses of sufficiency, their continuous incompletion, give the space and time of their collocation and condensation. Being-in-common is a matter of gravity, of drawing events of dehiscence, events that no one does, a *phusis* of eventful gravity marked by the deaths of subjects and the impossibility of immanent immersion. "A community is the presentation to its members of their mortal truth. . . . It is the presentation of the finitude and the irredeemable excess that make up finite being: its death, but also its birth" (*IC,* 15). It presents "to me my birth and my death"; it is "my existence outside myself" (*IC,* 26). In our communities we are continuously exposed, exposed in gravity's mortal exposure. This is not a matter of bumping into limits that define us but is rather, Nancy says, a matter of *being* finite. We are commonly singularities that are limited *in* dying and birthing, *in* multiple exposure in which hard things weigh us down and lighten us up in gravity's opaque, finite luminosity. Our singularity composes a *phusis*—an uprising—of unveiling mortality in a world of interrelations that composes us before and as we come to assert ourselves: composes us "at the end (or at the beginning)," Nancy says, "with contact of the skin (or the heart) of another singular being, at the confines of the *same* singularity that is, as such, always *other*, always shared, always exposed" (*IC*, 28). Singularities exist in "exposure to the outside" (*IC*, 29).

This gravity of finitude is not a work or a deed. It is more like the drawing incompletion of works and deeds. It is not like the effect of a vacuum or of a push or a pull. It is rather more like our exposure in pushes, pulls, and, perhaps, vacuums. Our flesh and blood belong to such gravity: they are composed of such exposure. Without it we would not be: without it, no motion, no organs, no sharing, no commonality, no death, no life. The gravity of thought is the same as the gravity of commonality—the physical, undone and undoing, generative and exhausting, vastly dense in the opaqueness of exposure, not a thing, shared beyond the meanings we attach to them, not quite a law, neither a ground nor a source, the physicality of time and place.

"Operative levity" suggests a kind of attunement that can accompany events of gravity. My purposes are not critical regarding Nancy's thought but are directed toward an implication of what Nancy, in the words of Bataille, calls exhaustion and that I will speak of with the word "levity." I do not need to remind you that levity can name excessive or unseemly frivolity. But it can also name buoyancy and is synonymous with lightness; that is, it means having little weight as well as releasing weight. It can suggest a dizzy or giddy quality—a certain light-headedness—but it can also suggest something easily endurable and gentle—a light touch, for example. To lighten something can also mean to make it clear, to let it shine brightly, or to release it from a burden. To lighten is to relieve. Levity, as I wish to apply the word, means a lightening aspect, a possible buoyancy that qualifies the meaning of exhaustion as it plays in Nancy's use of the word "grave." A thought's gravity, for example, releases thought from the weight of meaning while also collecting and collocating meaningful, thoughtful perceptions. In such release people may find that levity that comes when a burden of possession passes or when they come into a future of possibilities that release the weight of a totality of attachments. It is not a matter of total release. That would mean dispersion without identity or place. It is rather a dimension of people's existing that Nancy describes so well by the figurations of gravity—something like the dimensions of lapse in metaphoric functions that give metaphors lightness by ellipses and releases their references from the full weight of literal designation. We can emphasize death in such a dimension and thereby note the ethical and political importance of release from weighty totalizations, or we can highlight the levity of this dimension and note the ethical and political importance of a lightness of mind that is predisposed to affirmations with a light touch and with an attunement to the fragile, momentary quality in our feelings of loyalty and identity as well as in our collective and individual good sense. A thought's or a community's gravity is not totally grave. It is also susceptible to a buoyancy of spirit and a preparedness for affirmations with modifications, new beginnings, and that remarkable vitality that can accompany hearing again, answering again, and finding in our repetitions something uncommon and in-breaking.

Levity in gravity. "Gravity" that names cosmologically a force of collection, but a force that is mapped only abstractly and mathematically in a context in which it names its own possibility. For gravity is said to operate in all formations, and it does not appear to be any one thing. A relation of bodies? Yes. And how did the first little mass form? By gravity. And where and what was gravity before that? One more conundrum of origination. But a suggestive one in the sense that its meaning of force does not quite name a force, its definition of a law suggests a kind of regularity that explains itself—while I can say with conviction that we plainly know what we mean when we say gravity, that meaning seems to dissipate as we get closer to the density of what we are talking about. We are drawn to a collapse of the power of our meaningful explanation.

But the metaphors of gravity that I have been using with the suggestions of drawing, demise, collection, dehiscence, commonality, and opening up in thought and communities? I have said that gravity does not quite name a law when the meaning of "law" confronts the light density of what it is about. Nancy has helpfully used the word finitude at this point to name our being in our grave undoing, a name that also allows us to highlight the metaphors' lapses. And throughout the process of making descriptive claims we have found the lapses that Nancy wishes to speak of, lapses that are not done and that do nothing, lapses that nonetheless can operate by giving rise to lightened affections and to attunements of levity to, we might say, the operations of lapses.

These lapses and gravities and openings appear to compose our physicality, our physical events, not as structures of behavior or categories or essences—but appear as something like an operative, i.e., eventful, dimension throughout people's physical lives. Our lives do not seem to happen in a division of matter and spirit or of nature and subjectivity. They seem rather to happen interactively in a dimension of gravity that is inclusive of losses, impacts, and meanings in the events of which our hearts beat with quickened or slowed pace, our organs are vitalized by hope and affirmation, we are more or less attracted to various people, or our brains shut down their production of chemicals for neurotransmissions. Our lives— our physicality—seem also to happen in the gravity of differences with which we live and which we cannot overcome by meanings, with which we may experience panic or captivation or puzzlement or many other physical states. Our lives seem to be—is it not strange that we need to understand *our* lives?—in their interactive exchanges in a dimension of something like drawing effective gravity whereby we can find commonality without nature or structure or deed and whereby we can find a lightness of opening minds in the midst of grave events.

SEVEN

Lightness of Mind and Density

In his *Introduction to Metaphysics,* Heidegger prepares the way in his first lecture for his listeners to understand what he means by *Geist* and by a people's spirit. He speaks of the earth's and its inhabitants' place in the universe.[1] He points out that when we view our planetary home in terms of astrophysics and astronomy, it looks so minuscule in its spatial context as to obliterate any sense of significance that a person might attach to it. It is simply too tiny in all ways to count for much. In such a perspective the earth's inhabitants also seem useless, utterly without cosmological meaning. Our times and efforts, like imperceptible waves of light, blink out of nothing to nothing, evaporated in the moment of energy that produced them. Nothing like *Geist* appears before such a view. What appears in such a construction seems more like mere expenditures of force in rapidly passing shapes, rather like a particle in a moving cloud on a distant horizon. Nor do the formation and articulation of such knowledge themselves bear much witness to *Geist.* They lack awareness of the ways of life and thought that they comprise and to which they give rise. This knowledge composes a kind of objectivity that has little sense for its own event or for its basis in the very questionableness of *life* that it embodies.

Spirit, Heidegger says, happens as we experience the questionableness of our lives and their meaning. We happen in attunement to our lives as we recoil from and to uncertainty—when we happen as the recoil of uncertainty—uncertainty that is so profound that it can call appropriately for no knowledge to dispel it. We embody a questionableness that appears to happen as its own manifestation, not as the manifestation of anything else, and meaning is found in this coming out and uncovering of our lives' unavoidable, alert, self-articulating, highly productive, and caring fragility. No matter where we are in the universe, no matter our comparative dimensions, we *are* in question, and in that is everything that matters.

1. The following is a gloss on *EM* (see chapter 3, note 10), pp. 5ff.

You can see immediately how complicated and dense spirit (*Geist*) is in this context. Heidegger's use of the word does not suggest something that is reducible to anything else—not to fleshly matter or to an activity that is produced or caused by something else or to a point of view (such as a true way of viewing the world) or to something that is found to be like something else, or to anything that can be properly accounted as an object of knowledge. He is clear that *Geist* is not a specific subject or subjectivity in general. And although he sounds close to identifying *Geist* with a specific culture's specially gifted insight and self-expression (i.e., the whole of the ancient Greek tradition and that of the German language), such a culture's gift now would be found in its knowledge that it has lost touch with what is rightfully most important to it. For *Geist*, as Heidegger thinks of it, seems to be a kind of happening in which its own loss figures its presence—and *that* is dense. It is dense in the sense that *Geist*, as he considers it, cannot see through itself. It is thick with the distraction of insistent, everyday things, and obscured by a historically developed sense that it is grounded in and gives expression to deathless presence. *Geist* would be lighter if it could own its questionableness—its basic uncertainty, for in the context of the question of being, *Geist* is an occurrence whose very recoiling eventfulness is without a basis—although this being without a basis (being in question) is at least like a basis in the sense that being without a basis is as basic as things ever get. Dense! At this point *Geist* seems like a word that means neither heavy nor light, neither solid nor porous, neither subject nor object. I am thinking of "dense" in this sense: in this language we are up against something that we cannot exactly conceptualize or see through or walk through or reach through or around or understand in the luminosity of grammar and common sense. I would like to think of this density in terms of physicality and also think of it in connection with the function of the metaphor of space as Foucault works with it in *The Order of Things*. This is a kind of density about which we would not want to talk by reference to matter or materiality, a density that, while demonstrably dense, is opposed neither to luminosity nor lightness. And I would like to go on this voyage of thought for the purpose of exploring and refiguring, if only slightly, the way we often think of bodies. Physicality, the question of being, and space are the words around which this exploration will take its bearings.

Heidegger had several purposes when he contextualized *Geist* within the question of being in his 1936 summer lectures in which he introduced students to metaphysical thought. He wanted to counter with maximal energy a growing menace, one by which the question of language was losing what remained of its force in European cultures. By concerning themselves primarily with beings and issues that could be resolved, proved, answered, produced, used, and communicated with relative ease, people were losing a sensibility not only for the unresolvable, dark and opaque strangeness of life's event but also losing their sense for the astonishing opacity of language and thought when that strangeness pervades the meanings and references of things as they appear in particular linguistic and thoughtful enactments. Although this menace arrives with special emphasis in Russian and North American influence, it has been around for a long time, been around, indeed, within those two favorite cultures of Greece and Germany, and it is found by Heidegger's eyes in every faculty in the German universities. Heidegger, in fact, had little more patience with that pedantry that flourishes in German academies than many North Americans and Russians do, and he was strongly predisposed to blow the whole ship of German academics, including the "new" interpretations of Nietzsche, out of the water and start over with what he considered to be a more authentic curriculum—and all of that in the name of *Geist*! This approach to revolution by means of lectures and teaching might not be politics as a labor organizer or party fund-raiser would be inclined to think of it, but if we put these politicians in a debate with Heidegger, we would find, I think, that their opinions in this case were due to the fact that they were not all that familiar with *Geist* and might even unwittingly embody its antagonist, especially in their politics, in the form of a low-minded insensitivity to the lives they lead. *Geist,* the question of being, and a certain astonishment in and before life's questionability are terribly important political foci for Heidegger because, as he saw it, informed opinion was well on its way to thinking that scientific knowledge could tell us more truth about our world than anything else could and to thinking that the value of lives came down to a matter of serviceability, solutions for problems, and truths that can be understood objectively or commonsensically. All of this suggests to me that he wanted to reactivate in our most lively sensibility an awareness of density right where there is common sense and pragmatic, methodological clarity. "It" is not as clear as we tend to think it is when "it" means the occurrence of life.

Another purpose that Heidegger had in mind in these lectures was to join the question of being with a renewed understanding of what the Greek word *phusis* said and named. Even though the Latin translation of *phusis, natura,* suggests coming to birth, Heidegger is dissatisfied with it and its various cognates in Western languages. This word has a history that suggests the tensions in our knowledge of bodies that I want to highlight and that Heidegger wants to address. On the one hand *phusis* speaks of vital force. On the other, it names a created being in its essential character. In both of these senses it has been considered a synonym for being. And in yet a third connotation, *phusis* has been used to name creation as a whole. Amidst these differences of nuance I note especially the one between vital force and essential character. I believe that I can put the point by asking if the "inner fire" (an image some Stoics used for vital force) has a nature, in the sense of "composed by invariant principles" that define it? Does *phusis* as the springing up of life happen in a reasonable way? Is *phusis* nonrational and a basis for reasonable occurrences rather than happening under rational jurisdiction? If it were nonrational, it probably would be forever escaping rational grasp and frustrating reasonable people while at the same time suggesting, in an absence of principled universality or a status of any perceptible kind, that the rising up and passage of life does not necessarily happen in any definitive way, that our recognized necessities compose, strangely and perhaps irritatingly, only specific happenings of *phusis* and neither *phusis* "as such" nor a grasp of *phusis* "as such." I am approaching the possibility that *phusis* has more to do with the springing up of the image of nature as we usually visualize nature than it has to do with "having" the nature that an image or an idea might require it to have. Or, to speak in a way more like Heidegger spoke, *phusis* is not a being or a kind of being at all. That would mean that *phusis* names nothing specific at the same time that it names life's coming to pass.

"Nature" is like *phusis* in connoting both animation and identifying form. But "nature" is too firmly tied to images of invariant presence and definitions to allow conveniently for reference to nothing in particular that seems always to occur in happenings and in some vague sense lies with and in all mentation, lies in and with mentations not as a defined, rational predisposition, but as an indefinable sway that does not even suggest its own necessity beyond the locality of specific occurrences—a sway that seems to suggest that we need to rethink our own thinking in its inability to bring such density to thought. It might well be that *phusis* has the advantage of sounding more foreign and less ordinary than *nature* and that, in spite of the stresses of definition that it shares with *natura,* has the further advantage of not suggesting quite so strongly as *nature* does its own permanence (if it were an "it"). And it has the third advantage of pointing toward the word *physicality* about which this discussion is and about which I will say more in a moment.

The "second" complexity in the history of *phusis* that I noted above comes to the fore when we see that the word can name created beings in their essential specificity as a group or it can name life in general. It can name, in other words, beings as a whole and being as such, and in such naming it names the happening of lives or life's happening. This ability of the word in association with its suggestion of difference from anything that has a "nature" allows it, at least in Heidegger's language, to say that whatever is, as *is* (in being at all), happens beyond the reach of definitive grasp and that whatever happens happens in coming to pass. In happening, things do not bring to realization anything fully subject to definition.

When I think of *Geist, phusis,* and our tiny, tiny planet in this context, I am inclined to say that our spiritual (*geistige*) lives, as Heidegger thinks of them, have to do with perceiving things in pervasive awareness of the fragility of their and our lives, that something like fragility has within it, at least in "spiritual" events, a recoiling movement—a doubling dimension—in which whatever appears and the apprehending occurrence find indwelling connection: fragility in things (or inherent uncertainty in their being, or the questionableness of being) doubles back in the apprehension and shines through every appearing thing, provides a sense of relatedness in this fragility, and provides no sense of permanence. People react differently to such manifestations. They might care for things-in-their-fragility with profound empathy for them in the passing quality of their lives. They might be moved by a sense of beauty before the rising and fading animations of living things with all their hues and diversity. They might wish to find ways to present life to themselves with a good bit more permanence than is plainly apparent. However we react, the physicality of *Geist* on Heidegger's account—its *phusis*—appears as an enlivening dimension for people, no matter how painful or happy its manifestations might be, in the appearing of whatever appears, and in those appearances people often find interest and meaning in relation to everything around them without concern for the relative size or "objective" importance of their locality.

In addition to showing that size and permanence are not only not everything, as far as meaning is concerned, but also are inconsequential for meaning in our lives, Heidegger further suggests, largely by indirection in the introductory lectures, that the ways in which we give order to appearances and answer to the orders we find among them are highly consequential for our sense of life, our spirit. The ways a culture finds order, expression, and meaning with things comprise a large measure of the identity and particularity of their appearing. When we know things, for example, primarily by means of their functions and uses, their fragility is figured by their liability to breakage, malfunctioning, or contextual inappropriateness (their being unsuitable and valueless in many contexts). Or if things are determined by size, countable time, and metric distance (like, in Heidegger's example, the relative size of the earth and its inhabitants), their fragility is measured in comparative terms (lasts more time than . . . , has less mass and energy than . . . , has more or less force on other objects than . . .). When such ways of knowing come to define and order a people, they compose a thoroughly obscuring texture before what Heidegger identifies as an inherited Western spirit of fragility and question, and most things seem to happen pretty much objectively or subjectively and without much indication of their own eventful, immeasurable, thoroughly questionable, dense lives. Our orders of life and knowledge more or less make manifest the sense of immeasurable fragility and questionableness in

the lineages of our being and more or less give moment to astonishment
before the occurrences of lives, no matter whether we approve of them in
their details. I take this to mean that the ways by which the emerging
orders of our cultural lives form and endure for a time composes our physicality. The forms of things and their collections, as we live with and by
them, define our lives and the locales of our physicality. And the ways we
live with things *in* their appearing composes the physicality of our *Geist*,
the fully interconnected range of lineages, regulations, feelings, languages,
and thought.

With "physicality" in this context I would like to emphasize a transfiguration of the issue of bodies and their density. We have seen that
phusis, and hence *physicality*, has the considerable advantage of suggesting
physical, corporeal life and animation: the springing up and appearing of
lives with a density that people cannot fully grasp. I have pointed out that
when arising, persisting passage is conceived in the obscure light of the
question of being, on Heidegger's terms, we confront "something" dense—
really dense in the sense that there is nothing there clearly to focus on or
to see through or to pass through or to understand objectively and yet is
"there" in a pervasive sense of happening-without-finality-or-inevitable-
continuation. And such density "defines" (in a sense of defines that I cannot satisfactorily define because we're not talking about any *thing*, much
less about something that has a definable structure) physicality and hence
corporeal lives. I have indicated my doubt, however, that in Heidegger's
thought this density is conceived with sufficient attention to such corporeal things as bleeding, hunger, suffering, laughter, touching. I have not
found in Heidegger's accounts of *phusis* and the question of being an ex-
pressible, sensuous order among such things. His thought of *phusis* and its
density does not draw us to fleshly existence while it expands our horizons
for thinking about being and "spirit" in ways more satisfactory than those
we usually have available to us. I would like to think of orders of meaning
and influences as composing locales of physicality; I would like to think
of such orders in a way that complements rather than departs from sensuousness. But for now I wish to do no more than to follow the bend and
move toward an image of physicality that is without a suggestion of permanence while it embodies (Heidegger's word here is "say," *sagt*) a spirit
enlivened by the *question* of being and enlivened in such a way that the
word "physicality" means that question in the word's contextual life. In
that case we would confront an instance in which the question of being is
embodied in the meaning of physicality and we could ask about what the
question of being might mean in daily, sensuous, physical life. If this approach were to work out, the approach's own life would embody what it
addresses—a physically and sensuously oriented sense of the question of
being—and it would constitute a recoiling movement that could articu-

late love as well as desire and other basic moods and feelings within its own sensuousness.

In order to develop this thought further, I turn to some aspects of Foucault's thought, aspects that I find to be in concert with significant aspects of Heidegger's thinking, in striking ways given their considerable differences in style, lineage, and problematization. In this part of the discussion I will emphasize what happens—and I put this awkwardly now to stress a probability—in the arising and persisting, the physicality, of Foucault's thought in *The Order of Things*. I would like to be alert to a certain physicality in this work as I consider some of his study's implications for thinking about physicality.

An aspect of *The Order of Things* that is important for this discussion is found through two of its leading questions: how have orders arisen in our lineage, and how might we characterize the meaning and persistence of things in those orders? Putting the questions in this way allows me to underscore the importance of things' coming to appear in various orders as well as the importance of the appearing of different orders. When there are differences among dominant orders, "differences" (or "breaks" or "caesurae") refers to an exteriority vis-à-vis the orders, an outside that gives the orders and things in them to appear differently. "Appearing differently" here means that whatever defines an order and whatever status and value an order gives to things have validity that is limited by the order's own identity, by *its* difference. The phrase also means that Foucault is giving emphasis to processes of appearing in orders and to the limits and boundaries that define the integrity of a body of appearances and the regions of their appearing. The knowledge that he wants to develop in this book seems predisposed to descriptions, not to descriptions that look for some kind of pure origination that justifies their truth, but rather descriptions that embody a knowledge that their accuracy is based on the very lineage that they describe—*and* based as well on a quite determined departure from major aspects of that lineage. The differences among orders and their various departures not only from other orders but from their own, organizational identities—the differences that define conflicts and transformations among as well as within orders—is elaborated by Foucault by means of the metaphor of space. As this part of the discussion unfolds I will bring space and physicality into a close proximity of meaning in order to think of physical space and hence of physical times in a cultural context of both luminosity and density. If this effort succeeds, I will have taken a step toward seeing a concurrent contribution that Heidegger and Foucault make toward an understanding of worldly, historical, social, and disclosing lives.

"Nature," as we have seen, can name something essential in the origin of things that unfolds over a period of time. Knowledge of the unfolding, in continuous reference to its essential origin, can show, in this way of thinking of nature, an internal law of formation: if you know that law you have a pretty good handle on the essential truth—the nature—of whatever is developing, and in the case of conceptions of Nature writ large, you can in principle know the universal truth of everything that comes to rational disclosure. This conception of *phusis,* in other words, is one that finds constitutive of the springing up of life a definitive essence in that animation, and that knowledge has to be writ large because, as a conveyor of essential truth, it becomes such a momentous and lasting event: it becomes knowledge of being itself! And with this knowledge a person can understand the place of any particular order with respect to the laws of formation (the *phusis*) that govern all orders and ordering. *Phusis* is conceived as the Nature of all ordering and may properly receive the name of the Originary Order of orders.

It seems clear in many recent orders of knowing that the nature (or Nature) of all appearing things is found in the principle and laws of subjectivity, whether subjectivity is universal and necessary in its laws and principles or culturally or physiologically determined in its laws and principles. While people can read *The Order of Things* within this context and as presenting a theory of historicized subjectivity, I believe that a more considered reading of that book will find that the function in it of the metaphor of space combined with the archeological/genealogical accounts of orders of knowledge serves the observation that the very meaning of "subjectivity" derives from orders and not the reverse. In order to contextualize this observation, I shall return to Heidegger to see how he destabilizes subjectivity's priority by means of giving an account of the lineage of this prioritization. That should give us a basis for seeing in Foucault's thought an alternative to a position that privileges an historicized subjectivity. In this process of exposition, perhaps the viability will emerge of understanding thought and language as events of *phusis* that are not primarily composed either of principles or of some form of subjectivity. This move is preparatory to considering the metaphor of space in Foucault's discourse with emphasis on its density and luminosity.

One primary way by which Heidegger subverts the priority of subjectivity in *Introduction to Metaphysics* as well as in many of his other works is by addressing the lineage of that priority's development. In particular, in *Introduction to Metaphysics,* he shows that in early Greek thought *phusis* occurs with a sense of life's arising and enduring and without a sense that it is definable by principles. I use the word *sense* here because of Heidegger's claim that in the thought of some early Greeks the language of life's fragility—the language that arises from the sense that life itself is in danger and thus arises in the question of being—their language did not come to a fully developed conceptual expression. Their thought and language are pre-philosophical in that sense; they know the world through a language that arose with experience of the possibility that life might always bring as part of its happening destruction and death and that the very event of life might itself always be in jeopardy, that life as such might be subject to the destruction that it brings with the rising up and endurance of things.[2] This pre-philosophical sense is textured by a close affiliation of the jeopardized rising up and enduring of things with their unhiddenness—with their clear opacity as they happen and make passing differences.[3] This joining of the sensed fragility of being—its questionableness in Heidegger's terms—and the unhiddenness of things provides the setting which, he finds, gives to Western intelligence an impulse away from the dominance of subjectivity for an understanding of beings in their appearing lives. In their "language," things come to appear in their *phusis,* not because of the event of some agency, but in an unfolding—an unconcealing—that brings with the arising a limited enduring of things no other basis than the event of unfolding. This sensibility was no easier to bring to conceptual clarity then than it is now, and it is one that we can at best engage with as much allowance as possible for its difference from our very capacity for disciplined conceptualization. For our capacity for disciplined conceptualization arose with historical endurance in the Greek aspect of our tradition through concerted efforts to think in the astonishment, uncertainty, and incipient thought that permeates their sensibility. This strange non-thing, *phusis*! "It" appears as things come to appear, but "it" never seems to be captured by any definitive appearance. It's not as though *phusis* were something too big to fit into a finite mold or mode. It's rather that *phusis* comes to pass as appearing. And it's not as though *phusis* were something in which all appearing things participate. It's rather that there is neither a subject nor an object behind the occurrence of subjects and objects, nothing there to be defined in the occurrence of things as things appear in the utter commonality of appearing. What is same for all existing things as far as their existing is concerned is not an existing being at all. "It" is called *phusis.* So, whatever else we are going to say about

2. See "The Anaximander Fragment," in Heidegger's *EGT*, pp. 13ff.

3. He speaks of this fragility of being also in terms of being's withdrawal and hiddenness. We can read "withdrawal and hiddenness" as referring not primarily to "fragility" but as referring simply to being's ungraspability, its escape from designation and meaning. Being is in question because of its unavailability to intelligence, because of its dense opacity in its disclosiveness. People simply cannot know "it" or know even whether it "is" in any sense at all. I find this a questionable reading of Heidegger's interpretation, and I will hold the idea of being's withdrawal in close association with the sense that being brings destruction with arising to life in a being's appearance—I will hold together his study of Anaximander and his reading of Heraclitus and Parmenides—as I render the pre-philosophical sensibility that gives rise to classical Greek philosophy. Hence my remarks here concerning *EM* are informed by other of his writings on the Pre-Socratics. See especially the other essays collected in *EGT* referred to in chapter 3, note 11.

phusis with reference to this sensibility, we are not going to say that it is characterized by any kind of agency. Heidegger says that "it" is the happening of appearing, of unconcealing, that "it" is like the happening of an infinitive in the moods, modes, and voices of verbs, that "it" is the shining of what shines. But "its" lack of any it-quality and any character of agency leaves us perplexed when we attempt to think this thought in a disciplined way.

The aspect of Heidegger's account of the early Greek sense of *phusis* that I want to emphasize here points to its departure from those conceptions of nature that compose an image of a process that is defined by an original, purposive origin or that is sufficiently defined in principle by a series of interconnecting causes. The sense of *phusis* that Heidegger is attempting to bring to thought does not require that causal connections be denied. Far from such a requirement, one may well find all manner of causal complexes that seem to stretch far beyond observational grasp. But such complexes do not address what I have called a sensed fragility of living as such. That things happen, that they arise and endure for a time, that their living seems to require their dying, that complexes of causation happen at all—that appearing *occurs,* however it might occur in uncountable instances—*that* is the puzzlement that gives rise to a provocative mood that we call wonder or astonishment and that, Heidegger says descriptively, gave rise to efforts of understanding that we think of as philosophy in the Greek lineage. The sense is that the occurring of life as the appearing of things is not properly subject to explanation, that just where we might connect things by reference to something—be it law or agency—that means continuation of life, just "there" no definable or describable being happens.

This boggling point has so often been given in our Western tradition's determined focus by efforts of explanation, or by images of time-transcending participation in a being that holds things together, gifted by meanings that seam things together into a whole that the early Greek sense that gave impetus to thought has gone wanting in the thought to which it gave rise. People have posited some kind of order just where the noted sensibility found neither order nor orderer. I note here that the question of being, as Heidegger finds it operating in the Greek lineage of *phusis,* defines a limit to explanatory thought as such, that it means an endurance of question and uncertainty as they arose in that lineage, and that question and uncertainty endure as the meaning, the silent motivator, in any search for a way of being that gives transcendental meaning to the occurrence of life. Orders of beings are faced with the withdrawal of meaning in those orders as they provide meaning for the happening of life. Such meanings remain in question *in* the orders that provide assurance for life's continuance.

"I should not like," Foucault wrote in his preface to *The Order of Things,* "the effort I have made in one direction to be taken as a rejection of any other possible approach."[4] With these words and others like them (*OT,* xxiii, for example), Foucault articulates his proximity and difference vis-à-vis Heidegger. He turns away, of course, from any claim that suggests that the formations of orders are under the guidance of Subjectivity or Spirit or Law. But as a guiding preference, he also states that the knowledge (and the preferences) that guide his work should not function like a formation with universal authority for inclusion and exclusion of other manners of knowing. He is prepared for the knowledge that he presents to make differences, but he is not prepared to move from juxtaposition and encounter with other knowledges and values to justified dominance over them. This caveat by itself does not depose the priority of subjectivity, but it does function to put in question his own knowledge and as a caution before any predisposition toward an equation of knowledge, certainty, and truth with the privileges and dialectics that can accompany transcendental authorities. From the beginning of this study its own power is restricted to pointed and contextualized encounters and engagements, and whatever remains in his thought of a traditional inclination to fuse knowledge and Truth is put on notice that such fusion will be subject to something closer to derision and parody than obedience. This order—the order of this study—is without metaphysical comfort, and an expectation of its impermanence and limited jurisdiction constitutes a part of its texture. It appears in question.

There is nothing new in such a caution except, perhaps, its tone and style. It is composed in part of an alternative to the heroic sensibility that often accompanied traditional philosophical efforts, a sensibility to which Heidegger was not immune when he considered the importance of the question of being and his originality in its recall (not to mention the heroic status that he gives to classical Greek culture and the German language). The alternative is an orientation without a hero, without a desire to be a hero or to find one, and with a textured sense that with the demise of a positive sense for anything momentous and transcendental comes the demise of heroism with a positive value: exceptional accomplishments, certainly, but the extraordinary without the trappings of the quasi-divine archetype that our tradition often gives to the hero and with a sense for both the advantages and disadvantages, the opportunities and the dangers that compose extraordinary events and accomplishments. I

---

4. Michel Foucault, *The Order of Things* (New York: Vintage, 1973; henceforth *OT*), p. xiv. Page numbers for references to this work are given in the body of the text.

suppose that the passage of emotions that constitute recognitions of heroes marks also the passage of emotions that predispose people to worship. But the relevance of that passage here is found in Foucault's declension of transcendental elevation of either the knowledge that he presents, its methods and values, or its subject matter.

I used, of course, "declension" with purpose. I have in mind my reference to Heidegger's saying that *phusis* is to beings like an infinitive is to the inflections of verbs into moods, modes, and voices. In classical grammar inflection and conjugation were seen as a kind of decline from the infinitives, a compromise that takes place when something that is uncompromised (the infinitive in this case) becomes limited and diluted by determinations (like "to be" becoming "we are"). Something unlimited in its purity becomes tainted by the imperfections of specificity.[5] My observation now is that Foucault's turning aside from the complex lineage of heroism in his evaluation of the knowledge and approach that comprise his book is at once a spurning of the sense of perfect (or at least near perfect) instance that constitutes the hero. This refusal certainly bears witness to the heroic tradition but it also presents the alternative of a manner of thought and knowledge that are in relation to no model, image, or ideal other than those that compose their own paragenetic events. This is a preliminary formation of Foucault's concept of locality that he put to work during the 1970s, a fecund one, I believe, in which the appearing, eventful quality of thought, knowledge, and language is accented by reference to nothing criteriological outside of the space defined by them—it is not accented by a meaning of Nature. Knowledge does not fall away from and yet refer by decline to some "higher" or purer, infinitive-like life. The *phusis* of a discourse happens in self-disclosure and suggests its own truth in the dynamic structures of its appearance. "It"—*phusis*—constitutes the happening of the discourse's life. Or, as Foucault puts it in his preface, "there is order" outside of the archeological order that organizes what he says and knows (*OT,* xx).

This manner of thought that is so different in style and some of its moods in comparison to Heidegger's is nonetheless quite attuned in its sensibility to what I consider to be Heidegger's guiding thought with regard to *phusis:* the ground of existence occurs ungroundingly. We need not use this language of grounds if it feels old fashioned. We might say that the lives of things present no evidence for thinking that some origin or purpose or agency defines them other than those of the limited determinations that comprise them and their environments. Putting it that way, though, does not quite approach a relevant and forceful predisposition in Western cul-

---

5. See *EM,* chap. 2, especially pp. 68–74.

ture: a predisposition toward thinking with a more or less inchoate image of something that supports life's ephemeral transiency, something grander in scope and design that provides a transcendent context for our events, one that shines (or almost shines) around the edges of known realities, seems to shine enough to inspire belief in Something transcendental whether It is worshipful or simply magnificent in its splendid range of indifference. When they address this force of predisposition both Heidegger and Foucault find nothing like "Nature," not because they say that Nothing is There but because they turn to the historical roots of the predisposition and attempt to work descriptively on the traditional predisposition while at the same time turning out of it in the manner in which they describe its lineage—an effort to dispose the force of this predisposition by valorizing other orienting possibilities in our lineage. Such processes give rise to ways of thinking and speaking and to appreciating ways whereby things come to appear that are quite different from those spawned by the dominance of the predisposition that is in question. These processes give thought, language, and appearing a different kind of occurrence and hence a different sense of *phusis*.

This turn to history that in part grows out of nineteenth-century historicism, and also turns away from it, is facilitated for Foucault in *The Order of Things* by means of a metaphor of space. In this context Foucault proposes to come "face to face with order in its primary state" and "to show . . . in what way . . . our *culture has made manifest* the existence of order" (*OT* xx–xxi, emphasis mine). This basic sense of order and its meaning and the experiences of things in such a sense bring us to something like a site that he calls an epistemological field. He elaborates the image of field by the word "envisage"—it is a space of immediate envisagement; it happens as a vision of order as such in at least several spans of time in our Western lineage of knowing (*OT,* xxi). The field is a site of order for Foucault, although usually order has been taken to rest in itself—not, that is, to occur as an effect of anything and not as a part of transitional and describable processes, not even as *an* order, but as order as such. This would be a sense of order without chaos. The difference between Foucault and this sense of ultimate order is found in Foucault's placing such envisagement temporally and his naming it an episteme. An episteme is "a space of knowledge," but while fundamental senses of order have produced knowledges ruled by orders and connections of identity-governed differentiations, Foucault gives time a priority in his account of knowledges' spaces and introduces by this move something that is not ordered by Order. In this work of orientation that he carries out in *The Order of Things,* Foucault shows that the operations of an epistemological field have often functioned as a precognitive sense of the ultimacy of order as such, that such fields are temporally placed (they occur in designatable stretches

of time that we may call periods and that are characterized by the dominance of certain things in many cultural operations), and that their historical temporality, which is marked by all manner of showable lapses,
transitions, and mutations in their stretches of *continuity*, leads us to see
that "order as such" is quite mortal, quite without pure order, and quite
chaotic in its formations. This epistemological space that Foucault calls an
episteme is both the origin of many senses of the finality of order and the
site whose description destroys such envisagement. By cutting across many
historical corners I can say summarily, this study shows that *phusis* functions synonymously with "order" as Foucault thinks it; it happens as
historical organizing and is not properly subject to the priority of Order
when people speak of it.

The troubled camaraderie of Foucault's thought here with Heidegger's
guiding thought is apparent. Not only has he given time a place of primary importance in his metaphor of space (the implications of which I
will address in a moment), he has thereby put to work a thought that suggests the inseparability of space and time as he conceives the ungrounding
occurrences of grounds in our lineage.

So when Foucault says "there is order," he is, in the context of this
book, pointing out the space-time of the "there is," i.e., the space-time of
existential happening. Heidegger too concerned himself repeatedly with
the space-time of the "there is," that is, the space-time of *phusis*, and
concerned himself in ways that make impossible a convincing idea of
phusis—and hence of the "nature of things"—as an ordered, dynamic
principled process that is governed largely by a purposeful logos and by a
force of causation.[6] For space-time does not seem to cause its events, and
I believe that *The Order of Things* is as much an attempt to come to grips
with that possibility as are *Being and Time* and many other of Heidegger's
works. Space-time is a thought in which the idea of ungrounding ground
comes aborning, and it is one where the strange affiliation of Foucault
and Heidegger is most apparent.

I return now to the larger issue of this discussion, the interconnection
among density, luminosity, and physicality. You will recall that those words
come together for the purpose of forming a conception that elaborates
aspects of what has been addressed traditionally as "body." I have high-
lighted Foucault's and Heidegger's complementary ways of removing the
priority of subjectivity from the organizing values of their thought. I have
given emphasis to Heidegger's reconsideration of "nature" by addressing a
pre-philosophical sensibility concerning the fragility and question of being
and by putting in question the images and concepts of nature that arose in

6. See Heidegger's *Beiträge zur Philosophie* (GA 65), sections 96, 97, and 111.

the Greek-spawned lineage of Western philosophy. I found significant linkage between Heidegger and Foucault in the emphases they place on the disclosive, appearencial arising and passage of things in their orders (an emphasis that accompanies their removal of subjectivity's priority), and I indicated ways in which the thought of ungrounding ground plays a leading role in their thinking. Throughout I valorized the meaning of *phusis* with the intention of indicating that as I discussed these aspects of their thought I addressed the notion of physicality with its implication of luminosity and density.

Both density and luminosity in this context name dimensions (or aspects) of appearing. When appearing is freed from the context of subjectivity, the word can refer to and, in its thought and expression, embody and give to appear things in their presencing—in their rising and enduring for a time, in their coming to pass. Physicality names the happening of things and can mean neither materiality nor ideality in the usual philosophical senses of those words. The physicality of things is found in their coming to appear, or as some Greek writers put it, in the shining of what comes to shine. Appearing or shining is where the deeds, the works, the *pragmata* of things comes to happen: the space of the "where" and the time of "comes to happen" seem inseparable.

Density in this context names the unencompassable fragility of happening. The occurrence of what occurs does not seem to come from any other "where." Whatever contextualizes the happening of what happens and provides meaning for it appears as no less a happening. There is no defining presence that is transcendent to the happening of things. The imagery shifts from *something* dense, like a wall, or a rock, that one cannot see through; it shifts from something that is so much in itself or to itself that *its* occurrence is not presentable; and it shifts to a non-something that comes with appearing and that lightens the weight of images of a continuous presence.

When we use "light" in its derivation from *leukos* (white) we may speak of a source of light, like a star such as the sun, or to a standard (in the light of which we act), or even to a traffic signal. Or if we use "light" in its derivation from the Old English *leoht,* we may speak of someone's dismounting (he lit from the horse) or arriving by chance (she lit upon a solution) or attacking forcefully (the wrestlers lit into each other), or settling (the fly lit upon the wall). That sense of the word suggests a lightness of weight and movement, a sense that the German also carries when one says that the ship *lichtet* its anchor. It can mean that weight is lifted. The words suggest in their differences "to relieve of a burden," "to happen without heaviness," and "to make clear and brighten."

In Foucault's and Heidegger's thought the appearing of things carries these overtones, in their several nuances, of "light." Things appear in the light of their occurrences. Their coming to pass—their physicality—happens with lightness. They happen both disclosively and without the weight of substantial presence or purpose. Order as such for Foucault happens spatially and temporally, i.e., in seaming, limited stretches of continuity and mortality that allow a strange density to shine through—something like the appearing of mere space without pre-established or principled formation *in* the appearing of ordered things in specific orders. And beings occur according to Heidegger's descriptive accounts in the lightness of not-a-being-at-all, in a dense and lightening withdrawal of any possibility for permanent identification, meaning, and continuous presence. For both Heidegger and Foucault, their own interpretations arise in cultural lineages whose traditional explanatory accounts of themselves and their world—their narrative *historia*—bear a dense and usually obscure sense that things continuously appear in a lightness that lingers but does not provide assurance for any unbroken continuation.

Foucault often valorizes this sense of fragility by his concept of multiple, incompatible differences that compose ordered identities, in combination with his concept of the danger of axiomatic knowledges, ideals, and effective solutions to pressing problems. Values and knowledges may well address effectively specific threats to social vitality, such as poverty, disease, violent dissent, and environmental changes. But the identity-forming measures that instill character and recognition have *within* them severe conflicts that comprise the stabilities and hierarchies (e.g., oppression of some of their own constitutive parts, very different forces of desire with contradictory trajectories, experiences of conflicting values that constitute the ordered standards of placement, exchange, and recognitions). He finds danger in the limitations and exclusions that function silently to diminish such conflicts by means of a sense of purchase on Something where definitive presence is established, such as Order as such, Law, or transcendent purpose in Subjectivity, Nature, or Divine Word. In his well-known phrase, such resolutions and establishments are not wrong, but they are dangerous. The danger inheres in the weighty combination of assurance, limitation, and suppressed conflict, much like the quenching of inherent questionableness in the ways in which the question of being is carried out, according to Heidegger, in those concepts of time, space, truth, and reality that constitute the mainstream of Western thought. In such traditional turns of thought and practice the dense lightness of being is made heavy and dark by the values and patterns of thought that fix it into the *historia* of disciplined intelligence and understanding: Western values and concepts have tended to lose attunement with the physicality of their own events, at least with the physicality that seems to have been experienced by some early Greek thinkers. That is a loss, I am saying, the recognition of which is built into Foucault's image of the danger of our best cultural productions as well as into Heidegger's account of the question of being.

This way of thinking brings about a strange combination of density and lightness. The density is not only a matter of Heidegger's choice of words or Foucault's style of writing. It is something that happens in their unburdening, lightening movements of thinking. And it is in this movement that I find their thought to exceed considerably the limits of some of Heidegger's *Lederhosen* parochialism and Foucault's preoccupation with relatively recent forms of normalcy and deviation. Nor is the lightness of their work found in values that I can unambiguously affirm. There is, rather, in their thought a movement of unburdening, one that does not destroy values so much as it loosens them—"frees them" would say too much, I believe—loosens them from the moorings that hold them to tympanic authorities by virtue of which they resist, often with relentless subtlety and obsession, their own mortal placement. The values that function definitively in Heidegger's and Foucault's own styles of intelligence fall no less prey to the dense lightness of their thought than do those values and beliefs more foreign to them. I often lose sight and bearing in the loosening process, as though abandoned for a time in the dark, for I can find in neither philosopher's work a direction toward the function of a master or a director or even a guide for definitive thought, much less one of a seer of mysteries that can bring me to the truth. Each, I find, is glad to talk. In fact, each might be rather talky, profuse in the ways many remarkable, intellectual people seem to be. Each is accustomed to being heard and has something of the performer in him—although with Heidegger it's a fairly sober performance without the periods of levity that bubble up in Foucault's thought.[7]

But both Foucault and Heidegger address their reader, tell their interpretive stories, describe intentions and dimensions of life that no one else has described or perceived quite so well—describe them in the perceptiveness of styles of language and thought that often transform the good sense of current intelligence into the density of an obscure perceptiveness. My point is that both Heidegger's and Foucault's thought lift the burdens of eternity and universality from thought and allow in the process of thinking, for Western thought, the strange lightness of open, weightless encompassment.

I mean by those last three words that sameness is not any specific thing but happens nonetheless, that Heidegger and Foucault are thinking such happening in various figurations of ungrounding ground ("being," "space," "space-time," for example). Each finds open encompassment in

---

7. I have seen a photograph of Heidegger when he was "lit up" after a wine evening with Medard Boss. That side of him tends to be covered over and forgotten in his writings, in my experience.

the thought and knowledge of Western culture, in the eventful, physical dimension of meanings and in such images of enclosure as Order, Being, and Subjectivity. Each brings important aspects of our tradition to their own crises of falling apart in their designs that call for closed encompassment, and each thinks in and through such crises without requiring, either by knowledge or hope, a solution to the light of being's fragility in the density of existence.

I suppose that most of us have experienced with varying degrees of intensity the disappearance of something real, whether by death, loss of energy, mere silence, collapse of an order, or a simple change of mind. I believe that most of us have felt in such loss some distressed astonishment and a desire to fill what appears to be a vacuum with some kind of connection and meaning. In such experiences of disappearance many of us have wanted to reach out for a connection with something lasting that relativizes the void or to have a significant connection reach out to us—to feel connected and connected in such a way that the vacuum loses its seeming quality of over and finished. In Foucault's and Heidegger's thought, however, in the connections themselves inheres something like absence of presence, and in their thought that dense lightness appears that leaves us unguided in the very things that are most important and that guide us, leaves these things opened by loss, it seems, at their core, like a space of appearance that rises up without a Nature.

That dense lightness can appropriately be called physical, and Heidegger's and Foucault's thought join in bringing physicality to expression (in, among other ways, Heidegger's thought of the question of being and in Foucault's considerations of order). I expect that lives are composed of something like pre-conceptual awareness in their physicality, that they happen as alertnesses with their fragile needs as they, in their needs, move physically with their environments. Bodies seem to know that they require orders. The orders that comprise them appear to comprise as well an awareness of orders' need. Such need appears to happen no more as a cry of desperation than as a yes to ordering, no less as an urge to exist and flourish than as physical predisposition toward some kinds of cooperation for the sake of continuing. Looking on such elemental interests, like the astronomer in Heidegger's image of the universe within the limits of scientific conception and measurement, we might find in this needful struggle nothing more than a blind process without meaning or grounds for hope. Or we might find in Foucault's account of the mutational rising and falling of orders of axiomatic knowledge a mere replication of creatures' instinctual drive for survival by means of orders that embody the deathliness that they mean to forestall. But people might also find in Foucault's lightheartedness and in Heidegger's poetic thought—both without images of cosmic saving power or other enormities of universal proportions—a levity that Heidegger could call *geistig* and Foucault might name acceptance of divergence or a freeing of differences.[8] Each philosopher at his best has achieved a singular lightness of mind in spite of many instances of heavy prose and thought, and I find in their achievement a threshold for encountering lives in terms of physicality that can neither ignore the "materials" of which things are constructed nor reduce events to those materials and their functions. I have in mind the physicality of things in terms of which the dense lightness of finite occurrences and the incompleteness of any reduction directs our attitudes and interpretations regarding them.

This approach suggests a lightness of mind that is able, by virtue of its lightness, to encounter people and things less in terms of hierarchies of importance that are based on heavy foundations and doctrines and more in terms of the needs of the encountered one in *its* nonreducible event, its difference, its entree to another beginning and another encounter. There is, as far as I can tell, no necessary connection between lightness of mind and any form of compassion or community. But such lightness does seem to be without a need to spend energy to justify or redeem its occurrences and to be able to predispose a perceiver toward singular differences with singular clarity in their needful, ongoing occurrences. Such clarity appears to me to make less dangerous compassion and community, to unburden compassion and community of a measure of weight in some mythological and metaphysical purposes and justifications, to make possible alertness to dimensions of occurrence that are difficult, if not impossible to see when our recognitions are in the service of weighty Truth, Nature, or other capital meanings. Such claims appear to weigh down the physicality of things, to fix it in completions of designation, and to make extremely difficult affirmation of physical events in the midst of their often lightly nonresponsible, random movements in their continuing and never containable lives.

---

8. See *Language, Counter-Memory, Practice,* trans. D. F. Bouchard and Sherry Simon (Ithaca, N.Y.: Cornell University Press, 1977), p. 185, where he writes in a Deleuzean mood.

EIGHT

Feeling, Transmission, Phusis

A SHORT GENEALOGY OF "IMMANENCE"

I. THE INCESSANTLY PRESENT MOMENT

The Issue of Immanence

"Immanence" means to remain in, inhere, or indwell. In our Western tradition of thought the word often suggests the remaining presence of an absolute in two senses: divinity dwells in human beings so that any human enactment has within it divine life, a dynamic occurrence of divine presence that plays a part in all living events and provides an innate guidance for human action. Usually this immanent divine presence means that there is in human life a dimension of eternity that constitutes the possibility for wisdom and the possibility for fulfillment and violation of the divine. Because of divine immanence people are able to gain a living and embodied mindfulness of what is true and deathless in their lives, and they are also able to suffer when their ways of life are focused by values that disregard the imperatives of divine presence. In the context of this orientation, people can live more or less appropriately with immanent divinity in the occurrence of their being, especially if they have the help of people who are specially attuned to indwelling, divine guidance.

A second meaning in the remaining presence of an absolute or of absoluteness refers to the occurrence of the absolute or of divinity as such. The divine, whether it be figured as a God or as a dimension without a nameable identity, occurs immanently with itself. This awkward phrasing means that no matter how complex or mysterious the absolute is, it is purely absolute. We could say that in its event the absolute holds everything not absolute outside of itself. In a phrase, the absolute does not die, and there is within it no mixture or confusion with an absence of absoluteness. The absolute is immanent with itself even as "it" happens in human lives.

This latter observation can hold even if one thinks of the absolute or the divine as realizing itself in a process of history or as divided within

itself. Its own trajectory, its own inevitability, its own self-relation is immanent with itself, and it maintains a transcendence in itself with all of the
circumstances of its immanent disclosure.

I believe that these two senses of absolute immanence have had a range
of influence in our traditions that would be difficult to exaggerate. Even
when "divinity" is replaced by "universality" or "transcendence" or "withdrawal of the divine" or "nature," the double sense of immanence lingers.
It lingers in the thoughts of universal human community, human nature,
subjectivity, Dionysian ecstasy, and, I will emphasize in a moment, in what
we can call boundary experiences. People often conceive of the occurrences
of their lives in terms of indwelling immediacy. And we are all probably inclined to think of our consciousness as an immanent occurrence. In these
instances we can find a sense of immanent presence with people and a kind
of transcendence that is immanent with itself.

The idea of immanence suggests present enactment, and when it is attached to an image of a pervasive reality, that pervasive reality seems to be
present *in its pervasiveness,* in its transcending the instances of its mani-
festness. As immanent, the pervasive reality—human nature, for example—
seems to present itself as transcending its moment and as coming fully to
bear in its determined presence. So I may immediately violate pervasive
human nature when I act in certain ways, and I may be in immediate accord
with it in other actions. The transcendence of what is immanently present,
its inherent present excess in its specific determinations, gives it an authority over whatever is coming to pass. It has preeminence—priority—in its
inherent, transcending presence. When this precedence operates in our
thinking and knowing it tells us a considerable amount about who we are in
common and how we are obligated to live.

I expect that none of us is entirely satisfied with many of the images
of history and culture that accompany the precedence of immanent and
pervasive presence, especially those images that give originary authority to
ways of living that are opposed to our ways of living. And I also expect
that none of us is prepared to live without some sense of this precedence.
To live with only a sense of passing moments without some kind of immanent transcendence to unify those moments by meaning and order
sounds in our culture like chaos or at least like an absence of hope for a
human community. On the other hand, we are aware of the struggles—I
am inclined to say wars—that come with different authoritative images of
immanent presence. The orders of our lives and our sense of meaning are
at stake in these struggles. But the combination of images of an absolute
being and of its immanence often creates forms of authority and certainty that are stifling for other images of lives that operate in our
traditions. There is often a close association between authority and access
to essential immanence, and it might be the case that that association by

itself produces sensibilities from which we would do well to disassociate ourselves. In any case, I think that there is a developing sense of corporeal presence in our recent lineage that holds suspect figurations of nonphysical immanence, and I would like to intensify that developing sense. I will say that the idea of immanence is itself highly problematic, problematic in part because of its traditional combination with divine-like figures, inclusive of subjectivity, nature, and consciousness, that are immanent in themselves in their occurrences, problematic in part because of a conception of bodies that seems to inhere in our inherited, usually inchoate understanding of immanence, in part because the idea of immanence functions preeminently in our conception of translation and truth, and in part because of a conception of consciousness that seems to be an aspect of the figures of immanence.

The last phrase, "figures of immanence," is significant for the conception that guides this chapter. I wish to indicate that the idea of immanence composes a figuration that itself constitutes a massive interpretation of physical occurrences; that is, it constitutes a massive interpretation of generation, bringing forth, coming into being, being born, and "to be so and so by nature." These words come from Liddell and Scott's unproblematized translation of *phuo*. They translate *phusis* as "in nature, inborn quality . . . natural powers . . . disposition . . . natural order . . . natural origin." *Phuton* means that which grows, a creature, that which comes to breath. In the traditional figures of immanence we find interpretations and experiences of inception and origin, growth, physical disposition, and natural order. Immanence often suggests that we, as who we really are in our lives, begin in the immediacy of an unceasing and transcendent way of being, one that gives us the breath of life. It is the idea of body and physicality that is imbedded in some of our traditional senses of life, nature, and immanence to which I would like to give attention. Whether we speak of being, divine nature, human nature, lineage, or nature, when the idea of immanence operates, we usually name an incessantly present reality that has definitive power in all events.

Further, there is a double sense of translation that is suggested by this issue concerning immanence. I pointed out one of those senses when I said that "immanence" functions as an interpretation, a translation, if you will, of a traditional understanding of *phusis*. I do not want to say that the word "immanence" is an exact or adequate translation of the word *phusis*. But I do want to say that immanence carries over and, in that sense, translates in our lineage the inceptive meaning of *phusis* by giving it the suggestions of inherence, nature, and predisposition. And this conception is not only a translating interpretation of life, origin, growth, and nature. It also suggests another kind of translation, one in which one way of being translates into another way of being. Whatever is taken as immanent in our lives undergoes a transferal *in* its immanence in our lives from its own event—from its immanence with itself—to our specific and determined occurrences. Whether we consider some traditional, Jewish/Christian images of fall from the immanence of God's being or Kant's distinction between rational autonomy and heteronomy or Heidegger's conception of the ontological difference between being and beings, we find a sense of both removal and conveying that occur *in* the immanent transcendence with the particular human life. "Translation" and "transfer" both mean to bear from one place or event to another. The words in the instances of this discussion, say passing from ———— to ———— , from immanence with itself to immanence with another. From one perspective a translation can be enrapturing, as when a person is transferred from ordinary life to a Dionysian event of nonindividuation or as when Enoch, as scripture says, was translated into heaven. From another perspective the transferal can be to a more corrupted state, as when the moral law is translated into a specific decision or being is translated into ways of being together with other beings.

I would like to bring these two senses of translation close together, to see translation as an interpretive occurrence that transfers one event into another and to bring these two senses together without a suggestion that one event is necessarily "higher" or "lower" than the other. When we interpret our lives as characterized by transcendent immanence, we not only give a discursive form to our experiences. We also have as the object of our interpretations the figure of transferal and translation among "higher" and "lower" events; we have before us an interpretive occurrence, one in which an essential event bears itself forth in another inessential event, and this second event carries out the first occurrence in a transformed way. A particular individual, for example, carries out immanent divine presence or the presencing of being in a way that is quite distinct to divine self-immanence or to being when it is considered by itself. We will need to see how such a figuration of presence and transformation produces what we can recognize as truth.

Because the question of physical events is important in these considerations I will valorize feeling as the location of the draw of the concept of immanence as well as the location of immanent presence. After noting accounts of feeling, intuition, and immanence in Schleiermacher and Schelling, I will turn to Nietzsche in whose work we will find a complication of the thought of immanence as he gives descriptions of body, will, and affection. Before we finish we will need to ask if translation itself can be described as physically immanent. And if it can be considered that way, then the traditional thought of immanence might well be transformed insofar as a physical event of translation is not identical with any of its aspects or with their totality.

The process that I am forecasting is one in which we find that accounts of immanence cannot be justifiably separated from accounts of translation and interpretation. Because of this connection, the association of immanence with self-enacting transcendence is severely jeopardized, and we will find ourselves needing to pay attention to interpretive occurrences of translation instead of to transcendent entities that are immanent to us and themselves. In this process, I wager, we will encounter feelings in ourselves that predispose us toward some figuration of transcendence whether that figuration suggests its own utter undecidability, as it does in the thought of Derrida and Levinas, for example, or suggests a more describable occurrence such as human subjectivity or a divinity in its mysterious withdrawal.

II. BLIND LIFE:
"I AM NOT THE CENTER OF WHAT I KNOW NOT"
(Maurice Blanchot, *Writing of the Disaster*[1])

The context for the considerations in this section could be named with Nietzsche's phrase "cultural instincts" or, in a Merleau-Pontian mood, "habits of the body." I would like to highlight a few specific ideas about immanence in order to describe a predisposition in Western thought that I will call the axiomatic absolute. By this phrase I mean that an image or sense of something absolute functions as a grounding predisposition in our cultural formations. I do not know where or when this axiomatic absolute began, but I assume that its formation predates written texts, and I suspect that one of its major carriers into our lineage, in addition to scripture, is composed of Sanskrit words and values. I also assume that its lineage is primarily religious and only secondarily theological and philosophical, that ritual and sacrifice were significant in its formation, and that what we know as ontotheology is a late figuration of the religious feelings that inform the axiom. Given these assumptions I think of the axiomatic absolute as carrying feelings and intuitions that have to do with desire for meaning and at least minimal security in life, with fear and awe before the impersonal vastness of our environment, with terror that can accompany the savage mystery of suffering and death, with a need for communal authority and bonding, and with an anxious insecurity that pervades human certainty. I assume that such feelings and intuitions formed many ideas that have become definitive in our culture and that when we tap into the depth of those ideas we are in touch with affective dimensions that seem inherent in

---

1. Maurice Blanchot, *Writing of the Disaster*, trans. Ann Smock (Lincoln: University of Nebraska Press, 1986), p. 10.

our lives. It thus seems apparent to me that when we deal with translation and interpretation in the context of transcendence with immanence we are dealing with things that feel as though they remain with us by virtue of who we are as humans, by virtue of our being. Such feelings probably constitute the inception of meanings in some of our most compelling concepts and attitudes.

Or, to illustrate the point in Spinoza's language, "a true idea is distinguished from a false one not so much by its *extrinsic* object as by its *intrinsic nature.*"[2] Clear and distinct ideas follow from "the sole necessity of our nature." "The reality of a true thought must exist *in the thought itself* without reference to other thoughts. . . . [T]hat which constitutes the reality of a true thought must be sought *in the thought* itself and deduced from the nature of the understanding" (ibid.). I want to emphasize that Spinoza finds the reality of a true idea *in* the occurrence of the idea, in the enactment of a singular substance. What is absolute is conceived through itself. The absolute is the immanent occasion of its own conception, and in a move that separates his thought from the priority that I am giving to culturally inspired feelings, that means that nothing finite can cause an idea of the infinite. This idea of the self-enactment of the absolute in reason is a prime example of one kind of immanence. I find in these ideas the repeated sense that individual people are not the centers of their own enactment, that their very being enacts something they are not, that something happens in their experience and knowledge that they cannot know within the limits of finite subjectivity, that their being composes an event that is other to the limited perspectives of human physicality and history, and that their being is an active testimony to this nature-giving event. I also note in passing that a feeling of overwhelming connection with deathless substance runs through Spinoza's thought, a feeling that I will say in a moment Schleiermacher transforms and refines. Spinoza's idea of intrinsic nature is one of a remaining, continuous incipience, the occasion for everything that is alive, an *Ursprung* from which creaturely existence gushes and without which nothing would be the singular being that it is. He is thinking within the limits of his concept of reason the intangible unity of life that is felt in the existence of each embodied moment, the immanent *phusis* of life itself.

Whereas for Spinoza reason can happen as the self-aware occurrence of the absolute, for many early-nineteenth-century thinkers feeling is the site of the absolute's immanent, generative event. I will note Spinoza's influence on these people only by observing that his conception of the self-

2. Baruch Spinoza, "On the Improvement of Human Understanding" in *The Works of Spinoza,* vol. II (New York: Dover, 1955) p. 26, emphasis mine.

enactment of the one substance in reason's self-enactment, in combination with Kant's impact, provided a thought of immanence that exercised considerable force in the thought of Fichte, Schleiermacher, Jacobi, and Hegel. Even J. G. Hamann's observation that "experience and revelation are the same," that the absolute happens as a dimension of radical otherness to reason *in* people's affective enactment, figures a thought of immanence that has a troubled kinship with Spinoza's. Hamann moved the place of God's immanence away from rational formations to the affections and found principles, systems, and other constructions of reason to be nothing more than "crumbs, fragments, fancies, and sudden inspirations." But he nonetheless found the self-enactment of the absolute immanent in the enactments of human beings. Friedrich Jacobi, like Hamann, found reason to be empty in its formulations, but also described reason as characterized by a *Geistes-Gefühl* (spirit-feeling; feeling immanent in spirit) that bears testimony to God's immediate presence. That presence-in-feeling generates the real substance of ideas, and human freedom gives humans, in their being, transcendence of all physical necessities. God's immanence in human being produces the being in which God is immanent and physicality is transcended.

Friedrich Schleiermacher brings to fullest fruition, in my opinion, the early-nineteenth-century sense of the absolute's immediacy in feeling.[3] His thought brings us to the edge of contact between finite consciousness and the sustaining and creating *phusis* of the absolute, an edge that defines the limits of human agency in its life and the proximity to it of deathless life. This edge marks the wellspring of conscious life and is lived as feeling. There is a striking similarity between Schleiermacher's claim and one that Blanchot makes regarding Bataille: "Awareness of insufficiency arises from the fact that it puts itself in question, which question needs the other or an other to be enacted," although it differs decisively from Blanchot's further observation that "insufficiency cannot be derived from a model of sufficiency."[4] The similarity rests in the observation that a finite subject occurs in a definitive connection with an other to itself in being itself. "I would conduct you," Schleiermacher wrote, "to the profoundest depths where every feeling and conception receives its form. I would show you from what human tendency religion proceeds and how it belongs to what is for you highest and dearest" (*Speeches*, 11–12). Feeling in this context means a universal, constitutive, constant testimony in human beings to the imme-

3. I will restrict myself largely to Schleiermacher's *Speeches on Religion* (New York: Harper Torchbook, 1958; henceforth *Speeches*) and emphasize only certain aspects of his extraordinarily rich and subtle thought on religion, feeling, and history. Page references to this book are given in the text.

4. Maurice Blanchot, *The Unavowable Community*, trans. Pierre Joris (New York: Station Hill Press, 1988), pp. 15 and 8.

diate proximity of an absolute other on which a human being's life totally depends (43ff). For Schleiermacher, this absolute other—God—composes a perfect unity of being that is the condition for its own recognition, a unity of which we are individual parts and in relation to which we may act in more or less harmonious ways (36–37, 39). He understands the absolute to occur as a whole, fully inherent in itself, in relation to which humans are fragmented. In their fragmentation, however, people can find a dependent, partial, and individuated wholeness with God by proper response to the divine immanence (24, 27–28, 278–79). The absolute, then, does not come to its own self-realization in a translation to consciousness, but remains, as translated, other to the consciousness that finds, before the other, its own relative propriety (ibid.). Feeling, in Schleiermacher's terms, and only feeling, "sees God as living independently of man" (363; see also 40, 363ff). Feeling is the site of this translation.

Such feeling is subject to all manner of interpretations and never functions, according to Schleiermacher, like a body of teachings or pure insight into divine being. In that sense, the feeling of the Absolute's immanence is an occurrence that is never to be captured by systems of ideas or by definitive exposition. It can be described interpretively and responsively, but only within specific cultural contexts and perspectives: "Ideas and words are simply the necessary and inseparable outcome of the heart, only to be understood by it and along with it" (*Speeches,* 17. See also 24 and his *The Christian Faith,* sections 1, 2, 18, and 36[5]). And this means that we must, in our finitude, translate the feeling of God's presence into the language and values of specific places and times (103). In the final analysis, he says, feeling "can only be understood from within" (14; see also 14ff, 31, 45–54, 124, 144). It has many "true" expressions none of which may properly be given dominance over other expressions (see 111ff, 279). Even a concept of God is dispensable ("I do not accept the position, 'No God, no religion,'" 282). Or, we could say, concepts of God are translations of people's inherent feeling of connection with something absolute. And people are themselves "but an infinitely small part, a fleeting form of the Universe" (292). To put it in a sentence, no group of people and no history of experience and teaching can know the originary proximity of God, although this proximity is experienced in feeling as the originary source of consciousness; consciousness composes a continuous upsurge and translation of God's presence, a translation that both makes culturally present and also loses the whole of God's immanence. We can know that the absolute is immanent, but we cannot know it in its own immanent being.

5. Friedrich Schleiermacher, *The Christian Faith* (Edinburgh: T&T Clark, 1928).

I would like to consider further this dynamic experiential edge of human consciousness and life. The simultaneity of presence and loss holds my attention. Like so many claims about the immanence of an absolute, Schleiermacher's holds for certain that the immanence continues full and complete in spite of the restrictions that determine its appearance. The very occurrence of losing God's being in human experience of it includes, according to his descriptive claim, God's continuing immanence: God is the sustaining and creative force of life on which human experience totally depends. In a claim similar to Spinoza's, Schleiermacher says that the Absolute's unity is the continuing power of life in every aspect of existence. In Schleiermacher's language, every kind of thing in the world is fleeting. Only God remains eternally. In the Infinite-finite contact that constitutes human consciousness there is both the appearance and the disappearance of the whole, of the primordial, infinitely productive unity. Like the moon reflected in water, finite life wavers and quakes and passes as it, for a moment, reflects—bears—something so infinitely beyond its event that its event in its evanescence seems at once to be and not to be. And yet the moon *in* its reflection seems certain while it seems to be beyond the reflection that its casts. But in this strange situation of our uncertainty nothing definitive can be said of the source of the reflection. The watery, affective place of disclosure precludes the very being to which it gives an unsteady place for momentary holding. If in this analogy our lives are the moon-in-water and if the water is mortal time and if the moon is the absolute, we can see pictorially the site of immanence for this way of thought. It is an occurrence that loses "what" it holds in the hold, and its revelatory moment is so fragile that a passing cloud can extinguish its shining event. The absolute is known and yet not known at all in the moment of reflection. This aporia seems to constitute the immanence that is in question. The immanence that would translate the absolute to human awareness loses its full subject in an occurrence that is interpreted as a divine presentation. Hence the posited Absolute is in question by virtue of its declared disclosure.

Further, not only are we not the center of we know not what in this interpretation of immanence. We also do not compose the center of what we know. We are not the center of anything except our difference from the Absolute within this context of the axiom of the immanent Absolute. And since that axiom is a finite part of our uncentered finitude, we have with us an axiom that merely makes uncertain axiomatic certainty. This consequence arises from a physical occurrence, from feeling, and although Schleiermacher does not have a fully developed conception of physicality or the body, the door is left wide open for an interpretation of mortal physicality as the historically composed wellspring of the axiom of incessantly present deathless life, a site of translation not to eternal life but to historical figurations of feelings of anxious finitude. The possibility of a historiocorporeal *phusis* for images of absolute immanence seems to grow in places that are interpreted as feelings that belong to the immanent presentation of the absolute, although such possibility is not in keeping with Schleiermacher's intentions or convictions.

Schelling carries further than Schleiermacher could the image of division within absolute presence. Before him, in an account of consciousness contained entirely by the Ego, Fichte had described the self-enactment of consciousness as a unity of opposites: "In the unity of consciousness all the opposites are united."[6] Early and late in his thought the unity of consciousness dominates the differences that it produces, and this unity may come to a full, reflective awareness in which all opposites are brought under the jurisdiction of the pure ego. But he nonetheless understood consciousness as a field of oppositions in which the self is divided from itself. The play of syntheses and antitheses constitutes the pure act of consciousness that they presuppose and disclose. Or, to put the point technically, the Ego determines the limitation of itself (117). It determines what is not Ego (123). And the Ego is the "only one substance" (120). I note these initial, broad claims to indicate a point of departure for Schelling as he reflected on duality and difference in the Absolute's self-enactment.

One aspect of Schelling's thought begins with the observation that human consciousness occurs as an indication of the Absolute. For Schleiermacher a gulf exists between human awareness and a completely other divine presence that is never unified by either human being or a conscious act, and while Schelling could accept that general statement in large part, he is more directly moved than Schleiermacher by Fichte's thought that the self-enactment of consciousness composes an immediate intuition of a divided whole. I believe that Schleiermacher was able to think of the difference between human consciousness and the whole absolute as starkly as he did because his interpretation was oriented by feeling, that is, by an incipient conception of body and hence by an unovercomable sense of fallibility and mortality. He preserved a sense of radical otherness that accentuated our historicity as well as an absolute difference that wholly escapes human self-enactment. As a result he found Fichte's thought hopelessly centered by human selfhood. Schelling, on the other hand, accentuated the bifurcation of consciousness and valorized that bifurcation as an indication of the Absolute. In Schelling's thought, the Fichtean claim that the Ego is immediately and purely aware of itself in its presentation of other things becomes the descriptive claim that the immediate intuition of consciousness figures the transcendent and eternal

---

6. Johann Gottlieb Fichte, *The Science of Knowledge* (Philadelphia: J. B. Lippincott, 1868), p. 84. Page references to this book are given in the text.

truth of the Absolute. More specifically, human creativity in art and philosophy composes insight into the activity—the self-enactment—of the Absolute. And while he and Schleiermacher are in agreement that the self-enactment of the Absolute is incomprehensible for us, that incomprehensibility happens nonetheless as immediate intuition for Schelling, as, for example, people create ideas by means of conceptual speculation or, later in his thought, by means of mythologizing. A core idea of Schelling, and one whose subtlety and force would be difficult to overstate, is that an inconceivable insight happens in certain kinds of conceptualization and *geistige* figuration. The Absolute is incomprehensibly disclosed in Its immanence in finite activity. This incomprehensible dimension of human enactment forms the basis for the highest expression of philosophical endeavor. The "I's" enactment composes an encounter with I-know-not-what, and this encounter is composed by the most enrapturing possibilities found in human life.

In the rapture of creativity and thought people find themselves in an immediate, unovercomeable situation of difference. It's as though we were posited by we know not what, as though in the depth of our insight we are taken from ourselves and placed outside of the definition of our own enactment. No system of thought encompasses the difference from which it arises, and each system of thought drives toward another system because of its failure to say or think the *Ursprung* (origin) from which it arises and whose disclosure constitutes the system's obligation. The remarkable idea that comes to prominence in Schelling's thought is that the immanent *Ursprung* is characterized by radical conflict, and the conflict defines a whole that does not overcome it. Human consciousness and the systems that it spins articulate a radicality of opposition and conflict to which it cannot give reconciliation or coherent systematicity: systems of thought find their expression of an absolute immanence *in* their speculative creativity, an activity that falls infinitely short of a unity that systematic thought seeks. I emphasize that a search for unity constitutes a kind of creativity that fails in its intention. The immanent I-know-not-what is intuited in the failure of philosophical grasp.

"Something hindering, resisting, intruding obtrudes itself everywhere," Schelling said in *The Ages of the World,* an "eternal antithesis . . . in the primordial beginning of nature."[7] The absolute, in its immanence, is divided against itself and renders itself finite as an object to itself. Were the absolute perfect in itself it would be, Schelling wrote, "rounded, completed, finished" (98). With completion there would be "no motion, no life, no

7. Friedrich W. J. Schelling, *The Ages of the World,* trans. F. W. Bolman, Jr. (New York: Columbia University Press, 1942), p. 97. Page references to this book are given in the text.

progress" (105). The absolute would be dead and without the power of *phusis.* The absolute comprises a power of "no" to itself as it finitizes itself in immanent copulation with what it is not. Or, to put the point grammatically and from another angle, "the copula in judgment is the essential thing" by which life comes to expression in a process of simultaneous unification and disunification (100), and the unity provided by the "is," the copula, "is not more essential than each of the opposites by itself" (103). The point that I am emphasizing is that in its immanent self-enactment the absolute divides itself from itself and gives in its eternal "imperfection" continuing life (98). Unresolvable conflict in the absolute *and* in finite life is definitive of creativity.

I am not sure how to understand these words. Their accuracy is clearly an important issue for Schelling, and yet their copulative enactment as such, their fecundity in their insufficiency and imperfection, receives the stress of Schelling's attention. Were we to take his words as systematically definitive we would lapse into a dogmatism that would not be different for Schelling from intellectual death. Their errancy, their power of distortion and insufficiency, seem to be crucial for their truth. Or, I could say, errancy lies at the heart of their truth, a truth that escapes in its enactment both direct articulation and adequacy of figuration as well as completion of being. And in this errancy, on Schelling's terms, we undergo the immanence, the disclosure of the absolute. Were this the figure of errancy, we would be close to the errant claim that time is the figure of the absolute. And were time itself mortal we would be at the threshold of saying that the absolute reveals itself in its passing away. But Schelling did not want to go that far. The axiomatic absolute persists in his thought in the form of the claim that the continuation of the absolute is preserved in its infinite dimension of divided active power, and this claim appears to suggest an escape from the very limits of finitude that also define absolute being. That axiom means in Schelling's thought that the absolute occurs in a radical self-differentiation, and that means that all identities occur in retraction and refusal of themselves, that the enactment of identities composes a definitive and intrinsic connection with other finite identities as well as an intrinsic refusal of those intrinsic connections.

The persistence of the axiomatic absolute is further emphasized by Schelling's idea of Indifference: "primal nature is a life eternally revolving in itself, a kind of circle, since the lowest flows into the highest and the highest again into the lowest" (116). In the midst of the struggle of existing powers that negate each other in their self-enactment there is a unity of the whole without difference, a unity that pervades all differences—a potency, he calls it, that is indifferent toward positive and negative potencies. It is with them and yet indifferent to them. It composes an "eternal beginning" that "persists" and does not change, a "true beginning" that is without determining force and that obliquely allows perpetual beginning. It neither starts nor stops, has no teleology, but is like "an incessant wheel, a never resting, rotating movement in which there is no distinction" (116). He calls it "blind life," something like a disaster of determinations in determinations that grounds all existing things without will or nature or self, an indetermination that yields constant urge and desire. It is a "pure, primal, essential nature" that "is always apart from itself in its expression" (119). It is like a non-telos at the heart of willing that gives will to strive to return to its essence, its "pure freedom." But Indifference wills nothing (123). It is an indeterminate potency that is negated by determination and that occurs as a negation of determination in determination, one that is blankly definitive for both negative and positive powers. Indifference does nothing. It effects nothing. It composes neither a capacity for action nor a capacity to receive an action. It does not suggest an abundance of being. It offers no contracts for fulfillment and provides no mediation or transfer. It does not suggest strength, confinement, or coercion. It overcomes nothing. It is, as it were, pure indifference, pure freedom, pure and undifferentiated immanence. It is absolutely absolute we-know-not-what, the disaster of differentiation and occurrence.

And yet this figuration of no-figuration plays such an effective and enabling role in Schelling's thought! It has the power of a nonreducible axiom that informs us concerning the unity of positive and negative powers. It figures the priority of occurrence that belies expression, and describes, by the word "Indifference," a dimension of *phusis,* while at the same time, in its discursive power, it requires us to retract its name, its meaning, and its existence. And rather than freeing us for thought without the function of an absolute, it nails us to the thought of an empty absolute for any adequate interpretation of life and living things. Further, while not a power of transfer or dialectic, Indifference seems, in its immanence, to transfer itself by retraction, to happen like non-presence in presence, to transmit non-self without translation, and to require non-difference in the inception of whatever is. Indifference seems to happen as nothing, as necessary, and as an absolute empty of everything. I do not think that it happens like a black night in which all cows are black. That metaphor indicates too much. It happens in the withdrawal and disaster of life, in, that is, the continuousness of beginning.

Consider what Schelling is preserving with this suicidal concept. Not only is he preserving a sense of the absolute. He is defining the occurrence of the whole of all existing things, including the occurrence of divine initiation, self-withdrawal, and self-objectification. And he is defining by Indifference the occurrence of pure immanence in which translation happens as the withdrawal of anything to be translated. In this formulation the truth of translation is at once absolute and devoid of content.

We can say that Schelling presents a double immanence in his thought. There is the immanence of the determined absolute—God—who is active, infinite, passive, and finite all at once and who is immanent in creative spirituality and mentation. And there is the empty immanence of Indifference. In regard to both kinds of immanence disclosure occurs in *geistige* enactments rather than in the coherence of systematic thought or in the accuracy of descriptions and statements. The translations of immanent occurrences, in other words, constitute enactments in which something pure in its own event both connects with an other and retracts in and from that connection. The immanent event is composed of the connection and the retraction as well as by the occurrence of the event—its eventuation, which is the way I am interpreting Indifference and which is not subject to any appropriate expression or effective retention. In phenomenological language we can say that Indifference is not subject to any form of intention. And we can say that it is without dialectic or history. But it is, as it were, immanent, and, as I have said, the word "Indifference" figures immanence in its event. This is not to say that the figure of Indifference is without history or intention or that Schelling's language on its own terms should be heard as establishing itself with proposed finality. I am saying, rather, that the originality and mortal struggle found in Schelling's language in its lively movement composes, on its terms, an intuition of the absolute in the failure of language and figuration before the incipience that gives them to arise.

Further, we can see that the axiomatic absolute comes to a remarkable expression in Schelling's thought as that axiom reaches a dimension of absolute nondetermination. In this context immanence is not a being. It is totally without subjectivity or objectivity, and it opens Schelling to a dimension of creativity and spiritual life in consciousness that is without consciousness and agency. That is a dimension that he calls pure freedom, and I have described it as the truth of translation in Schelling's thought.

Notice what we cannot say or believe in this combination of immanence and the axiomatic absolute. We cannot say that the truth of immediate events is found in the history of the development of the figures of immanence. We cannot say that the insufficiency of systems of thought is found by primary reference to changes in what and how we know—Foucault's concept of problematization, for example, is not a constructive possibility within the context of either Schleiermacher's or Schelling's thought. Neither way of thinking can tolerate a Nietzschean genealogy of the origin and development of our axiomatic concepts and values. We cannot believe, in either context, that the origins of our sense of ultimacy are found in cultural histories. We cannot find our pervasive kinships primarily in our languages, customs, and genes. We cannot avoid transcendental, ontological explanation of our existence. We cannot speak creatively and truly without a sense of eternal life. We cannot find final value in the existing singularity of things. We cannot understand ourselves without religious attitudes and references. We cannot think well without reference to a transcendental absolute. We cannot encounter things by sole reference to their mortal lives. We cannot experience our physical selves by sole reference to how our historical, cultural bodies occur. We cannot think of our worlds without a sense of disastrous loss of something more important than our worlds. We are unable to experience reflective joy and hope without a sense of a transcendent absolute that lifts our experience out of the limits of our lives into a wellspring of life that occurs, whether empty or full, as deathless and originary for our most valued states of mind. We cannot think without a deep preoccupation with absolute otherness. I suspect that in this context thought also has at its core a definitive sense of helplessness, of something like a cry for help, perhaps of despair. And with that sense of helplessness comes a sense of being alone in our human difference, a feeling not unlike pre-reflective mourning that colors our thinking and emotions with a tint of need for something more than we are. It carries a sense that, without the eternal, our power of affirmation would fail.

III. "I HAVE AS YET FOUND NO REASON FOR DISCOURAGEMENT"[8]

I have suggested indirectly that a contemporary preoccupation with sickness, depression, loss, anguish, and hopelessness (in a state of mind approximate to what Nietzsche calls "pathological irritability," *WTP,* 79) has something to do with an often inchoate thought of the axiomatic absolute in combination with that of immanence. Recall that "immanence" means "continuous indwelling," and with the axiomatic absolute it means that the events of our lives are infused with a continuously originary wellspring of beginning life, even if that wellspring is devoid of content. It carries the rhetorical question, "Surely there must be more to life than what is offered within the limits of utterly finite existence." And it carries as well the sense that meaning for life has its origins in an immanence that no matter how impersonal or conflictual connects us with a transcendent more-than-we-are. This "more" functions as a measure of our vitality as well as of our deaths. Even if it means disaster it translates nonetheless into a continuous indwelling of we know not what that does not seem to die. Some traditions carry on active arguments and discourses with it. Many pray to it. Others

---

8. Friedrich Nietzsche, *The Will to Power,* ed. and trans. Walter Kaufmann (New York: Random House, 1967), p. 128; henceforth *WTP.* References to this book are given in the text according to sections.

translate it into commanded practices or into other forms of immanent presence. Some retain a sense of it by obsessed, elliptical thought regarding transcendence or by the sense of a lost other. But in all such instances there seems to be the figuration of a border at which we find both disclosure and a retraction of disclosure as well as the figuration of immanence in presence and loss of presence. At this border of transcendent immanence occurs a loss (many people say) of subjective power and often an accompanying sense of overwhelming passivity and immanent disaster. They require our attention for the sake of human community and understanding as we speak, write, think, and establish hierarchies of values.

In this context I shall turn to Nietzsche in whose work we find a struggle with the axiomatic absolute and the possibility of an idea of immanence that could reshape its figuration in comparison to the ideas of immanence that we have been considering. I begin with the observation that people can read his ideas on will to power as having in them a sense of immanence and transcendence. We can see the will to power in its explanatory functions as naming an impersonal force of nature that is immanent in every living event. By it, Nietzsche seems to have hoped to define at least in part the essential movement of life, the meaning of scientific knowledge, the essence of thought and action, the bases of human violence, the origin of the lie of truth, and the death of God. We can see will to power as also providing an alternative image for divine intentionality and for the very idea of divinity. In the context of his thought, worship is a completely inappropriate response to the will to power. It does not require a specific ethics or moral code. It does not even justify Dionysian festivals. It is faceless, without subjectivity, and could be named with Schelling's phrase "blind life." Most significantly for Nietzsche, the will to power means that truths, meanings, values, and religious feelings do not originate the self-enactment of anything that is characterized by such words as truth, meaning, value, or divinity. But will to power nonetheless can be taken as immanent in all living events. And although Nietzsche would not use a word like "dependence" to describe people's immediate relation with it, we might say that in a Nietzschean world nothing would exist were the will to power removed.

Further, the will to power is disclosed in its retraction. No figuration or idea (including the idea of will to power) grasps it, and all figures or ideas fail to disclose it with definitive completeness. The world is the fragmented, differentiated continuous witness to will to power's eventful presence. It is merely and totally the enactment of life, the enactment of urge to be, *the* qualitative dimension in the occurrence of all quanta, and its conception loses it in expressing it.

"Force is to be found in quality" (*WTP,* 660). With this claim Nietzsche made clear that he thinks of will to power as an event of differentiation, not

as a self-subsisting substance. Indeed, his thought holds bodies primary and
dispenses with the "myth" of causality, and we recognize from the outset
that will to power cannot name for Nietzsche either a primordial cause or a
kind of being that is separated from bodies. Will to power is not a self-sub-
sistent anything. He elaborates its event in differentiation in terms of
command and strength (*WTP,* 490), a quality, he calls it, that is not reducible to any "in itself" (*WTP,* 563). The word force names "a play of
forces and waves of forces, at the same time one and many . . . a sea of
forces flowing and rushing together . . . with an ebb and a flood of its
forms" (*WTP,* 1067). It does not name something that could be immanent,
although Nietzsche's language at times certainly indicates a quality of absoluteness.

    In the last quotation I left out these phrases that describe "our world":
"eternally changing, eternally flooding back, with tremendous years of recurrence." In this description of the world, he writes that it is a "firm
magnitude of force that does not grow bigger or smaller, that does not
expend itself but only transforms itself; as a whole, of unalterable size."
The world is "not in a definite space *as a definite force*" (emphasis mine),
and not a space that might be "empty" here or there, but rather as force
throughout. "The world," as he describes it, is "enclosed by 'nothingness' as
by a boundary." The world is composed of plays of forces and constitutes
a place of forces, and the suggestion is that this play and place have neither
beginning nor end and compose a site "of firm magnitude," a monster of
radically altering intensities that produces an infinity of ensembles of
forces each with characteristic orders of command and submission. Nothing causes the world and its bodies. Rather, they are there like a moonless
tide that rocks and rolls with nothing causing or doing the rocking and
rolling.

    How, then, are we to hear these claims? On their own terms, as ensem-
bles of forces, as passing aspects of the rocking and rolling. Nietzsche's is a
discourse that continuously calls itself in question by the claims it makes
regarding its own site and temporality. Were we in a Schellingean mood we
might say that the nonseriousness that the spirit of Nietzsche's thought
often suggests regarding itself composes an intuition of the nothingness
that blanks out obliquely at the world's border, an intuition of the nothingness that "encloses" the world and infuses it with a formlessness without
meaning or jurisdiction. In such a mood we might say that an absence of
system and even an absence of a will to system constitute a striking clarity
of intuitive perception regarding the very event of the world's occurrence.
But that would be more Schellingean than Nietzschean because Schelling
was looking for a kind of immanence that Nietzsche was not looking for.
Schelling had a way of turning even nothing into presence, no matter how
obliquely, by thinking of immanent borders in terms of intuitive percep-

tive events. But there is a powerful sense in which Nietzsche does not think that way. Qualities of powers are composed of shifting relations among forces that are themselves qualities of powers. They do not suggest anything beyond their own singularities and singular interactions. And on these terms, the dominant value that Nietzsche gives to power and force is itself a complex quality of power that is in various intensities of conflict as it moves with and against other *geistige* forces. The idea of the will to power, in other words, does not mean or perceive anything beyond its own events.

Just at this point human emotions in the figurations of cultural instincts come into play. Nietzsche does not find the borders of living events, taken either as individual ensembles or as a whole, to be infused by anything other. Not even the thought of "disaster" can indicate appropriately the border of life, much less a thought of being. This is the moment when Nietzsche's thought without God is most forceful. This thought does not come most powerfully with his account of will to power, an account that eliminates all thought of a personal or purposeful God, but rather with the eradication in his thought of the affections, images, and concepts that would suggest I-know-not-what at and in the extremity of lives' occurrences. And this move happens not so much as he undercuts most of the traditional concepts of an absolute by his image of will to power, but as he develops his surrogate concept of an absolute *in such a way* that it suspends all inclinations to encounter it in any way other than in singular cultural productions. People meet something in their histories that has been embossed in their bodies, hidden in their genes and habits and capacities, something that gives them to feel in specific ways, as they encounter images or experiences of an immanent absolute. I shall go in a moment into more detail about this process as Nietzsche figures it, but for now I wish to mark the site of his strongest and most challenging enactment of departure from an axiom that has formed most philosophical thinking. In this enactment in his thought, the possibility of an absolute or absoluteness fades out, and where seriousness has traditionally collected regarding the immanence of radical alterity, we find instead, he says, a singular playfulness, a joy without a goal, a voluptuous delight—an undulating circularity in his image, one that is affirmed without purpose (*WTP,* 1067). Were I to say that nothing is immanent I would have said too much in this context, because in such phrasing "nothing" becomes too close to something to allow Nietzsche's thought its moment. If we must speak of immanence we can say only that a group of bodies are immanent with themselves as they enact habits of mind that have traceable histories of physical formations. Bodies are sites of relatively enduring imprints of practices and values that appear to have in their formations a drive to survive, and that drive describes their force of movement. And the claim, of course, has its meaning as a short-lived constellation of affective, reflective images.

When he says with obvious pleasure that "this world is the will to power—and nothing besides, and you yourselves are also this will to power—and nothing besides," he articulates, I believe, a physical transformation that springs out of a vacuity left by departed images of an immanent absolute. When I say "pleasure" I mean that there is a dimension in Nietzsche's thought that is not characterized by mourning or even sadness over this vacuity. He is glad to feel no need to look for resonance or assurance or grounding or alterity or depth or agency or presence or even transcendence at the border of lives' occurrences. And when I say "glad" I mean that the physicality that composes the formations of the immanent axiomatic absolute have changed, that the mood of his thought composes a physical transformation, a different wellspring for images, values, and interpretations. I speculate that out of this experience came the image of a way of being that is no longer defined by many of the feelings that people have considered inherent in human beings. The image of the *Übermensch*, perhaps, articulates the experience of finding joy and no discouragement in the loss of the site that has generated a considerable measure of hope and a sense of cosmic connection in our tradition, no discouragement over loss of the feeling that his life is constituted by the happening of an absolute, transcendent other, primarily joy in the realization that life may not eternally overcome death.

This sense of no discouragement composes a considerable physical transformation of cultural instincts. It generates the sense of the possible emergence of a new kind of body. This thought carries the further implication that when it is recognized as nihilistic it is recognized by a body that has not undergone this transformation.

This feeling of joy in "the circle itself," of pleasure with the forces of life and with a sense of being a constellation of some of those forces appears to me to suggest that we should not read Nietzsche's claims primarily as discursive teachings about the way things really are. As those claims are made, the ways in which they are made undercut their own suggestion of universality. They take themselves to be enactments of a specific physical transformation. That transformation is figured in Nietzsche's thought by forces—by valences, values—that accentuate the importance of growth, initiation, formation, and productivity without transcendent justification (and wherever people find transcendent justification the axiomatic absolute is probably in play). It is figured by the value of life, by the value of *phusis* in its multiple forms without transcendent justification, by the enactment of lives that are free of the feeling of having fallen from something greater, and by a feeling of happiness without guilt. This accomplishment constitutes a physical transformation of the bodies produced by many of our dominant traditions, an accomplishment whose force is probably still difficult to appreciate. "Qualities [of lives]," Nietzsche wrote, "are an idiosyncrasy peculiar to man; to demand that our human interpretations and values should be universal and perhaps [ontologically] constitutive values is one of the hereditary madnesses of human pride" (*WTP,* 565). He might have added, the hereditary fear of being alone in the universe.

I believe that we should say that Nietzsche understood his own claims to be interpretations that express "a different consciousness, feeling, desiring, a different perspective" from those that have defined major portions of our lineage (*WTP,* 563). He measures this difference by "strength" to depart from the lineage, by "growth" that expresses "a desire to be more," by the creation of a body that turns its history into an enactment of origination that feels good in its departure from images of absolute immanence (*WTP,* 563). That is like a body that is able to transform what comes into it into energy for qualities of movements that what comes into it could not themselves perform.

IV. TRANSLATION AND PHYSIOGNOMIES OF MEANINGS

I have been speaking of translation with an emphasis on the first syllable "trans" that describes the sense of carry that the "late" of "translate" expresses. "Trans" has the senses of entering, over, across, beyond, and on the other side of, as well as senses of completeness of change, transcending, and surpassing. This syllable links "translation," "transfiguration," and "transcendence." It brings together the ideas of both being beyond (i.e., surpassing, completeness of change) and being present (i.e., *going* across, *carrying* over), of going *beyond* and definitive changes. These senses and their associations suggest a differentiation in immanence as distinct from simple or "pure" identity. They suggest that immanence by transcendence happens as differentiation. "Trans" suggests presenting occurrences in which definitive changes happen by means of a transfer, not by unmediated presence. The transfer happens in translation as a way of being changes to another way of being and in that change and carrying over, one way of being is disclosed to another as a consequence of occurring by means of the change. Translation thus suggests that what is translated comes to be lost to its own event and that it persists only by way of losing its own way of being in another kind of event. I have called those events of transfer border experiences that have been described by the word "immanence." A transmigration of absoluteness to mortality, for example, seems to occur in many traditional images of the absolute's transmission. And the image of such transmission and transformation has opened the field of judgment to many, often opposing interpretations of what gets transferred and the effects of such transferal. The translation of the absolute in human being suggests both a bearing of an absolute and its removal, although many people have interpreted the removal by giving dominance to the absolute's continued bearing in itself and in withdrawal from the mortal being with which it is immanent.

The site of the absolute's translation according to Schleiermacher, we saw, is feeling, and according to Schelling, it is intuition. Whereas Schleiermacher emphasized an occurrence (feeling) that is charged with mortality and physicality, Schelling emphasized conflict and self-loss within divine immanence and found absolute unity in the Indifference of the divine event, an Indifference that appears in intuition and that seems to be completely unaffected by either bodies or mortal temporality. But for both of them any translation into conceptualization, meaning, story, and other forms of experience includes loss of absoluteness.

With Nietzsche we find "body" and "physiology" to compose "the starting point" (*WTP*, 492) for interpreting images of absoluteness, and while his thought of the will to power might seem to suggest an absolute with immanent transcendence, we found in the affective performance of his thought the requirement that we think of will to power as outside of the organizing power of the axiomatic absolute, that, as he puts it, "the whole 'inner experience' rests upon the fact that a cause for an excitement of the nerve centers is sought and imagined . . . [but] this cause . . . is a groping on the basis of previous 'inner experiences,' i.e. of memory" (*WTP*, 479). I have interpreted such memory by reference to his concept of culturally generated, physiologically composed, transformable states of mind. And I have said that both traditional states of mind and the occurrence of their transformation in Nietzsche's experience are *phusis*-like in the sense that they happen as the arising of powerful, controlling images, feelings, intuitions, and conceptions concerning the world and the way things happen. Bodies compose the *phusis* of figurations of an absolute.

In the context of Nietzsche's thought we can also say that bodies occur as sites of translation and that sedimentations of organizing values and their lineages both constitute the site immanently and compose what is translated. When I say that bodies are composed of the immanent processes of forceful, traditional ways of estimating and valuing things, I mean that bodies, for Nietzsche, are both translational and traditional. They are the sites that happen when traditional ordering powers are effective in their transferal of images and possibilities before people are able to speak of them or address them. And they are also effective *and* transformed as people speak of them and address them. Bodies for Nietzsche are extensive in the sense that they compose pre-reflective expressions of traditional forces of order, recognition, and evaluation. These forces "grow" the body in specific ways. Bodies are transformative sites of linkage with past events and practices that form the body's enactment of itself. This pre-experiential dimension comes to compose "inner experiences" "only after [a person's] consciousness has found a language that the individual understands—i.e., a translation of a condition into conditions familiar to him" (*WTP,* 479). And this manner of translating diminishes the singularity and newness of everything because of the ordering power possessed by repetition of the familiar. Nothing that people understand is totally new. "'To understand' means merely: to be able to express something new in the language of something old and familiar" (*WTP,* 479). The powers in this kind of memory give dominance to a past that is inscribed in our languages and values, and hence in our bodies, and a past is lived in feelings of familiarity and significance. The site of generation of these feelings is physiological memory, the place of a culture's primary transmission. Nietzsche called the operation of these powerful memories fictions insofar as they undercut what we traditionally expect truth to be. They provide no basis for the positive value of universality or a self-enacting absolute or an unchanging constancy of presence of purely objective facts.

A body also provides in its immediacy a moment that is not determined by interpretation. In *On the Advantages and Disadvantages of History for Life,* Nietzsche describes this moment as *unhistorisch,* unhistorical (as distinct from *ungeschichtlich,* uneventful).[9] A body's immediate moment, in its full determination, is not fully controlled by the stories and accounts by which we interpret and narrate what has gone on before the moment (i.e., by histories). A body's contribution to immediacy is pre-reflective and uncontrolled by the meanings that inhabit it. This immediacy of a moment composes a time of change, creation, and originality, a time of generation of new images and forms of power. It is a moment of translation, of full determination without the complete determination of an overriding interpretation. An interpretation would be dominant only if it were thematized and repeated in the moment. Nonhistorical (*unhistorische*) but eventful (*geschichtliche*) mutations of determinations occur nonvoluntarily and physically in a moment, but people can also enact themselves voluntarily and interpretively to provide a different determination in relation to those that compose the moment.

I wish to emphasize that the moment for Nietzsche is not an empty event or one disclosive of being, and it is not like Schellingean Indifference, in the sense that for Nietzsche the moment happens physically within a culture and with all kinds of limits and powers. A moment does

---

9. Friedrich Nietzsche, *On the Advantages and Disadvantages of History for Life,* trans. Peter Preuss (Indianapolis: Hackett, 1980).

not transcend power formations and form a separate event. It is rather the finite, physical happening *of* power formations with limited possibilities of transformation—not transcendental possibility but particular possibilities within specific formations. A moment is a happening of transferal, but I believe that we would misread Nietzsche if we interpreted this happening in terms of an ontological difference between beings and being or between event and events. That kind of distinction has its inception in interpretations that grow out of the axiomatic absolute. The possibilities for transformation and translation inhere in the formations and their conflicts and not in something ontologically different from them. Mutability does not have the condition of its possibility in another dimension but rather in the struggle of the elements that are occurring. This is one of the reasons why Heidegger finds nihilism in Nietzsche's thought and why I find in Nietzsche an admirable rethinking, more transformative than Heidegger's thought of ontological difference, of immanence without the power of an axiomatic absolute. Or, to put the point in language closer to Nietzsche's, the image of another dimension, whether that dimension be called time, being, Indifference, or God, would be a fiction bred of inheritances that have become forceful patterns of intelligibility in our nervous systems.

Nietzsche says that "we gain the correct idea of the nature of our subject-unity, namely as regents at the head of a community (not as "souls" or "life forces"), and also [the correct idea of the nature of] the dependence of those regents upon the ruled and of an order of rank and division of labor as the conditions that make possible the whole and its parts. In the same way, how living unities continually arise and die and how the "subject" is not eternal; in the same way, that the struggle expresses itself in obeying and commanding, and that a fluctuating assessment of the limits of power is part of life" (*WTP,* 492). This statement is "correct" in what sense? In the sense that a group of transforming values now carry out their force in Nietzsche's thought, and his observations express that transformation. He begins the section from which I took the last quotation with the words that I quoted earlier: "the body and physiology as the starting point. . . ." Why, he asks, does he begin there? "The most important thing . . . is: that we understand that the ruler and his subjects are of the same kind, all feeling, willing, thinking— and that, wherever we see a 'divine' movement in a body we learn to conclude that there is a subjective, invisible life appertaining to it. Movement is symbolism for the eye; it indicates that something has been felt, willed, thought" (*WTP,* 492). One implication in this statement is that "invisible life" names a conclusion, an evaluation on the basis of what is familiar to us in our inherited intelligence. Another implication is that "invisible life" does not exist except insofar as we fail to perceive movement in a given instance. A third implication is that forces that are in some sense perceptible rule perceptible bodies. And a fourth implication is that subject-unity, wherever it is attributed to something, is an image that expresses a body of familiar presuppositions. Change the body of presuppositions and you change the field of orders and accuracies, and hence you change the field for correctness of observation.

Within Nietzsche's thought no moment is characterized by subject-unity if the meaning of "unity" suggests simple identity. Bodies are not unities but sites that are composed of a variety of more or less dense elements and of conflicting forces that are ruled, more or less, by parts of the conflict. Bodies compose a fluid constellation of interacting forces in which the rule is always up for grabs in any moment. Within this perspective a moment is a digestive process that has as its aim the continued movement and activity of the body. Activity slows or inverts on itself like a developed food allergy when the mutational process is grasped solely by repetitions or by an effort to shut down transformations.

The physical site of translation is thus one for Nietzsche that has its singularity in the ways constellated parts contest and fuse with one another. It is neither a site of unity nor a place of absolute immanence. Fluid orders of forces are immanent in the body's activities. They form the conditions of people's existence. The passing away of some figurations of power by changes into other figurations is immanent in a body's life. The spaces defined by conflicts and ruling and subservient figurations are immanent. There are many processes, many conflictual variations, many harmonies, and there is nothing absolute with it. That is what Nietzsche shows us in the mirror of his transformation of the immanent absolute.

We have in these reflections the image of a site of translation that belongs to translation. I suppose that we could say that translating is immanent to translating if we mean that nothing occurs outside of translating, that the translated is itself a translation, that forces too are translations, and that Nietzsche's "correct" descriptions are translations of translations. The primary value of activity for living organisms that operates in Nietzsche's thought is also a translation of aspects of a vast tradition. The word "tradition" means an act of delivering something into the hands of another, and this delivery has in it, in the word "tradition," a sense of surrender, almost of betrayal—"tradition" in its history is associated with "traitor." This meaning is prominent in Nietzsche's connection with his tradition, and for his thought the hands into which traditional values and ideas are delivered are those of moments. In the moments of this thinking many of our past images are handed over to the physical, mutational process that a moment is, and in *his* moments the values of lives lose the power of the value of absoluteness and become compositions of the powers of organisms that struggle to continue to move.

V. THE JOYS OF KNOWING AND THE FOOLS FOR RHYTHMS WHO HAVE NO SENSE OF THEFT[10]

You will have noticed that Nietzsche, in contrast to many philosophers in this century, gives priority to bodies over language and texts. Bodies live with flesh and blood, and texts have flesh and blood only in their embodiments. Textual copulation is vastly different from the tissues, juices, and spasms of bodies. For Nietzsche, languages are secondary to many other physical functions, do not happen with vitality when they live primarily like grammatical signifiers, and are characterized by nonlinguistic perceptions. Meanings are secondary to many other vital activities, and physical activities other than signifying are often more important than signification is. In their lives, languages are physical occurrences that are under the jurisdictions of drives, fears, satisfactions, enjoyments of organic survival, dyspepsia, quirks of incidental experiences, psychological configurations, bowel and erotic functions, diseases and good health. And yet on Nietzsche's accounting, bodies are extensive and traditional as well as innovative. They are not defined solely by a singular material thing or by any grouping of quanta. They are, in his language, *geistige* and intangible, if "tangible" is understood in purely materialistic terms. They are *geistige* like digestion is *geistige* as they become what they are by the infusion of all manner of contents and as they turn those contents into something else that belongs to bodies. Bodies are characterized by willpower, by urges that are not reducible to a quantity of anything. And the transformations and translations that occur as and in bodies, we saw, are themselves physical occurrences. It is just at the point of translation that multiple stories, images, and ideas arise concerning what happens and who or what is there. Translation is a thoroughly *geistige* moment, and on Nietzsche's terms it is not necessarily linguistic, but is rather an occurrence of many different forces. The plays of languages in such translation are often inhibiting and destructively conserving of what is familiar as well as originating and creative.

Even when we recognize that language is most strange in its happening, that it too offsets and translates what it would say, that it too does not compose a unity, that it is more like an ellipsis than it is like a straightforward presentation of things, that it continuously defers what it would disclose—even then the priority of language for thought nonetheless has a fictitious, vaguely transcendental scent to a Nietzschean nose. In its priority, language is often judged as housing too much, preserving too much in spite of its elusive qualities, as too distant from the bodies that give it to live. Languages are often closer to translations of bodies, translations that

---

10. Friedrich Nietzsche, *The Gay Science,* trans. Walter Kaufmann (New York: Random House/Vintage, 1974; henceforth *GS*), sections 83 and 84.

appear to lose their own physicality and the physical things that they translate, than they are to disclosures of something true. And the danger when a
language turns toward itself and speaks of itself is one of self-enclosure,
one of transcendentalizing itself by the priority that it gives to itself. That
would seem to be a danger even for a language that finds itself divided
from itself and a perpetuator of perpetual conflict and error. Unless enacted languages live in the truancy and fragmentations of their physical
occurrences, they cannot bleed, and if they cannot bleed, they are not fully
alive: words at their best are physical enactments.

The words of the previous paragraph articulate a suspicion, a caution
regarding the force of language when it is prioritized. In its priority it can
submit the *geistige* aspect of translation to its dominance and become, as it
were, the image of translation's stomach and gastrointestinal tract. It can
even give itself the image of the heart and lungs of comprehension and inchoately install a kind of intellectualism at the center of philosophy's life.
Of course all this that I am saying and writing is in a language, and of
course I and Nietzsche are making claims that function linguistically. But
if I translate this activity and this medium into something absolute for
itself, if I make language a self-enclosed, self-legislating kind of event by
which all perceptions, all knowledge, and all experience are measured, I
will have turned language into a kind of event that diminishes its own
physicality as well as diminishes the forces of bodies and establishes a
regime of special disclosure or one of signifiers. Nietzsche is interested in
the silent, nonlinguistic motivations for that establishment, the stakes of
power in such a creation, the lineage and interests of lives that want such
governance.

This caution and suspicion arise, at least in part, from the intention to
give bodies priority for their own lives. They arise in a language whose interests are in returning languages to their lifeblood, in giving them to
collapse before feelings and drives, physical moments, and constellations of
forces that do not speak—such as physical drives and draws, sunlight, blind
collisions, wordless transformations, retractions without images, and sound-
less figurations. The *geistige* for Nietzsche often occurs without word or
sign, as plays of forces that we can translate into images (as I have done)
but that are not reliant in their force on such translations. *Geist* for him is
far more than meaningful events and closer to digestion than to "wisdom."
It is at this juncture of word and wordlessness, of image and imagelessness
that I would like to consider joy.

When Nietzsche addresses high culture in *The Gay Science,*[11] he looks
for "forms of conquest" (83), robustness of energy, feelings of power (13),

11. Ibid. References to this book are given in the text.

sympathies, measures of delight, movements of decay, contexts of usefulness, bodily effects of rhythms, "unconquerable urges" (84), excitations
and tranquilizations, instincts, enforcements, forms of deception, manipu-
lations, expressions of pride, incorporations, expressions of desire, and
capacities for pleasure and joy (12). He looks for, in other words, the nodal
points at which unworded and unimaged physiological occurrences come
to word and image, points of radical translation at which physical occurrences are converted into other physical occurrences that bear the descriptions of "cultural." The direction of his attention is not fixed by the
produced signs and their organizations but is defined more by the physical
transformations in which the unworded and unimaged occurrences remain
attendable. The great mistake is to take so-called cultural works with that
seriousness born of a forceful, traditional image of truth or goodness or an
absolute—an image that bears no sense for its own physicality. In *The Gay
Science* he also occasionally considers possible descents in our traditions to
find the values that are given to cultural expressions. Consider one such de-
scent in this context that is found in the section entitled "On the Origin of
Poetry" (84).

In this section Nietzsche departs from some of the more serious claims
found in *The Birth of Tragedy* concerning Dionysian excess, especially the
implication that one can stand outside the complex determination of one's
own physical occurrence. I can summarize part of the difference with the
example that when one says "my body" or when one says "I"—using Nietzsche's terms from the time he wrote *The Gay Science*—one's body is
coming to the physical expression of speech. By this time, identifying determinations are not something one must stand out from to be enmeshed
ecstatically with one's body, and form is not an opposite to the physical.
Identity is bodily, and form is bodily, and the issues have to do with the
ways in which identities and forms express their flesh; they have to do with
degrees of subjugation, ignorance and sensitivity, fear, and what we can call
sublimation if we are careful with that word and do not give a complete
control of it to the Freudian tradition. This change in Nietzsche's thinking
is manifest in the more intense and wider appreciation that he gives to
Apollo in the section before us, and in his avoidance of an exaggerated account of ecstasy and oblivion. Now the emphasis falls on the usefulness of
ritual and poetry for bodily interests.

Early in our lineage, he says, rhythms of speech and sound functioned
at the behest of superstitions. "Rhythm was meant to impress the gods
more deeply with a human petition, for it was noticed that [people] remember a verse much better than ordinary speech. It was also believed that
a rhythm's tick-tock was audible over greater distances; a rhythmical prayer
was supposed to get closer to the ears of the gods. Above all [people] desired
the utility of the elemental and overpowering effect that we experience in

ourselves as we listen to music: rhythm is a compulsion; it engenders an unconquerable urge to yield and join in; not only our feet follow the beat but
the soul does too—probably, one surmised, the soul of the gods as well!"
The use of rhythm was an attempt to "compel" the gods by "forcing their
hand." "Poetry was thrown at them like a magical snare." By this act people
could achieve a stronger divine hearing for what they desired and perhaps
have their desires met, perhaps even become godlike in ecstatic closeness. In
the context of Nietzsche's thought we may surmise that this intention is
not altogether lacking in the arts today—hence the frequent beliefs that
there is something connected to divinity in fine art and that art and religion
enjoy a close association in their approximation to something "higher" for
our lives.

But there is an even stranger utility that "may have contributed most of
all to the origin of poetry." The Pythagoreans used rhythmical sounds not
only as an aid to education but also as an instrument to achieve truth and
eternal life. Music in its rhythm was considered most helpful in "discharg-
ing the emotions . . . purifying the soul," and easing ferocity of mind. In
such release one then danced as a culmination to the therapy. The Pythagoreans used such measures to reach beyond time to Mnemosyne's eternal
being, to join her, and to escape an endless cycle of ignorance, separation
from the eternal, and consequent suffering and death.

In some cults rhythm was used to intensify the emotions "to the ultimate extreme, making those who were in a rage entirely mad; and the
vengeful, frenzied with lust for revenge." And "all orgiastic cults aim at dis-
charging the ferocity of some deity all at once, turning it into an orgy, in
order that the deity should feel freer and calmer afterward and leave
[people] in peace." In these cases rhythm is used to tranquilize or excite to
battle. In all instances the function of poetry and music was to spellbind
bodies and to transform them, make them hurt less or achieve more or find
greater satisfaction or allow one to leave them. And from these experiences
people supposed that the gods too could be spellbound or persuaded to fa-
cilitate their wishes so that divinities underwent the pleasures and modulations of rhythms. In these paragraphs Nietzsche uses "utility" as a medium
to connect rhythms with physical interests and to illustrate the bodily incipience in some of our most ethereal and poetic accomplishments. When
we attend to this incipience we are disinclined to give priority to a supposed
nonphysical immanence in such occurrences, and we are predisposed
to find in bodies the *phusis* of religion and art. The line of association that
Nietzsche follows is this: a bodily state, such as despondency, forgetfulness,
ferocity, or boredom, experiences a measure of relief in its release by means
of rhythmic experiences. People's enthusiasm for battle or sexual excitation
or the security found in a sense of bonding found support in rhythmic beats. Rhythm "discharges the emotions" and produces, as aftereffects,

altered states of feeling such as tranquility or fearless confrontation of danger. Just as rhythms "reorder all the atoms of a sentence" when one lets them permeate speech, they also reorder the atoms of experience when they permeate the body. The products of such strategic reordering—the rituals, beliefs, prophecies, poetry, narratives, dances, theaters, establishments of orders of mediators with the divine, temples and other structures, statues, paintings, music, practices of purification and recollection, patterns of belief and evaluation—such products form both a large portion of cultures, and they compose cathexes of emotions—retentions of emotions—in their very formations. There is a striking connection of emotional purgation (catharsis) and retention (cathexis) in these structures, a combination of emotional investment and release in them. Their force and hence their value (valence), in other words, arise from the emotions that are translated and immanent in them.

And what is the site of the origin of cultural forms like? The site happens as a finite generator of energy, a magnitude of force that expends itself and transforms itself, something blurry, set in a definite space as a definite field of forces, set in a space that itself is constituted as plays and waves of forces, at the same time one and many, increasing here, decreasing there, changing always, undergoing periods of recurrence and periods of traumatic change with an ebb and flow of its forms, striving to move out of simple forms to highly complex ones, striving to move from the stillest of moments to the hottest and most turbulent, most self-contradictory ones, returning occasionally to the joy of concord, and returning always to the simplicity of death.[12] The site of cultural formations are bodies in their worlds. Cultural formations (and here we speak of the power of Apollo) compose cathected emotions whose trajectories arise in the physical benefits of their release.

And the feelings that governed the entire process? The moving forces toward and in culture as we know it? The drives that produced those ancient formations that gave birth to many of the sophistications that now describe unwittingly their origins as ancient and superstitious? Rhythms that were expressed as useful "superstitions" "enable one to do anything— to advance some work magically [as when we find something more than ourselves speaking back to us in our creations]; to force a god to appear, to be near, and to listen [as when we worship, confess, and pray]; to mold the future in accordance with one's will [as when we find purposes in something absolute]; to cleanse one's own soul from some excess (of anxiety, mania, pity, or vengefulness)—and not only one's own soul but also that of the most evil demon [as when we expect wisdom or beauty to transform

---

12. These words constitute a gloss on lines in *WTP,* 1087.

bad people or destructive events]: without verse one was nothing; by means of verse one almost became a god [O divine Shakespeare, divine Goethe, divine Mahler, most divine Plato, and Hegel—forgive him!]. Such a fundamental feeling can never be erased entirely, and even now, after [people] have fought against such superstition for thousands of years, the wisest among us are still occasionally fooled by rhythm—if only because insofar as we sometimes consider an idea truer simply because it has a metrical form and presents itself with a divine skip and jump. Isn't it rather amusing that to this day the most serious philosophers, however strict they may be in questions of certainty, still call on what poets have said to lend their ideas force and credibility?" The feelings that govern the process are ones that sought energy, satisfaction, release, and power, that cathected themselves into cultural forces, and that led to the reinforcing power of the values of truth. But watch out, Nietzsche says, for "as Homer says, 'Many lies tell the poets.'" And when we believe the poets, truths are in trouble. And when a poet is called upon by a philosopher to tell us that poets lie, we are in double trouble because we don't know whom to believe, especially when the philosopher who quoted the poet has just lampooned the use of poetry to support philosophical claims. It's as though we can't trust anyone with the truth, nor trust that mistrust. It's as though we have little more than our bodies and their interests to go with. And being bodies, do we know that they don't lie? Could they experience joy by stealing truths from a fund that has no truths to keep?

I hope by this last play to indicate that even bodies collectively cannot function for Nietzsche as an axiomatic absolute. He often treats them as though they were an absolute beginning for everything that has meaning and is right or good or true. Physical life appears to be central for his thought. In his thought bodies are like we know not what that have no true center even in their regard for themselves. But the idea of a central immanence slips away into an image of transformative constellations of shifting forces that makes useless an image of centrality—there are centralities but no center for them all outside of their own productive centering energies. The feeling of joy in this knowledge appears to define Nietzsche's accomplishment as he followed the disconnections of traditional senses of immanence from an image of absoluteness that exercised the power of an axiom. Joy is not a feeling that we can trust. It is not free of the powers of rhythms. It is a feeling beholden to Hermes, the god of thieves as well as of divine intuition. It is attached to moments with little foresight; it is completely affected by its own moment; it does not necessarily suggest love, tenderness, or kindness; and it can come to the killer as well as to the creator, to the fool as well as to the wise one. Joy is known by the religious as well as by those without religious affections. It does not necessarily mean the presence of any immanent being. It means neither more nor less than a moment of "concord." It is subject to further justification only on the basis of what we have heard Nietzsche call lies masquerading as truths. We can mold our lives around it only at the costs of absurdity and sentimentality. Joy justifies nothing. I think that Nietzsche knew that and that is why he described his knowledge by "joy": a knowledge that disciplines itself—hence its *wissenschaftliche* character—by seriousness and nonseriousness at the same time; his knowledge energetically seeks at once to establish itself. It is a knowledge that finds a concordance in its physical moment, whatever the fate of that moment might be, a knowledge that releases a few emotional vibrations into figurations that have their values only in their expressions and in the possibilities to which they give rise. Joy may forecast disaster or happiness, an increase or a decrease of suffering, moments of discord or relative harmony. But bodies seem to like joys and will seek them even at the expense of themselves and other bodies. In his moments, Nietzsche found joy in that knowledge, and in that experience I believe that he knew how little our traditional wisdom and truth knew of the bodies that they guided and that constituted them.

NINE

Psalms, Poems, and Morals with Celestial Indifference

I would like to address the issues of this chapter by presenting three options. One is clearly theistic, one figures a loss of faith, and one arises outside of a sense of divine presence or of loss of divine presence. I use the word "address" in order to indicate that I do not have a final judgment to make regarding the advantages of one option over the others, although I find myself oriented by the third. My purposes are broadly descriptive and intended to indicate three kinds of attitude, three affective awarenesses, each exclusive of the other two and each viable now for various people. Only the first option is distinctly religious, but all three are formed in part by attitudes regarding humans' "place" and meaning in the universe. One persuasion that guides these observations is that a religious response to the vast expanse of our setting and to the challenges that that vastness presents to human significance is optional in the sense that such a response is not "natural" to humans. Nothing "material" or necessary for humankind is articulated in any of the attitudes, and each figures the present-day optionality of the other two.

Consider the sense of distance and empty space that can accompany our experience of starlight. On a clear night we look up to see uncountable shining lights surrounded in darkness and silence. They shine on us in our raptures and can give us to feel awe before sheer expanse, vastness beyond narration. They also shine as the infant dies, people cry out in agony, and unrecountable injustices are performed without care and without witness. A vacant coldness can be found with stars even when they lift our hearts and inspire us to sing, and taken by themselves they speak to us of nothing moral or right or just even when we are inclined by their shining glory to bow in reverence before the universe. They are not witnesses of human lives. The writer of the Eighth Psalm seems to have been aware of something like this ambiguity in people's experiences of starlight:

Oh Lord our Lord, how excellent is thy name in all the earth! Who hast set thy glory above the heavens.

Out of the mouth of babes and sucklings hast thou ordained strength because of thine enemies, that thou mightest still the enemy and the avenger.

When I consider the heavens, the work of thy fingers, the moon and the stars which thou hast ordained;

What is man, that thou art mindful of him? And the son of man, that thou visitest him?

For thou hast made him a little lower than the angels, and hast crowned him with glory and honor.

Thou madest him to have dominion over the works of thy hands; thou hast put all things under his feet. . . .

The poet addresses God in this psalm in the form of an encomium: you, Lord, are above the heavens, above the light of stars, above all that is overwhelming in the shining expanse of the sky. Your glory, *your* shine, outshines all the shining hosts. And from that brilliance you heed us; you have given strength to the weak and have immobilized the powerful who fail to heed you.

But the poet is not immune to the power of the starry heavens and their indifference to people. Even when he incorporates a recognition that God is the creator of the universe—"the work of thy fingers, the moon and the stars which thou hast ordained"—even then he finds an incipient insignificance before the vast, nonreflecting, unresponding sky: "when I consider the heavens . . . what is man, that thou art mindful of him?" I do not mean to suggest that his faith falters. Far from it. But I do find that within the context of his faith and the sense of goodness that it provides, the poet also feels a sense of diminishment and insignificance before the sidereal vastness of night. And it is to God that he looks for the investment of importance in humans, not to the stars, for God, the creator of people and stars and their orders, comes to humans, "visits" them, and gives them also to shine with significance, to have a place of power, even of dominion, in a world in which human beings could seem, without divine attendance, out-gloried and underappreciated within the awful reach of celestial indifference. The difference that God makes for this poet is absolute. Because of God, and only because of God, are the starry heavens upbuilding for human spirit. Because of God's "mindfulness" of humans, the glory of stars sheds light on the glory of the One who sheds his light on his creation.

Recall some of the facts and theories that are current in our knowledge of stars. It takes light from the star Eta Carine 10,000 years, traveling at 186,273 miles per second, to reach the earth. The light from it that people now see began its travel across space when Homo sapiens were just beginning to learn how to raise food instead of foraging for it—5,000 years before the earliest pyramids were built. That light—those photons—that strikes our eyes and that is absorbed by our rods and cones has been traveling at a blinding speed while all the events of what we know as human culture took place. The universe itself is probably 15 billion years old, and astronomers expect to be able to see the light that marks the beginning of the universe, light that for all practical purposes comes from beyond the reach of our imaginations. We figure it only to lose its meaning, only to cancel the power of our position to know it, only to stand in awe of its extent and power.

We use peculiar metaphors to speak of the beginning of our universe: "big bang" to speak of its origin, "cosmic egg" to speak of "the mote," the condensed "thing," out of the explosion of which the universe came to be. Before our universe came to be, there was no past, no present, no future, no space, no time, no vacuum, no individuated thing—not even dark, which cannot "exist" without light. There was an eruption, perhaps, by which trillions of units of force—of sheer energy—burst forth, originating something else that was also brand new: direction. Energy burst forth as heat, light, pressure, and electromagnetic and nuclear forces "where" there had been no "where" and no time a microsecond "before." This event is thought to have happened in an instant too small to measure: something so huge occurred in a billionth of a second. Out of that billionth of a second emerged the regularities and patterns of reality.

By means of relativity theory, we are reasonably sure that nothing can travel faster than light—186,273 miles a second—because as something increases its speed it increases its mass. And when it reaches the speed of light, the mass of anything becomes infinite—beyond all measurement— and then it needs infinite or unmeasurable energy to accelerate its speed. But that amount of energy does not exist, so the speed of light is as fast as a mass of energy can go. But no one knows for sure whether light itself has infinite mass and can travel faster than what we now measure as the speed of light, because light changes back and forth from mass to pure energy. In fact, no one knows if light has either infinite mass or no mass at all as "it" travels at 186,273 miles per second. It is at least possible that at the Big Bang energy traveled much faster than the speed of light. But no one is sure about that because no one knows when the limiting laws of velocity came to be.

Early in the universe's expansion, stars did not exist, but gravity did exist, forcing the swirling clouds of subnuclear gas to form huge clumps of elementary matter in space. These clumps grew larger and larger as the force of gravity merged and smashed together subatomic particles. These larger, heavier clumps pulled in more and more particles and swirling gasses. Subatomic particles formed atoms, atoms formed molecules, the pressures and pulls increased over unmeasured time, and these larger and larger masses themselves began to turn from the effect of the forces by which matter collected into compacted, highly energized centers. This is the way we know stars to have been born.

This knowledge, "our" knowledge, is filled with gaps, hypotheses that push toward their own overthrowal by other hypotheses based on further discoveries, by sheer ignorance, and by a tentativeness that on its own terms requires in a pursuit for knowledge neither reverence nor a being that gives meaning to a figure of gigantic wholeness. In this knowledge there is a stark absence of metaphors of personality in relation to the starry heavens and no suggestion of witness to a moral law, a greater subjectivity, or a definitive teleology. Such values, if they interpret this knowledge, must come from a different metaphorical source. There are nonetheless plenty of "scientific" beliefs in it as well as methodological trust, but both the beliefs and the trust do not have, on their own terms, either an eternal object or an eternal life expectancy. I shall say later that this tentativeness and the assumptions that call for it—this epistemological boldness with a good bit of self-doubt and expectation for radical transformation built into it—can be and indeed have been relevant for attitudes toward morality as our perception of our place in the universe shifts out of a religious and theological lineage. I will say that recognition of spaces bereft of connection and meaning and hence bereft of possibility for divine connections among them can play a constructive role in the formation of moral attitudes that do not require divine mystery or authority to compose the world's occurrence. But first, I would like to return to the psalmist.

The psalmist set the context for his consideration of the heavens outside of scientific grasp with the words, "O Lord our Lord how excellent is thy name in all the earth! Who hast set thy glory above the heavens." He knew, as I noted, that stars and starry space do not, when taken solely by themselves, give moral or religious meaning. They do not, when taken by themselves, provide Lordship, covenant, inspired human laws, or the glory of God. God's glory comes from above the heavens. Otherwise we would be without help before our enemies, and our lives would seem hopeless. So the entire psalm is given in the context of a God who provides for humans' glory, honor, and a basis for a true way of life. Without God we are as nothing before the beautiful, silent, cold distance of the starry heavens; we are minute beings who are lost in the midst of forces and immeasurable vastness if we do not have guidance and testimony beyond ourselves. The absence of God would mean for the psalmist, I believe, a despair that itself is immeasurable and that is bred of human anarchy, violence, meaningless pain, and unrecountable loss.

My thought is that God provides for the psalmist and for many other people a source and basis for morality and meaning that is beyond the reach of nonhuman nature and the stark absence of human care in the constantly originating, nonhuman energy of the universe. With God as our creator and guide, we are not alone among the overpowering forces of nonhuman energy. We rather find the space and silence of the heavens to be the sites that disclose God's creative glory. In this thought we find recognition that the vastness, perhaps the enormity and mystery of the universe provide no adequate basis for religious attitudes. Without God there is nothing true to worship. The universe does not mean anything intrinsically worthwhile for people. "God" alone gives true meaning to the universe, and without God the "universe" would be a place without hope for the dominion of human significance. Values would be ours alone. That would leave us prey to all the horrors that occur under the day's sun and the night's sidereal carelessness.

Consider part of a very different, but perhaps obliquely complementary poem: Matthew Arnold's "Dover Beach," written in 1867:

> The Sea of Faith
> Was once, too, at the full, and round earth's shore
> Lay like the folds of a bright girdle furled.
> But now I only hear
> Its melancholy, long, withdrawing roar,
> Retreating, to the breath
> Of the night-wind, down the vast edges drear
> And naked shingles of the world.
> Ah, love, let us be true
> To one another! For the world, which seems
> To lie before us like a land of dreams,
> So various, so beautiful, so new
> Hath really neither joy, nor love, nor light,
> Nor certitude, nor peace, nor help for pain;
> And we are here as on a darkling plain
> Swept with confused alarms of struggle and flight,
> Where ignorant armies clash by night.

This poem expresses a genre of experience that is now thoroughly familiar: like the psalmist, I believe, Arnold found no ultimate basis for hope, love, or enlightened truth in a world without God or in a life without faith in God. But in contrast to the psalmist, he finds no wisdom or truth that transcends the world and the universe and that gives us that transcendence that turns bright what otherwise would be a darkling plain. Faith in God is now heard by Arnold only in the vacuum and night of its withdrawal. In the withdrawal of faith he finds as his best moral option a true relation with the one he loves, a relation, I assume, that struggles to be free of betrayal or cruelty, one in which his experience of human love provides him with knowledge of the way people can live at their best. Deeply satisfying human love—a small measure in the enormity of the universe and of faith's withdrawal—such love in this context of faith's abandonment is the measure for human circumstances at their best.

The dark sadness in this poem expresses, I believe, the pain of *lost* faith. I do not hear Arnold's sadness as nostalgia for a time of faith. I hear it arising out of his nonvoluntary and experiential knowledge of life without faith in God, without certainty before the universe's vastness, but with some hope in faith's failure, and with a small measure of meaning with suffering. I hear in his sadness his experiential and nonvoluntary knowledge of a world that no longer manifests the glory and presence of God. I believe that he did not choose to be without faith and that he did not choose his experience of the impossibility of faith. He found himself in a world without God and with only the memory of the power of faith. In that sense his despair was a way of being true to this world instead of running away from it by means of nostalgic images from a time that was passed. But he nonetheless suffered faith's loss and experienced the loss in mourning and depression.

I view the option of welcoming the world's appearance without faith as one for those people for whom faith in God is not a living possibility, not a possibility that arises in their deepest experiences. For those people who, when faced with the possibility of faithful belief in God, find that they do not have any sense of God's "real" existence, or find that they do not need even to deny the existence of God in order to be true to their predispositions and experiences, or those who simply remain indifferent or silent before the question of God or no God and look in other directions—for such people as these, I believe that there is the possibility for affirmations of life that are free of Arnold's sadness. Here is one option among, I am sure, many others for a kind of affirmation that constitutes a basis for a morality without a sense of "Nature" or some specific Being that bestows meaning on the lives of things. We can describe it as one in which an individual releases the appearance of the universe to its enormity with no requirement for further meaning and releases people to their relative smallness and singularity before the celestial vastness. I use the word "release" to mean that a person, in experiences of sheer vastness, simply allows it to happen as it happens without further meaning. One does not draw conclusions about it and does not look to it for signs or symbols of something else but rather perceives vastness simply as something that is there: a sort of well-there-it-is encounter. And in the perception of human tininess, one might be astonished that we are and experience astonishment—not *at* something but astonishment in the experience of being here in the midst of incalculable movement and space (instead, for example, of feeling a need to find by way of confirmation that other humans are "out there"!). In this situation one does not find the "work of thy fingers" or a feeling of the mournful withdrawal of faith. People rather find a lot of emptiness and a lot of existing things and know themselves to be here now and to be astonished and to find their meaning and endurance thoroughly in question in the astonishment. All the facts, explanations, and existing things in the world bear no witness to the force of astonishment, and all the astonishment in the world, piled high in one place, would not compose an important counter to any fact or explanation—nor would all that astonishment constitute even a gesture with theological or religious meaning—at least not in the mentation that I am describing. People can be quite amazed before starlight with no sense of its meaning anything "in itself" or by virtue of a creator. And people can find themselves and their kind singular in the universe and enjoy their singularity, amazed at how huge it all is, in the midst of knowledge that says how things appear in terms of energy and quanta without a larger purposefulness. Appearances in a context of amazement do not need to mean anything more than appearing, specific lives in the context of their happening.

This sensibility, we have seen, can be lived in everyday situations as people find emptiness among all things. Like the starry heavens juxtaposed with the earth and its inhabitants, "emptiness" with things does not do anything. "It" is something like an experience of seemingly empty and immeasurable space—not anything in particular, not the trees that "it" pervades or the humans who find themselves with "it" or the consciousness that "it" infuses. Emptiness is not even "something" that we are in. In alertness with "it" a person can find things strangely both apart *and* connected by nothing at all in addition to all the specific occurrences that hold things apart and connect them. Events seem to matter only in their happening and to matter considerably at the same time that nothing transcendental fills in the gaps and gives them an immanent backdrop of full and unbroken presence. This sense of emptiness with things can prompt people to live on this tiny planet with passion in the midst of a gappy and spaced-out universe that is without human passion and is not the earth at all. Or being with things and emptiness together can be like concentrating on something intensely so that in the spasm of concentration something comes to a prominence that only the concentration sustains.

A person can become lost in experiences of emptiness just as one can become lost in the midst of demanding things and everyday preoccupations. The art in this instance is one of perceiving both at once, both emptiness and what is present in its connected particularity. Losing either would constitute a lapse of attentiveness that has implications for the ways we live.

I am using "emptiness" as a sign both to indicate the loss of an absolute for human orientation and to indicate a sensibility that can give rise to values and attitudes that embody affirmation of the world without an absolute that gives it value and universal continuity. Things do not appear that way to many people, and in a sense of emptiness an undespairing positivity toward living and beings can arise. People can find the world appearing with no intimation of an absolute and find in such appearing motivation to discover what most enhances their lives together.

With the introduction of the word "moral" at this point I introduce the possibility of a morality without a trans-sidereal Lord or an attitude expressed by Arnold's words, "Ah, love, let us be true to one another." I am considering an attitude that is generative of values and evaluations, an attitude that is informed neither by theological reference nor by despair over a loss of faith's vitality.

I suggested that losing either a sense of emptiness or a perceptive association with things in their connected, concrete particularity could constitute a lapse with moral implications. A sense *solely* of emptiness, which can come with despair as well as with serene contemplation, is without care or concern or attachment in relation to things. By itself this sense is without love or initiative or a sense of right and wrong or even amazement. It is profoundly inactive, and it composes a sense that nothing ultimately matters, that everything is the same. Nothing seems to happen, and that has a correlate that everything and anything that happens is allowed with something like indifference. When one is lost in emptiness nothing else is taken care of or nurtured or resisted or changed. Nothing makes a difference.

But when the sense of nothing—or emptiness—does make a difference, when it is countenanced in a conscious relation to the singular, active lives of things, we are taken out of either a depressed or a serene disposition that is governed by attunement to inactivity. And we are also taken out of a sense that the world is composed exclusively of useful things, whether those useful things are only mundane or are holy as well as mundane. Things stand out in their singularity. They stand out in their "just-so" quality, their nonreducibility to anything else, in the simultaneous palpability and impalpability of their events. They are connected in their own epiphanies, and that recognition, I believe, can be significant for a morality—although elaboration of that significance is beyond the scope of this book.

When things are known in their pervasive emptiness *and* their singularity, our moral conduct, the ways whereby we connect with things and use them or value them, is always in question. People and things are not knowable *primarily* by means of an anchoring generic commonality: "*It*," for example, is known as *this tree*, not merely as an instance of a larger genre. And "*she*" is known as this one, in *her* life and feeling and needs and possibilities, with *this* history and *those* abilities, as *this one* who comes to pass in these specific ways. She does not occur in this perceptive happening primarily as an instance of the type female or as one of the larger class of citizen or as valuable because someone else values her. All of these things—female, citizen, and value because of another—belong to her and determine who she is. But she is also this singular individual who stands out now from the emptiness that connects her to and separates her from everything else in the world. Questionableness also happens in such singular events. Not only is her event always in jeopardy. My connections with her too are always in jeopardy. As I encounter her, I face the question of how I am to be with her in this moment. How am I to receive and address her? How am I now to be with *her*? These are questions that open to a full range of moral considerations, and here they are questions and possibilities that are based on intense experiences of presence with emptiness (and presence with emptiness is a questionable basis for anything—a basis that is without basis). Undergoing this kind of uncertainty and certainty at the same time is something like finding the earth quite singular in its tiny and uninsured presence in a vast universe and being struck by the question: "Since this is all we have, how are we to be with it and with each other in our time on it?"

Should I call this option moral? Or should I look for another name for an ethos—a way of making a dwelling place—that arises out of mindfulness of emptiness with communal singularities? Whatever we decide to call it, in speaking of it I wish to speak of an affirmation of things as we find them appearing, an affirmation of what we find of the world by our most determined and experimental knowledge, and of the ways we find things occurring in the world. These affirmations occur in a release of people and things to their epiphanies with emptiness—in an absence of expectation for meanings or glories that transcend worldly occurrences. These affirmations happen in the discovery that life without a religious faith is affirmable in both the absence of infinite meaning and texture and in the interactive singularities of living things. These affirmations have a quality, a metaphor for which we might find in the image of the earth's life, turning with vast and empty space, space that we do not grasp, traversed by immeasurable, nonhuman energies without which the earth and its inhabitants could not be.

TEN

The Phusis *of Nihil*

THE SIGHT AND GENERATION OF NIHILISM

The word "nihilism" in its many meanings usually has such a negative and even hostile connotation! In popular academic culture, if you can make "nihilistic" stick to a name, you have pretty much ruined that name as far as wide influence is concerned. People who appreciate Nietzsche's thought have gone to a lot of trouble to show that at worst "nihilism" describes only a temporary and productive phase of his thinking and that at best it names something that he recognized as pervasive in Western culture and that is overcome in his thought—what is *really* nihilistic is something like globalization, consumerism, and a Disney World popular culture. There is so much interest in nihilism and its avoidance right now in both the United States and Europe that I would like to pause with the meanings of the word, the generative force of "nihil" and consider what nihilism-anxiety might be about. My hypotheses are that the origins of meanings for nihilism show the very conditions that many of those meanings condemn, that those origins figure "something" like nihil and that Nietzsche seemed to understand that. I hope to be constructively responsive to an aspect of Nietzschean thought by taking pleasure in uncovering the "nihilism" of the charge that Nietzsche is nihilistic, and enjoying a kind of sight that arises from positive attention to nothing with things.

THE WORD

Nihilism has many meanings.[1] It was coined in the eighteenth century, not much more than a hundred years before Nietzsche used it, and sug-

1. In the following discussion I draw from *Webster's New International Dictionary,* Hermann Paul's *Deutsches Wörterbuch,* Klein's *Comprehensive Etymological Dictionary,* Grimm's *Deutsches Wörterbuch,* and *The Oxford English Dictionary.*

gested positions and actions that denied the existence of real and true substance, a use that is quite different from the way Nietzsche applied the
word. It has been used to name a doctrine that no reality exists, that there
is no objective or real ground for truth and moral principles. It can name
a position that seeks the annihilation of desires and self-consciousness. It
can name a zero-sum-game politics that seeks the destruction of institutions without constructive alternatives, or simply a politics of terrorism
and assassination. It has named, variously, doctrines that say Christ had no
true substance, people who refuse beneficial medical treatment, a pathol-
ogy of delusion in which everything seems unreal, doctrines which are
taken as generally negative in their intent, rejections of or nonbelief in
current religious beliefs or moral principles, extreme forms of skepticism,
life in separation from divinity, atheism, modernist rejections of traditional values, and postmodernists' rejection of modernist values.

I especially like one of the definitive references provided by the OED:
"Nihilism in Russia is an explosive compound, generated by the contact of
the Slav character with Western ideas." People have used the word to describe Fichtean thought, Humean epistemology, and Buddhist teachings.
In an early usage, Turgenev wrote of nihilism in *Fathers and Sons* to name
the idea that only sensuous experiences are real. Jacobi said, in one of the
word's earliest usages, that any position is nihilistic (and for him this included Kant's and all other "idealists'") that leads to a view of the human
subject as everything and the world as nothing. He thought that transcendental subjectivity is an unworthy candidate for the a priori, substantial
basis for worldly reality.

The word has suggested a prioritizing of the abyssal instead of a transcendent reality, thought that is not organized by the primary value of unity
and unified identity, the prioritizing of the human, anti-foundationalism, a
breakdown in the prioritizing of the human, and above all, a loss of meaning for life regardless of the cause of that loss.

Recognitions of the loss of the value of life bear witness to an enormous range of different beliefs, passions, and perspectives that give rise to
those recognitions. I think that I would be most true to the word's wide
range of suggestions and descriptions if I said that its meaning is governed
by what a discourse finds most valuable and most reprehensible: it usually
names a perspective, thought, or program in which people see other people
to lose what, according to the accusers, makes life valuable and losing as
well the authorities and experiences to which they give highest credence.
So if I believed that static forms constitute the essence of life and you were
to say that all forms are only relatively stable patterns of dynamic
processes, you could well appear nihilistic to me. Or, if you were sure that
the highest values for life originate only in Chicago, and I were sure that
they originate in Oklahoma City and exclude many of Chicago's highest

values, we could begin to appear nihilistic to each other. That's because the meanings of nihilism have much to do with where and how our highest meanings and values are generated.

I have located the probable generation of the meanings of nihilism in specific discourses, which means, I suppose, that if one believes that meanings require a generator that transcends mortal time, the very meanings of nihilism, as I see them, are nihilistic. They are circumscribed by the discourses that generate them and do not appear to have their basis in something transcendent.

Probably, for the word nihilism to hold much intrinsic meaning, something definitive, transcendent of historical processes, and knowable has to be implicated. And as my last observations indicate, the meanings of nihilism seem to be intrinsically temporal and historical. They seem to originate in discourses when something of highest value for life appears to be threatened or left out in another discourse. If those observations are correct, the meanings of nihilism lack the unity and basis that is necessary to avoid nihilism as it is often understood.

The palpable absence of such a basis, however, does not mean that people cannot affirm that a transcendent basis for the value of life exists. Whether they hope there is one, or know by faith that there is such a basis, or think that one must exist if life is to be worth living, or have experiences that indicate to them that one does exist, people may certainly know that within the perimeters of their values they must have a transcendent basis for life if life is to be genuinely worthwhile for them. And within these perimeters we may construct all manner of arguments, appeals, practices, laws, and confessions to confirm the perceived necessity. For the basis of the meanings of nihilism rests in discursively formed feelings—extremely powerful feelings—that are violated only at the cost of a sense of fundamental identity, security, and purpose.

It is such discourses and feelings as these that Nietzsche addresses when he confronts what he calls nihilism.

NIETZSCHE'S EXPERIENCE

One sense of nihilism for Nietzsche names the site and aftermath of the death of God and with them the death of a sense of transcendent meaning for life and lives. This site of divine passage and sense of loss carries *a consequent feeling* that life itself has lost its meaning and value. It names an historical *process* whereby the meaning of the death of "God's" power is expressed by a sense that life itself has lost its worth. This was a time for Nietzsche of transformation, of possibility in which despair over life figures an insistent retention of God as the basis for any value that life might have. This description on Nietzsche's part constitutes a move through such nihilism and the emergence of an option to it, the option of affirming the death of God and one that I will elaborate by reference to eternal return. It is the option of trans-valuing all values in the force of this affirmation of God's passage. This option describes a region of thought that arises from a history that affirms God's transcendent gift of meaning, that suffers the growing impotence of that affirmation, and that allows new and different envisagements of the value of being alive. "The death of God" for Nietzsche, names a region of metamorphoses. It is in this description that we find a hopeful dimension in Nietzsche's thought, one that is excessive to the kind of sickness and sorrow that characterize what Nietzsche calls nihilism, and one from which springs the joy that is one hallmark of Nietzsche's reflective and outgoing affections.

"Nihil" in the context of his thought can refer to the sheer absence of intrinsic worth in life for those who are attached to the passing God. I think of people who have told me that without a divine and transcendent Life, whether that Life be directly known or indirectly perceived through scripture, to provide standards of conduct, a reference for meaning, a present certainty before the relativities of earthly existence—without such transcendence we are without a basis for peace, hope, and sustaining faith. Nietzsche's spirit echoes: Have you not heard, have you not noticed? You live in a culture that lacks an agreed basis for moral values, a culture that has lost spirit, a culture of resentful punishments and exclusions, one that looks for pale forms of redemption, one that recognizes God's revelation as past. We also live in a culture in which God appears as an epiphenomenon of insistence to provide value-added meaning to the ways we do things, a culture whose texture is made of economies of exchange, constitutions, and contracts, a prioritizing of information, multiple efforts to give priority to humans, and efforts to find economies that will make life better than tolerable. We live in a culture that intends to find life's values *in* life, a culture in which religious passions play on the borders of the texture that composes the economies and systems of lives. Or, such passions inspire efforts to overturn the culture in the name of what at one time might have defined another era of Western life. The power of God does not make the operative meanings of primary connections in our cultural life. Other powers are at work. We are in a time when the values of our lives do not have to have a transcendent basis in order to be genuine values. We do not have to lose a sense of the value of life and be nihilists in the absence of God's power.

Nietzsche did not reach easily his movement out of nihilism. One indication of the considerable struggle that marked the shift in his attunements in the late 1870s and early '80s can be found in the shock he experienced when the image of eternal return began to form. Lou Salome's account of her conversations with him when he first spoke of eternal return are consistent with Zarathustra's horror before his emerging vision of this "abysmal thought." Salome wrote:

> Only with a quiet voice and with all the signs of deepest horror did he speak about his secret. Life, in fact, produced such suffering in him that the certainty of an eternal return of life had to mean something horrifying to him.[2]

Whether or not we accept her interpretation that Nietzsche could never reconcile his experience of eternal return and the affirmation of life that it came to mean for him with the suffering and terror of life as he experienced it, or Pierre Klossowski's interpretation that eternal return's vicious circularity meant in a terrible way to Nietzsche the continuous loss of his self to the selfless force of time, Nietzsche in any case found at first terrifying the imagery and experiential basis of eternal return. In that terror I believe that he knew the meaning of one kind of nihilism in the wake of God's loss: if there is no transcendent meaning for self and world, given the suffering, radical injustice, and tragedies that come with ordinary living, life is worthless. He was within the reach of traditional values that were forceful and in an orientation that was centered on transcendent being. That reach inspired terror in him when he experienced a vivid alternative in which lives either had their own time-limited values or no value at all.

In *Thus Spoke Zarathustra,* Nietzsche writes of the confrontation with eternal return and the foreboding that led to it. Through *Zarathustra* he describes the cultural conditions in which he existed as deeply fatiguing, crippled, unendurable, in need of recreation and liberation, filled with revenge, distorted and sick.[3]

Zarathustra required solitude, separation, *Scheidung,* to confront with clarity—with genuine sight—what he found most unendurable in cultural life. To see how destructive were Europe's highest values, to see how dispiriting was the soul of Western humanity's best accomplishments was, for Zarathustra, an extremely demanding, wrenching, and lonely effort. This process of coming to see clearly the stagnation at the heart of Western religion, art, education, and thought required Zarathustra to find the wasteland in himself, to survive that knowledge and the loneliness its discovery required, and to develop the leonine energy needed to fight off the reductive powers of cultural amalgamation and the blindness that composes that amalgamation. He had to find the energy to envision constructive exits from the wasteland to new options. At first, Zarathustra

---

2. Quoted in Pierre Klossowski, *Nietzsche and the Vicious Circle* (Chicago: University of Chicago Press, 1997), p. 95. (French edition, 1969.)

3. The following two paragraphs are a reading of parts of section II, 20–21, "On Redemption" and "The Stillest Hour."

thought he could make that move himself by the force of his mounting energy: he could see clearly, he could be alone, he could dream a new world. At first he did not know that he could dream and struggle only by re-instituting the very values he intended to overcome. He did not know that a life-denying situation's greatest power is that of transformational possibilities within the life-denying values themselves, possibilities that would overturn those values that harbored them.

This separation and solitude did not compose simply a meditative withdrawal. It turned into his "stillest hour," absent of joy, in which "the ground gave way under me," "the dream began," and "my heart took fright."[4] As the possibility of eternal return begins to emerge, Zarathustra's face blanches. The new dream does not arrive as *his* conception. He will not say what he is coming to know—*"Ich will es nicht reden."* What he heard was not a voice—what he confronted was *"ohne Stimme,"* yet too demanding and beyond his power to control or assimilate. He cried and trembled. It felt to him as though something awful and unclear were to be said, given word, and it felt as though bringing it to expression would break him apart. He was facing, I believe, an experience that was outside of the region of *his* recognitions, outside of his own self-conscious identity, beyond his ability to affirm, and yet it was "something" that was preparing to be said and before which his refusal to give it words was like stubbornness and defiance (*Trotz*). He felt in his stubbornness attached to the self that he knew himself to be, and thereby attached to a moralistic and theistic culture that he knew to be pathological. He lacked, however, "humility," *die Demut,* for such a transfiguration of himself. He was leonine and strong, and did not want his familiar and reliable self to fall apart. He knew the shadowed and diseased valley of his cultural self, but he did not know how to reach the heights of a qualitatively different kind of affirmation. He was fixed to a kind of nihilism in which life seemed awful and without exit by which to reach an entrance to life-affirmation.

The voiceless communication told him that he needed a new innocence, one without shame, a rejuvenation that could come only if he underwent the terrible transition of identity-loss. Zarathustra's answer confirmed his nihilistic attachment: I am ashamed: *I* do not want to die, to go under. The uncompromising response? Laughter. A laughter that was unavailable to Zarathustra at that time, but a promise of celebration when his self, and with it his shame and terror, died. The laughter left him to

---

4. The Kaufmann translation loses a measure of the poem's emphasis in this section and other sections by turning the short, divided paragraphs into longer ones that suggest less breakage and division than the original.

"his loneliest walk" without a map or a cleared path (III.1). Everything around him seemed "drunk with sleep" and groaning "with evil memories" that were embedded in the very texture of somnolent consciousness. He was angry, filled with longing, and bitter (ibid.). He was in the thick of what he recognized as nihilism.

If you agree with me that this account arises from Nietzsche's own experiences, you can appreciate how difficult was his full movement into the state of mind that produced his most mature and far-reaching work. You can see that the meaning of nihilism as he found it happens in a body of feelings and attunements that defined a significant segment of his culture and hence himself. And you can see that the nihilistic life that composed him was the only place of departure that he had, that its sickness in combination with his cleared vision of that sickness pushed him to the extremity of a self-overcoming that was not entirely voluntary. This nihilism was generated by a dying segment of cultural life, and it—this nihilism—also generated, in a strange hermaphroditic mating with its own destructive limits, both a death and a rebirth for Nietzsche. Not only are many meanings of nihilism generated by what those meanings identify as nihilistic. The energy and trajectory for movements out of nihilism, in Nietzsche's experience, are generated within nihilistic situations. This transformative aspect is possible, I believe, because cultural situations have within them many trajectories of life that, when given increased force, radically transform the organizing hierarchies, values, and meanings—and hence the feelings and attunements—of a culture—as when the value of equality within a society gains prominent force over other values of enslavement, or when the value of information becomes more forceful than the value of manufacturing.

However we understand the huge number of conflicting forces in a cultural complex, we can see that Nietzsche's experience makes viable the observation that a pervasively nihilistic culture, by virtue of its margins and suppressed aspects, gave impetus to his departure from it.

Eternal return figures an attunement to an absence of transcendent, meaningful life, to what Nietzsche often referred to as chaos. But for him the nihilism was not housed, as it were, in chaos. It is housed in a sense of valuelessness that arises when a sense of chaos replaces a sense of meaningful transcendence—the very sense of meaningful transcendence that seems to motivate those interpretations of Nietzsche's thought that find it nihilistic.

Consider what Zarathustra says happened on his loneliest walk (III.1–2). He met the embodiment of a major component in his lineage and his self, his "devil and archenemy," the spirit of gravity, the very spirit that would hold him in the valley of nihilism and weigh him down and disable him with depression. Zarathustra met the force of his own stubbornness and defiance before the call of self-overcoming's possibility. When he speaks of the spirit of gravity, I believe that Zarathustra speaks of a dread that often drives people back to where they were before they experienced an immanent possibility of transition and transformation, back to the abuser, back to old familiar ways, to the village's security and the community's creation-less protection. Back to the same. Back to sites of predictability and certainty. Back to life as it has been. That return might not sound stubborn. It might sound like good sense when a person's or a group of people's sense of identity is seriously threatened.

Zarathustra's response? *Mut* "slays dizziness at the edge of abysses: and where does man not stand at the edge of abysses? Is not seeing itself—seeing abysses?" (III.2, trans. modified). It is a question of seeing or not seeing that again confronts Zarathustra. Is he to deny what he is coming to see, what in some sense, at the border of his awareness, he knows? In this instance something is emerging that he did not and was not able to construct, a little ecstasy of configurations that enacted in its articulation and meaning an exit from nihilism. With this envisagement Zarathustra feels as though he were standing on the edge of his cultural subjectivity and seeing nothing that he can identify, as though he were seeing possibilities in an abyss without transcendent support.

An abysmal thought is thus what is at issue for Zarathustra. The spirit of gravity does not know and "could not bear" this thought, this prospect of spiritual transformation. For such knowledge and bearing would destroy the downward pull and give this gravity to move toward lightness of heart. The meaning of this thought is that temporal processes enjoy only those meanings that define them in their passing, that people look beyond their lives and lineages in a projective vanity when they look for meaning in addition to those meanings that are generated in meaningful practices and knowledges and their mutational interplays. If you are going to affirm *life* and *lives* then you will have to let them occur in all the details of *their* unredeemable horror and beauty, in their passage, as though they would return mindlessly just as they have been and are in a movement with no other purpose.

But this spirit of gravity, this depression of spirit that would keep people small and in need of transcendent assurance of life's ultimate meaning, became lighter. This "dwarf" jumped off of Zarathustra's shoulder down to the ground and presented Zarathustra with a choice. It lost its weight on Zarathustra and began, by its demotion in importance, a process of transformation that would accomplish an eradication of much of its own force. As Zarathustra brings to articulation the imagery and meaning of eternal return—the story in which everything that happens will happen again and again—and brings it to articulation with the passion of someone who is undergoing a cure, a relief from great pain—in this process of expression he experienced a jubilant release from what he knew to be nihilistic. Nothing in his culture was, as it were, solved, but he felt released from a measure of its overwhelming power in his own awareness. He felt that he did not have to be so aggressive—so leonine—that he could in his activity be far more playful and childlike, that he could laugh freely and without bitterness, that his work could have an edge of open uncertainty and happy exploration, even when he was suffering. He felt attuned to chaos beyond and within the worlds of specific values and meanings. Through his experience of eternal return he felt, I believe, a love for life, regardless of its terrible aspect, that had not been previously quite so available to him. What he identified as life's exhaustion in the dominant moralities and religions of his lineage was replaced in some measure by the energizing, enlightening conception of eternal return.

Nietzsche was excited about his discovery, and like many people who find release from pain and openings to new and better ways of life, he wanted to make his medium of release—eternal return—into a factually based medium for everyone who could take it. That probably shows how much under the sway he was of what he knew to be nihilism—he would have liked to show—to prove—that eternal return is the fundamental truth of physics, to make it an indisputable, authoritative fact.

I would be happier to call eternal return a strategy of envisagement that surely worked for Nietzsche and might also work for other people who are transcendentally beset. The issue at hand does not need a careful account of eternal return, but rather the observation that a different generation of the meaning of nihilism comes into play in the awareness that is expressed in Nietzsche's embodiment of the idea of eternal return. This is a kind of generating and creativity that is different from the knowledge that springs from his critical accounts of his culture and is especially different from the "nihilistic" production that is provided by transcendentally oriented theories and values. The differences between those generative orientations are huge, because they show not so much that nihilism has been defeated by Nietzsche's departure as they show that its power is limited and subject to self-overcoming, that the essence of nihilism is a conflicted and changing field of attunements, attunements that compose recognitions within histories of anxieties and affirmations. "Nihilism" means multiple discourses, multiple regions of recognition, and multiple efforts to live well, usually made under adverse circumstances. Each of these discourses engenders its own sense for what enhances lives, each, in its sensibility, recognizes what is destructive for lives, and each discourse might also engender a meaning for "nihilism." That meaning in its turn generates the nihilistic "thing," the states of affairs *in* experience and recognitions that reduce the discourse's most cherished values to virtually nothing.

I return to Zarathustra's observation to the grave dwarf of despair: "Ist Sehen nicht selber—Abgründe sehen?" I interpret him to mean that the occurrence of seeing is accompanied by nothing to be seen, that in addition to the recognition, experience, and admission that is sight, there is also at once nothing to be held, like void, or chaos—mere absence of presence. This weird, and for some people awful, accompaniment is not reasonably subject to articles, does not even compose a void or the void. Nothing. The experience he has in mind is something like being at the edge of an abyss when whatever orients a person is also shifting and unstable. That dimension of experience seems to happen whenever people recognize something; it composes a giddiness with the coming of determinate things. When you pay attention to this dimension of occurrences, clarity of sight brings bewilderment with the definiteness and concreteness of whatever is seen.

I expect that Nietzsche experienced something like that anxious lightheartedness with the arrival of the imagery of eternal return and that he was looking for a language and metaphors to receive and welcome such nihil. It's not that nihil generates anything. It's that nothing also happens when things appear. When such welcoming occurred he was able to see both that he was held by nothing and that when he accepted his sight the life-exhausting dimension of his self and culture became most clear. The cultural nihilism did not happen due to the nihil-dimension of experience. It happened as an attempted escape from nihil in life and produced ways of life that refused to see clearly that as people suffer and prosper they find their meanings here, always here where they are in a stretch of time and place, circumscribed by nihil and founded on shaky ground. Nihil, as it turns out, names, paradoxically, a highest value for Nietzsche, for by welcoming attention to the nihil-dimension of experiences, people can come into their own and find avenues to life-affirming creations in values, art, and thought.

Zarathustra then gives a little paean to *Mut,* a word that strikes me as saying a good bit more than "courage," unless that English word is heard in the full range of suggestion that is in its older meanings, those of mind, heart, and disposition, as well as fortitude, refusal to give up regardless of the odds, a certain grit and pluck when things are really dangerous and hard. With *Mut* before *Abgrund* Nietzsche was enabled to say, "as deeply as [we see] into life [we] also see into suffering" and "was [what I saw] life? Fine! Let's see it again!" (III.2.2, trans. mine). But his strongest, most mature confirmation comes in the next lines: in my words, he says, "there is a lot of brassy play" (trans. mine). His abysmal thought in affirming nihil is as shaky as the disabled affirmations of life that are produced by his nihilistic culture, except that he sees abysmally that his thought and sight are abysmal, and he welcomes that sight. This confirmation composes, I believe, a meaning in his words that some people call nihilistic, a meaning by which he could recognize their nihilism and by which, on his terms, he could undergo and affirm a non-nihilistic experience of the value of nihil.

INDEX

Alberts, Bruce, 91n5
Ananke, 41, 42
Animality, 88–93
Appropriation, 118
Arnold, Matthew, 179, 182
Astonishment, 3–22, 57, 60, 75, 130, 134;
    appearance of astonishment, 9; astonishing
    factuality of hearing, 7; everyday quality, 12;
    in meaning and non-meaning, 7, 14–15;
    and physicality, 6–9, 16, 22, 60; and
    recognition, 9

Barbree, Jay, 104n1
Bataille, 150
Beginning, 36, 40–44, 73–76; and *phusis,* 42;
    and returning, 45
Being and Time, 14, 97
Being-in-common, 121
Beston, Henry, 22
The Bible, 107–108
Blanchot, 109, 148
Body, 16–18, 54–56, 116–18, 162, 164–65,
    168; and immanence, 162; and gravity,
    116–18; and Nietzsche, 165; and physicality,
    18, 56
Boss, Medard, 141n7

Caidin, Martin, 104n1
Calvino, Italo, vii–ix
Cells, 91–93
Chora, 36–53; and *ananke,* 41; as *hupodoxa,* 43,
    52–53; and *logos,* 45–46; and nature, 48; and
    nous, 41, 42; and *phusis,* 36, 41–42; and
    place, 46; and *techne,* 41
Community, 113, 120

Density, 114–16, 119, 125–43; and lightness,
    141; and physicality, 139
Derrida, Jaques, 148
Dewey, John, 67–73
Dionysus, 147, 159, 170

Ears, 6–10; heard meanings, 7; physiology of
    hearing, 6–8; and spatial siting, 10
Eidos, 3, 7, 43–44; and *mimesis,* 44
Embodiment, 89
Eternal Return, 192–94
Eyes, 100–103, 107

Faces, 100
Facts, 3–22; of ears, 7–10; engendering
    astonishment, 4; and metaphors, 9; and
    poetic experiences, 3; in science, 3, 5
Fichte, J. G., 150
Flesh, 93, 109
Foucault, Michel, 131–43, 157

Gadda, Carlo Emilio, vii
The Gay Science, 169
Geist, 125–29, 143; and density, 126
Goodenough, Ursula, 91n5
Gravity, 116–24; and levity, 122–23; and
    meaning, 122

Hamann, J. G., 150
Hegel, G. W. F., 114, 150
Heidegger, Martin, 13, 14, 18, 57–67,
    72–73, 85–98, 125–34, 141–43, 166; and
    animality, 88, 89; and astonishment, 13; and
    being, 18; and Foucault, 141–43; and
    Geist, 125–34; and *phusis,* 57–67; and
    time, 97
Heraclitus, 87
Heraclitus' Fragment B16, 85
Hesiod, 39
History, 137–40, 161
Homer, 85–86, 89, 93–94, 98, 173
Hupodoxa, 43–44, 51
Husserl, 58–59

Immanence, 25, 114, 144–76; and *phusis,*
    146–76; and translation, 147–76; and
    truth, 147
Introduction to Metaphysics, 66, 125, 132

Jacobi, F. H., 150

Klossowski, Pierre, 188n2

Language, 167–74
Law, 79, 131, 135
Levinas, 18, 99–100, 107, 109, 148
Levity, 122–23; operative, 122
Light, 93, 103–107; and eyes, 103–107
Lightness, 19, 140, 141
Limit, 51
Logos, 45, 46, 118; and *chora,* 45

Mann, Thomas, 72n25
Memory, 80, 87–89, 91–95, 98, 165; and animality, 89, 93; in cells, 91–93; as cultural embodiment, 89–91; and Heidegger, 87; physiological memory, 165; and time, 98; without a subject, 89
Merleau-Ponty, 148
Metaphor, 6–9; erasure of, 9; in physiology of hearing, 7, 8
Mimesis, 39, 40–42, 44
Mystery, 11, 12; and astonishment, 12

Nancy, Jean-Luc, 18, 100, 113–24
Nature, 17, 22–26, 34–36, 43, 48–53, 54, 57, 59, 68–69, 80–81, 120, 131–38, 142, 180; and abstraction, 23; and *hupodoxa,* 43; as immanent cause, 25; and orders, 80; and origin, 36; and *phusis,* 17, 26–34; and wholeness, 24
Nietzsche, 100, 118, 127, 147, 158–60, 164–74, 184–85, 192; and ascetic ideal, 118; and eternal return, 192; and immanence, 164–74; and nihilism, 184, 185
Nihilism, 162, 184–94
Nous, 37–41, 44, 47

The Order of Things, 131, 135–43
Orders, 79, 80, 134, 137, 138, 145
The Origin of the Work of Art, 14
Otto, Rudolph, 12–13

Phaedo, 36
Phenomenology, 23
Phusis, 17–21, 26–27, 29, 34–53, 57–68, 75, 80, 92, 121–22, 127–35, 162, 164, 171; and *chora,* 36–53; and Heidegger, 57–67, 127–35; and immanence, 162; and nature, 26, 27, 29; and physicality, 17; and *ta panta,* 34, 35
Physicality, vii–viii, 6, 16–21, 56, 67, 73, 81, 87, 115, 121, 130, 131–40, 143, 150, 152, 162, 170; and astonishment, 6; and body, 16, 56; in Foucault, 131, 139, 140, 143; and Heidegger, 67; inoperative dimension of, 121; and organic functions, 20; and *phusis,* 17–19; in Schleiermacher, 152; and spatial siting, 17

Physiology, 164
Place, 10, 46, 51
Plato, 36–52, 103
Poetry, 170

Rensberger, Boyce, 91n5
Rhythm 167–74

Sallis, John, 36–51, 57
Sartre, 29–32
Schelling, 114, 147, 153–60; and freedom, 157; and indifference, 155–60
Schleiermacher, 147, 149–53, 164
Science, 55, 62
Shining, 85, 86
Socrates, 38, 39
Space, 135–43
Space-Time, 138
Spinoza, 149
Spirituality, 16
Systems, 79

Ta panta, 34, 35
Techne, 36, 37, 41
Technology, 63, 64, 90
Thomas, Lewis, 91n5
Thus Spoke Zarathustra, 188
Timaeus, 36–52, 103
Time, 86–87, 97–98, 155
Transcendence, 107
Transfer, 11, 147; and translation, 147
Translation, 146–74; and immanence, 146–74; and physiognomies of meanings, 163–74
Truth, 146, 147

Ungrounding ground, 138–39

Vision, 100
Void, 52

Weight, 117–19

Zamenes, 85
Zao, 85
Zapuros, 85
Zatheos, 85

CHARLES E. SCOTT is Edwin Erle Sparks Professor of Philosophy at the Pennsylvania State University. Among his books are *The Question of Ethics; On the Advantages and Disadvantages of Ethics in Politics;* and *The Time of Memory.*